Richard Falk, the former UN Special Rapporteur for Human Rights in the Occupied Palestinian Territory, wields the sharpest of word-swords in the legitimacy struggle that shapes today's search for justice for Palestinians. In this extraordinary collection, he once again provides us with the tools to forge a path through the thicket of lies, propaganda and cruelty that mask the real basis for achieving Palestinian rights: international law, human rights, and equality for all. Global civil society has joined Palestinians to embrace that path; Falk's groundbreaking work challenges governments to do so as well.

—**PHYLLIS BENNIS**
Director, New Internationalism Project
Institute for Policy Studies

Palestine: The Legitimacy of Hope is the writing of a great mind with a brave heart and a moral compass.

—**MARWAN BISHARA**
Senior political analyst, Al-Jazeera English

This book is a gem of brilliant clarity. In his years as Special Rapporteur on Palestine for the UN Human Rights Council Richard Falk in his bi-annual reports consistently provided "a truthful witness to the unspeakable ordeal of the prolonged and harsh Israeli occupation." This collection of his blogs will bring his painstaking research to a wider readership, drawn by the combination of moving reports, simple style and deep insight.

Palestine: The Legitimacy of Hope, gives us Professor Falk's coherent thoughts about how he has seen Palestinians evolve in tactics and aspirations as door after door closed to them, and they understood that neither international law or diplomacy, or the United Nations, or the Arab world, or their own military capacity, was going to bring them relief from the Occupation. "Legitimacy struggle" is Falk's phrase to describe today's "Palestinian grand strategy of resistance and liberation"—non-violent and based on morality as well as international law and international human rights standards. The author's own courage, affinities with those suffering injustice, and his unflinching moral standards shine through every chapter and make this a book that inspires as well as informs.

—**VICTORIA BRITTAIN**
Author, *Shadow Live*   *)r*

GH00566860

Professor Falk's mandate as the UN Human Rights Council special rapporteur on Occupied Palestine has given him a front row seat in observing the tragic reality of the lives of the Palestinian people over recent years. This book comprising blogs that he issued over this period provides important and timely commentary into the multiple facets of the situation, as they arose. His often unconventional thoughts are expressed in a frank and fearless, frequently controversial manner. But what shines through is his belief in the 'legitimacy struggle' of the Palestinians and in the importance of non-traditional ways of seeking their objectives, notably in the actions from below, those of ordinary people. It is an important read for those who believe in the solidarity of global civil society and their wielding of soft power as instruments for social change.

—CHRISTINE CHINKIN
Member, UN Fact Finding Mission
on the Gaza Conflict, 2009

Richard Falk writes that he has sought to be a "truthful observer." He has succeeded admirably, and gone well beyond. The essays collected here are perceptive and informative, rich in insight and understanding, inspired by just sympathy for the oppressed and their legitimate struggles, above all by the determination of Palestinians to resist the dismal fate projected for them by criminal Israeli policies conducted with unremitting US support. It is an impressive record of Falk's remarkable contributions during the difficult and fateful years of his dedicated and courageous service as UN Special Rapporteur for Palestine.

—NOAM CHOMSKY
Political theorist, media critic,
and linguistics scholar

This volume, like Richard Falk himself, is equal parts brilliance and compassion. What began as blog posts blends into a distillation of a lifetime of thinking about and working on Palestine and Israel. This book has no peer.

—LISA HAJJAR
Chair, Law and Society Program,
University of California–Santa Barbara

This is the voice of reasoned outrage. The blogosphere and legal scholarship are combined in an extraordinarily moving, detailed, and perceptive account of what Richard Falk calls the 'legitimacy struggle' of the Palestinian people. Anyone who cares about human solidarity and wants to understand what is happening now in Gaza must read this book.

—**MARY KALDOR**
Professor of Global Governance,
London School of Economics

This book reflects an extraordinary lifetime of scholarship, political engagement, and intellectual brilliance. Richard Falk's blend of universal principle, forensic critique of power, and sensitive appreciation of the challenges faced by Palestinians makes him uniquely placed to advance a liberation strategy for Palestine. He does so here with his typical grace, intelligence and commitment. Always at the forefront of struggles for justice from Vietnam to Palestine, *Palestine, the Legitimacy of Hope* sets out a radical solution that is courageous, gentle, and full of humanity.

—**KARMA NABULSI**
University lecturer in politics and
international relations, Oxford University

Professor Falk has an unbroken record of speaking forthrightly about Justice and in particular on Palestine. Both as a scholar and practitioner he has gathered an impressive understanding and detailed knowledge of the mechanisms of control and the exercise of power by the strong against the weak. He has used his high academic standing to seek justice and insist on the exercise of rights. He provides an important model for the engaged academic who is willing to suffer the harsh consequences of taking an unpopular position in his defense of principles he believes in.

In a world permeated and controlled by cynical powers pitting the strong against the weak, Falk's erudition and voice is an important one that gives hope by paving the way for a new kind of struggle for Justice.

—**RAJA SHEHADEH**
Founder, Al-Haq
Author, *Occupation Diaries*

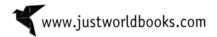

PALESTINE
THE LEGITIMACY
OF HOPE

Other works by Richard Falk

Law, War, and Morality in the Contemporary World (1963)

Legal Order in a Violent World (1968)

This Endangered Planet: Proposals for Human Survival (1971)

A Study of Future Worlds (1975)

Revolutionaries and Functionaries: The Dual Face of Terrorism (1988)

On Humane Governance: Toward a New Global Politics (1995)

Predatory Globalization: A Critique (2000)

Human Rights Horizons (2001)

Religion and Humane Global Governance (2002)

The Great Terror War (2003)

The Declining World Order: America's Neoimperial World Order (2004)

The Costs of War: International Law, the UN, and World Order after Iraq (2004)

Achieving Human Rights (2009)

(Re)imagining Humane Global Governance (2014)

PALESTINE
THE LEGITIMACY OF HOPE

RICHARD FALK

JUST WORLD
BOOKS

CHARLOTTESVILLE, VIRGINIA

Just World Books is an imprint of Just World Publishing, LLC.

Cover design by CSTUDIODESIGN for Just World Publishing, LLC.
Cartography and typesetting by Jane Sickon for Just World Publishing, LLC.

Publisher's Cataloging-in-Publication
(Provided by Quality Books, Inc.)

Falk, Richard A.
    Palestine : the legitimacy of hope / by Richard Falk.
    pages cm
    Includes bibliographical references.
    LCCN 2014944991
    ISBN (pb.) 978-1-935982-42-5
    ISBN (hc.) 978-1-935982-48-7
    ISBN (e.) 978-1-935982-47-0

    1. Arab-Israeli conflict--1993---Peace. 2. Human rights advocacy. 3. Falk, Richard A.--Blogs.
    I. Title.

DS119.76.F35 2014   956.9405'4
                                    QBI14-600130

For Zeynep & Andre

who got me this far—with love

Contents

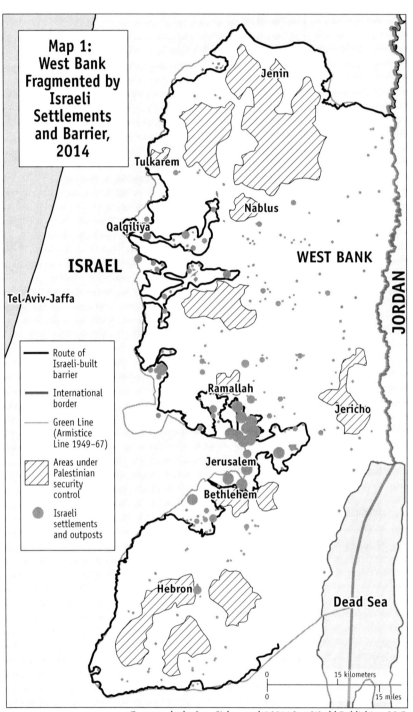

Map 1:
West Bank
Fragmented by
Israeli
Settlements
and Barrier,
2014

Jenin

Tulkarem

Nablus

Qalqiliya

ISRAEL

WEST BANK

Tel-Aviv-Jaffa

JORDAN

Route of
Israeli-built
barrier

International
border

Green Line
(Armistice
Line 1949–67)

Areas under
Palestinian
security
control

Israeli
settlements
and outposts

Ramallah

Jericho

Jerusalem

Bethlehem

Hebron

Dead Sea

0   15 kilometers

0   15 miles

Cartography by Jane Sickon and ©2014 Just World Publishing, LLC.

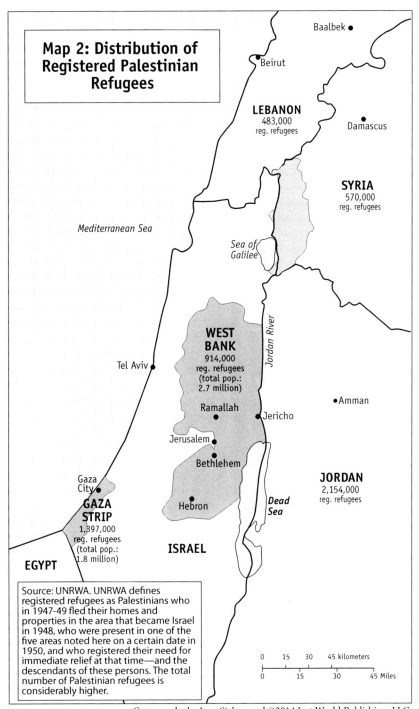

Map 2: Distribution of Registered Palestinian Refugees

Baalbek ●

● Beirut

LEBANON
483,000
reg. refugees

● Damascus

SYRIA
570,000
reg. refugees

Mediterranean Sea

Sea of Galilee

Jordan River

WEST BANK
914,000
reg. refugees
(total pop.:
2.7 million)

Tel Aviv ●

Ramallah ●

● Jericho

● Amman

Jerusalem ●

Bethlehem ●

JORDAN
2,154,000
reg. refugees

Gaza City ●

GAZA STRIP
1,397,000
reg. refugees
(total pop.:
1.8 million)

Hebron ●

Dead Sea

ISRAEL

EGYPT

Source: UNRWA. UNRWA defines registered refugees as Palestinians who in 1947-49 fled their homes and properties in the area that became Israel in 1948, who were present in one of the five areas noted here on a certain date in 1950, and who registered their need for immediate relief at that time—and the descendants of these persons. The total number of Palestinian refugees is considerably higher.

| 0 | 15 | 30 | 45 kilometers |
| 0 | 15 | 30 | 45 Miles |

Cartography by Jane Sickon and ©2014 Just World Publishing, LLC.

Introduction

From March 2008 through March 2014, I acted as Special Rapporteur on Occupied Palestine for the UN Human Rights Council. It made me acutely sensitive to the ordeal that has confronted the Palestinian people in their struggle for human rights. It also brought me into contact with an extraordinary array of Palestinians, who inspired me by their spirited embrace of life despite the extraordinary obstacles they face on a daily basis. This combination of engagement and admiration is what sustained my work relating to the Palestinian national movement in the face of a determined campaign of defamation and dirty tricks, which unfortunately comes with this territory.

Becoming convinced that mainstream media and publishers rely on a rigid ideological filter to avoid lending credibility to progressive views, I took refuge in the blogosphere, which has no censors and is an open forum for expressing views. This turned out to be especially valuable as what was being assessed went generally against the grain of conventional wisdom. In my experience, especially here in the United States, no discussion is more distorted by the constraints of political correctness and ideological bias than that on Israel and Palestine and their apportionment of responsibility for the costly political, legal, and moral failure, now stretching over the course of more than six and a half decades, to find a solution that would enable Israelis and Palestinians to live securely and justly in historic Palestine.

In my UN role and as a commentator on the realities I perceive in relation to the question of legal and moral rights that I have devoted my adult life to studying, my efforts are premised upon being a truthful observer and a progressive interpreter. This means, in relation to Israeli policies and practices, allowing inquiry to enter zones declared "off limits" by the many avid defenders of what is called "brand Israel," including many of the most prominent and influential American liberals. It means exposing the cruelty of the occupation, the lawlessness of the settlements and the violence of the settlers, the illegality of the separation wall, the brutality of arrest and detention procedures, the multifaceted humiliation of the Palestinian populace, the abuse of children, the reliance on excessive and vindictive force, and the discriminatory administration of laws. Beyond these wrongs associated with the occupation is an inherently dangerous situation, especially in Gaza, where there are risks of acute poverty and disease, unsafe and scarce water, and severe threats to food security and overall economic viability.

Being a truthful observer also means taking a close look at Palestinian governmental behavior in response, including the compliant international postures adopted often, although not always, by the formal leadership of the Palestinian Authority. It means also taking account of the role and political evolution of Hamas, especially its recent attitudes toward long-term coexistence with Israel and its support for nonviolent resistance—an evolution it has undergone without renouncing options of retaliation and without taking responsibility for the actions of nonaffiliated but allied political actors, such as Islamic Jihad. I believe that the time has long passed for Hamas to be treated as a political actor and no longer stigmatized as a "terrorist organization." To be sure, firing rockets indiscriminately, which Hamas has done on occasion and its militia allies have reportedly done more frequently, is a serious violation of the laws of war and of human rights and should be condemned as such.[1] Yet the use of military means by Hamas and its allies should also be viewed in the context of the internationally supported right of peoples to use all necessary means to resist foreign military occupation, as well as that of the unlawful blockade, collective punishment, and regime of state terror that Israel has imposed upon the people of Gaza for many years. Israel has launched frequent violent provocations against both Gaza and the West Bank, ranging from targeted assassinations and disrupted truce arrangements to the massive air, sea, and land attacks against Gaza in 2006, 2008–9, and 2012.

This book draws on material taken from my blog, "Global Justice in the 21st Century." The book is organized around seven thematic clusters of posts; the entries selected for this book were written between 2010 and 2013 and have not been substantively altered. The shift in Palestinian tactics

---

1. Western readers should understand, however, that when rockets are fired from Gaza, many of them are targeted against, and fall within, Israeli military bases, though Israel's military censorship forbids any reporting of these impacts, thereby contributing to a distorted image of the violent interactions between Israel and Gaza.

and aspirations that has taken shape in this period is notable. Palestinians have long understood that their rights under international law, despite being overwhelmingly confirmed by formal action at the United Nations, are not self-implementing. They have also come to appreciate that they will not be liberated or even protected by their Arab neighbors and will have to depend upon their own self-empowerment. This shift is also reinforced by disillusionment with both Palestinian armed resistance and conventional international diplomacy, most recently dramatized by the collapse of direct negotiations on April 29, 2014, after nine months of fruitless and frantic efforts orchestrated from Washington. Such disillusionment also coincides with the spreading awareness that the so-called "two-state consensus" has reached a dead end.

I have tried to give coherence to this recent shift in Palestinian tactics by using the term "legitimacy war" in a thread that runs through much of the book. Friends and critics have suggested to me that any reliance on the terminology of "war" as a positive element in Palestinian strategy is misleading and regressive. I am persuaded by such suggestions and will from now on refer to this turn in the Palestinian grand strategy of resistance and liberation as a "legitimacy struggle." Legitimacy remains at the core, as this most promising phase of Palestinian self-empowerment rests on nonviolent forms of mobilization and on taking control of the commanding heights of international law and morality, as well as international human rights standards. This embrace of legitimacy struggle as the path to realizing the Palestinian right of self-determination was creatively prefigured by the intifada of 1987, which shook the foundations of the Israeli occupation of the West Bank. Palestinians showed the world the explosive potential of massive nonviolent resistance. It was an unexpected manifestation of leading from below that has had the effect of transforming the leadership of the Palestinian national movement, although not as yet its formal governmental face, presented to the world by way of the Ramallah-based Palestinian Authority.

The essence of this legitimacy struggle is its reliance on soft-power initiatives that draw on the capacity of people to serve as the principal agents of historical change. This reliance goes against a still-prevailing "political realism" that regards the experience of historical change as fundamentally a hard-power narrative, given formal contours by governmental diplomacy that ratifies battlefield results. A few months ago at a private dinner attended by a dozen or so UN ambassadors, I had an exchange with the French ambassador, who took the occasion to say, "Forget about the Palestinian struggle. Israel has won. The Palestinians have been defeated. I may not like this result, but to think otherwise is to dream idly." Such a view was the perfect embodiment of a cynical view of history that ignores the role of people and overlooks the striking reality that most of the outcomes of the political struggles of the last seventy-five years have been won by the side with inferior military capabilities.

This generalization includes the outcomes of the anticolonial struggles of the 1960s and 1970s, the indigenous resistance against the huge high-tech American military intervention in Vietnam, the 1980s movements challenging Soviet rule in Eastern Europe, and the global campaign against apartheid in South Africa. Analyzed from the perspective of legitimacy struggle, the pattern is clear. Such evidence suggests that the geopolitical optic on which "political realists" rely has lost its claim to comprehend the real. Such a conclusion should not be understood as being deterministic. It is by no means assured that the side that prevails in a legitimacy struggle will also prevail politically. For instance, the experience of the Tibetan people goes against the trend, as do several other struggles of "peoples" entrapped in multiethnic sovereign states.

It is from this perspective of legitimacy struggle that I comprehend this latest phase in the Palestinian national movement. The outcome of this struggle cannot be foreseen. Although the winners of legitimacy struggles have eventually prevailed in many political encounters since 1945, this cannot be taken for granted in any specific case. Sometimes legitimacy struggles succeed and yet an oppressive set of circumstances in defiance of law and morality persists, as a reflection of the capacity of the territorial state to sustain illegitimate forms of governance or to be assisted in so doing by external geopolitical forces. This is arguably the case in relation to Tibet, Kashmir, Chechnya, and many other situations where existing state structures, often with assistance from geopolitical forces, entrap captive nations that occupy a distinct geographic region and have persuasive grounds for claiming a right of self-determination. Whether the Palestinian legitimacy struggle can alter the situation on the ground sufficiently to garner respect for Palestinian rights cannot be known at present.

What is known is that the Palestinian people, living under occupation and worldwide, are being reinforced by a growing global solidarity movement that is part of a legitimacy struggle that is building momentum and enjoying increasing success. Its main arena at present involves various fights around the issue of boycott and divestment and edges closer to formal, government-backed endorsement of sanctions: more commonly known as the boycott, divestment, sanctions or BDS movement. The Israeli pushback against these developments contends that BDS backers are "anti-Semitic" and intent on destroying the state of Israel. Such political slander is diversionary. The Palestinian legitimacy struggle is inclusive and nonviolent. It affirms rights under international law for both Israelis and Palestinians on the basis of equality and respect for other ethnicities. Its target is not the sovereign state of Israel, but Israeli policies and practices.

What follows in the selections that comprise this volume is a running commentary on various facets of the overall situation, both criticism of the "old thinking" that looks to traditional diplomacy or armed struggle as the sole path to a solution and explorations of the "new thinking" that rests on nonterritorial militant nonviolence as a liberation strategy.

Richard Falk
Santa Barbara
May 28, 2014

1

Resolving the Conflict

The mainstream view that the road to peace depends on intergovernmental negotiations in which the United States government serves as the hegemonic intermediary has held firm ever since the Camp David negotiations between Israel and Egypt in 1978, during the Carter presidency. For Israel and Palestine such a process has dominated the diplomacy of the conflict for decades, although the UN Security Council initially tried to set forth a conception of peace based essentially on the 1967 borders and on a fair resolution of the refugee issue in the unanimously adopted Security Council Resolution 242.

The Oslo framework agreement was reached in 1993 and sanctified on the White House lawn by a handshake between Yitzhak Rabin and Yasser Arafat, with a smiling Bill Clinton standing between the two leaders. What has been evident all along has been the accentuation of the hard-power disparity by a "peace process" heavily slanted in favor of Israel, dramatized by the Palestinian willingness to indulge the fantasy that the United States can be trusted to act as an "honest broker." This fantasy was revived by U.S. secretary of state John Kerry, who exerted muscular diplomatic pressure on two reluctant political actors, the government of Israel and the Palestinian Authority, in 2013-14 to make one last effort to resolve the conflict by negotiations carried on under the watchful eye of the U.S. government.

The chronologically arranged posts in this chapter consider, at various times during the last three years, this flawed approach to reaching a sustainable and just peace for both peoples based upon the rights, security goals, and sovereign equality of the negotiating political actors. Several offer skeptical commentaries on this unpromising peace process.

Attention is also given here to various Palestinian efforts to alter the diplomatic context, particularly by way of a UN acknowledgement of Palestinian statehood. "The Palestinian Statehood Bid" highlights the interaction between the efforts of the Palestinian Authority to gain voice and presence in the world, and the combined efforts of Israel and the United States at the UN to make sure that the Palestinians remain a mute and humiliated, occupied, and dispersed people until the outcome of diplomatic negotiations certifies them as "legitimate." But suppose, as has been evident for many years, that Israel has no interest in reaching such a finish line and is willing either to extend the status quo indefinitely or offer the Palestinians a paltry remnant of historic Palestine on a take-it-or-leave-it basis?

Three posts in this chapter discuss alternatives to this Camp David–Oslo approach from various angles, with the objective of nurturing what I would call a "genuine peace process." "UNESCO Membership and Palestinian Self-Determination" introduces the motif of hope that pervades this gathering of commentaries on the Palestinian struggle. It sets forth two essential arguments: that at the core of the struggle are contesting visions of what is morally right and legally correct, what I call "legitimacy war" (or, for reasons explained in the Introduction, "legitimacy struggle"), and that the side that prevails in the legitimacy struggle has generally—although not always—controlled the political outcome of the conflict in the decades since the end of World War II.

"Khaled Mashaal and Prospects for a Sustainable Israel–Palestine Peace" cautiously supports the controversial view that Hamas has come to share this outlook: not because of a conversion to nonviolence, but for tactical reasons of resolving the conflict. This interpretation of Hamas's evolving approach to resistance and peace ventures the opinion that a credible Israeli commitment to reaching a solution via diplomacy would be disclosed by Tel Aviv's willingness to treat Hamas as a political actor rather than adhering to the exclusionary insistence that Hamas is a "terrorist organization." Israel's prime minister, Benjamin Netanyahu, continues to insist that the Palestinian Authority must choose between what he calls "unity" (as between itself and Hamas) and "peace" (as between itself and Israel).

"The Palestine National Movement Advances" articulates and advocates this strategy of legitimacy struggle as the most desirable path for Palestinian resistance and solidarity to follow at this time. This post considers why the present approach is deficient and what kinds of changes would have to take place to give statecraft the prospect of playing a constructive role. The essence of the argument is that the political climate in Israel, and to some degree the United States, would have to change sufficiently to enable fairness between Israelis and Palestinians. This seems almost certain to be an unrealizable goal without a Palestinian solidarity movement, conjoined with Palestinian resistance activities, exerting much greater pressure on

Israel. The boycott, divestment, and sanctions (BDS) campaign has been growing in this period and epitomizes the kind of militant nonviolence that has the best chance of creating a diplomatic atmosphere conducive to peace with justice and to equal security and sovereignty for both sides.

On the Peace Process
November 21, 2010[1]

The mainstream discourse is preoccupied with whether a deal can be struck, and worries not at all about such a deal's fairness, or about the process that features a partisan mediator, or about Palestinian representation (which is neither inclusive nor legitimate). It speculates that maybe it will be possible to strike a bargain because Israel regards Iran as an existential threat and because the Palestinian Authority is weak and badly wishes to solidify its claims to lead some kind of Palestinian entity. The U.S. government is most eager of all, because President Obama needs some kind of foreign policy success and it would be a step toward reducing anti-Americanism in the region.

At the moment, Palestinian Authority president Mahmoud Abbas insists that unless the settlement freeze for the ninety-day period is extended to East Jerusalem, there will be no resumption of negotiations. Netanyahu is beset by settler militancy but has been gifted such a bribe by the United States that it is hard to imagine that he will accept some sort of ambiguous freeze arrangement. It still seems likely that U.S.–Israeli leverage will revive a negotiating process beset with obstacles from a Palestinian perspective.

An almost-condition of the negotiations is that whatever is agreed upon is final so far as any future Palestinian demands are concerned. This reinforces the importance of assessing the adequacy of the process and of Palestinian representation. It also shows how impossible it seems that anything will emerge that can be reconciled with even a minimal construction of Palestinian rights or expectations.

There are three severe shortcomings of the peace process as now constituted: (1) the excessive influence of the United States, due to its dual role as unconditional ally of Israel and self-appointed "honest broker" for the negotiations; (2) exclusion of any assessment of contested issues by

---

1. Originally published as "Comments on the Peace Process," http://richardfalk.
   wordpress.com/2010/11/21/comments-on-the-peace-process-xi212010.

reference to international law, including borders, Jerusalem, settlements, water, refugees—on each of these issues the Palestinian claims accord with international law while the Israeli position does not, and thus excluding international law guidelines from the peace process profoundly impairs prospects for achieving Palestinian self-determination by way of inter-governmental negotiations; and (3) exclusion of any consideration of the historical context that, if considered, would imprint a colonial character on the Zionist project from at least the time of its endorsement in the London Balfour Declaration of 1917 and which, over time, has turned the Israeli governing process into one that combines ethnic cleansing, the crime of apartheid, and settler colonialism.

A further observation: the likely presentation of a land swap in exchange for the incorporation of settlement blocs into Israel is both deceptive and sets a trap with regard to Palestinians' search for self-determination: what Israel seems prepared to offer is either desert wasteland in the Negev, Palestinian communities situated in the Galilee region of Israel, or some combination. The latter would really achieve two Israeli goals in exchange for essentially nothing: it would somewhat legitimate Israeli sovereign claims with respect to the settlement blocs and, at the same time, contribute to the ethnic cleansing of Palestinians currently resident behind the green line.

The Palestinian Legitimacy Struggle versus "Lawfare"
December 15, 2010[2]

There has long been advocacy of the idea that judges in national courts could help strengthen the implementation of global norms by extending the reach of national law, especially for serious crimes that cannot be otherwise prosecuted. The authority to use national courts against piracy on the high seas was widely endorsed and constitutes the jurisprudential basis for what has come to be known as "universal jurisdiction": that is, regardless of where a crime was committed or the national identity of the alleged perpetrator or victim, a national court has the authority to attach its law.

This reliance on universal jurisdiction received a strong shot in the arm as a result of the war-crimes trials at the end of World War II against

---

2. Originally published at http://richardfalk.wordpress.com/2010/12/17/
the-palestinian-legitimacy-war-versus-lawfare/.

surviving German and Japanese political and military leaders, a legal framework institutionalized internationally in 2002 as a result of the establishment of the International Criminal Court. The underlying rationale is that aggressive war, crimes against humanity, and severe violations of the law of war and international humanitarian law are crimes against the whole of humanity, not just the victim state or people. Although the Nuremberg judgment was flawed, "victors' justice," it generated global norms in the form of the Nuremberg Principles that are considered by international law consensus to be universally binding.

These ideas underlie the recent prosecution of geopolitical pariahs such as Saddam Hussein, Slobodan Milošević, and several African tyrannical figures. But when it comes to the lead political actors, as understood by the U.S.-led hegemonic hierarchy, the leadership of the rest of the world enjoys impunity, in effect, an exemption from accountability to international criminal law. It is a prime instance of the double standards that pervade the current world order, perhaps most prominently illustrated in relation to the veto power given permanent members of the UN Security Council or the nonproliferation regime governing nuclear weaponry.

Double standards sever any link between law, as administered by the state system on a world level, and pretensions of global justice. The challenge for those seeking global justice based on international law that treats equals equally is to overcome, in every substantive setting, double standards and impunity. The world of sovereign states and the United Nations have not been able to mount such a challenge. Into this vacuum has moved a surging, global civil society movement that got its start in the global fight against colonialism, especially the Vietnam War, and moved forward dramatically as a result of the South African anti-apartheid campaign. This movement has relied upon various instruments, including BDS solidarity movements, informally constituted citizens' war-crimes tribunals (starting with the Russell Tribunal during the Vietnam War, and extended by the Permanent Peoples' Tribunal in Rome and, in 2005, by the Iraq War Tribunal, which held twenty sessions around the world, culminating in a final session in Istanbul), and civil disobedience in various forms, especially refusals to serve in military operations that violate international law.

A coalition of civil society actors created the political climate that somewhat surprisingly allowed the International Criminal Court to come into being in 2002, although unsurprisingly without the participation of the United States, Israel, or most of the senior members of the geopolitical first echelon. It is against this background that two contradictory developments are to be found: the waging of an all-out legitimacy war against Israel on behalf of the Palestinian struggle for a just peace and a backlash campaign against what is called "lawfare" by Israeli hardliners.[3]

A legitimacy-war strategy seeks popular mobilization on the basis of nonviolent coercion to achieve political goals, relying on the relevance of international law and the accountability of those who act on behalf of states in the commission of crimes of state. The Goldstone Report illustrates this interface between a legitimacy war and lawfare, reinforcing Palestinian contentions of victimization as a result of Israel's use of force, as in the notorious Operation Cast Lead (December 27, 2008–January 18, 2009), and driving Israel's top leaders to venomous fury in their effort to discredit the distinguished jurist Richard Goldstone, who headed the UN mission responsible for the report, and the findings he so convincingly reached.[4] With Israeli impunity under growing threat, special pressures have been placed on the United States to use its geopolitical muscle within the UN to maintain the mantle of impunity over the documented record of Israeli criminality and to make sure that the UN remains a selective sanctuary for such outrageous grants of impunity.

These issues of criminal accountability are on the front lines of the legitimacy war and provide the foundation for efforts throughout the world in relation to the growing BDS campaign. The lawfare counterattack at one level acknowledges the strength of civil society efforts, but it is also cynically and polemically undertaken to discredit reliance on international law by those who are victimized by abusive and oppressive uses of military and police power. The Palestinians have been victimized in these respects for more than sixty-two years, and their efforts to end this intolerable set of realities through an innovative reliance on nonviolent resistance and self-defense deserves the support of persons of conscience throughout the world. Whether this reliance on a legitimacy war can finally achieve justice for the Palestinian people and peace for both peoples only the future can tell, but there is no doubt that this struggle is the best contemporary instance of a "just war."

3. In *The Battle for Justice in Palestine* (Chicago: Haymarket Books, 2014), Ali Abunimah sums this up as "the use of courts or the legal system in an attempt to criminalize or repress legitimate advocacy" (166).

4. The full text of the Goldstone Report is available at the website of the UN Office of the High Commissioner for Human Rights: http://www2.ohchr.org/english/bodies/hrcouncil/docs/12session/A-HRC-12-48.pdf.

The Palestinian Statehood Bid

September 20, 2011[5]

Even if nothing further were to happen, the proposed Palestinian initiative, combined with the furious negative response in Tel Aviv and Washington, has given much-needed visibility to the ongoing daily ordeal of the Palestinian people, whether living under the rigors of occupation, consigned for decades to miserable refugee camps, or existing in the stressful limbo of exile. The only genuine challenge facing the world community of states and the UN is how to end this ordeal, which has lasted now for an incredible period of sixty-three years, in a manner that produces a just and sustainable peace. It is the entanglement of geopolitics with this unmet challenge that signifies the moral, legal, and political inadequacy of the contemporary world order. The Israel–Palestine conflict, along with the continued presence of nuclear weaponry and the persistence of world poverty, exhibits the failure of international law and morality, as well as of common sense and enlightened realism, to guide the behavior of leading sovereign states. In the face of this failure, the frustrations and extraordinary suffering experienced by the Palestinian people, the intolerable injustice of their situation, has come to dominate the moral and political imagination of the world. No issue has generated this level of solidarity among the peoples of the world since the anti-apartheid campaign toppled the racist regime in South Africa more than twenty years ago.

To the surprise of many and the comprehension of few, it is not only Israel that opposes this initiative of the Palestinian Authority. A crucial part of the background is the division among Palestinians as to the wisdom and effects of the statehood initiative at the UN. Palestinian critics consider it diversionary and divisive, possibly shrinking the dispute to territorial issues, placing approximately seven million Palestinian refugees and exile communities in permanent limbo, and allowing Israel to treat the outcome of this UN shadow play as the end game in their long effort to transform what was to be a temporary occupation of East Jerusalem and the West

---

5. Originally published as "Statehood versus 'Facts on the Ground,'" Al Jazeera English, September 20, 2011, http://www.aljazeera.com/indepth/opinion/2011/09/201191992257436181.html.

Bank into a condition of permanent, if de facto, annexation.[6] The question that underlies this debate is whether the diplomatic claim of statehood in this form *legitimately* represents the Palestinian people in their several dimensions or merely fulfills, at a price, the ambitions of the Palestinian Authority. In the background is the organizational complexity of the Palestinian community, with the future of the Palestinian Liberation Organization (PLO) drawn into question. Whereas the councils of the PLO includes representatives of the Palestinian diaspora, the Palestinian Authority is a political formation intended to address the circumstances of occupation in the post-Oslo period and has as its primary goal promoting the withdrawal of Israeli occupying forces. To carry out this mission it has been seeking, with some success (achieving favorable progress reports from the World Bank and International Monetary Fund), to demonstrate that it possesses the institutional capabilities needed for stable governance, including maintaining security and preventing anti-Israeli activism. How this sense of political priorities relates to the claims of refugees confined in camps in neighboring Arab countries, as well as the several million Palestinians living around the world, seems to be the deepest issue dividing the Palestinian people considered as a whole. A closely related concern, but one that is more widely appreciated, is Hamas's refusal to lend support to this initiative, despite the fanfare surrounding the unity agreement brokered by Egypt in early June 2011.

What Palestinian opponents of the statehood bid most fear is that the issue of representation will be wrongly resolved from their perspective. This issue of representation lies at the political core of the internal Palestinian struggle to achieve their rights under international law and, above all, to define the Palestinian "self" that is entitled to claim a right of self-determination.

There are worries among Palestinians living outside of the occupied territories that the statehood bid, whatever its outcome, will have an adverse spillover effect on the still-unresolved representation issue. In addressing this concern, the nonparticipation of Hamas in this kind of Palestinian diplomacy cannot be ignored, nor can it be facilely dismissed due to Hamas's alleged refusal to accept even an Israel that lives within its 1967

---

6. From the perspective of international law, Gaza remains occupied (despite the Israeli "disengagement" in 2005) because Israel continues to exert control over exit and entry, as well as airspace and access from the sea. It is treated separately politically because Israel has no territorial ambitions in relation to Gaza and would appear to welcome either an autonomous Gaza or its absorption into Egypt.

borders. It should be appreciated, without necessarily being accepted as reliable, that Hamas leaders have periodically indicated a willingness to sign onto a long-term coexistence agreement of up to fifty years if Israel withdraws completely to the green line that was treated as Israel's border until the 1967 War. Such an agreement is highly unlikely to overcome genuine Israeli anxieties or correspond to Israeli perceptions of Hamas and its intentions; as well, its implementation would certainly thwart Israel's territorial ambitions by entailing dismantling the settlements. At the same time the realization that what has been tried has not worked, nor is it likely to do any better in the future, suggests that this admittedly imperfect alternative to negotiations in the search for a sustainable peace should not be unconditionally rejected.

Against such a background, how can we explain the furious Israeli and U.S. opposition to this Palestinian initiative? Should not Israel and the United States welcome, even encourage, this as a way of reducing the conflict to its land-for-peace dimensions, maybe getting rid of the right-of-return issue once and for all? Joseph Massad has perceptively analyzed the statehood bid as if it presents Israel with a win-win situation. Even so, the intensive U.S. diplomacy leading up to casting an alienating veto or transparently using its geopolitical muscle to secure a blocking majority in the Security Council is easy to understand. On any question that comes before the UN in which Israeli policy is seriously questioned or its behavior is subject to criticism, the United States leaps to Israel's defense regardless of the merits, whenever necessary using its veto power in the Security Council to shield Israel. This has been true during the Obama presidency on UN efforts to censure unlawful settlement expansion, to carry forward the accountability recommendations of the Goldstone Report, and to allow civil society to break the unlawful blockade that has entrapped the people of Gaza for more than four years. Casting a veto here or working behind the scenes to cobble a majority, as the respected international law expert Balakrishnan Rajagopal has noted in a recent column in the *Huffington Post*, is both politically imprudent and unmindful of the responsibility of a member of the United Nations to uphold the legal rights of every political community to enjoy the privileges of statehood if it qualifies as a state.[7] It is a tribute to the UN that the most important of these privileges is now access to the United Nations system with the status of a sovereign state. It should be observed that another highly regarded international jurist, John Quigley, in a scholarly book published by Cambridge University Press,

---

7. Balakrishnan Rajagopal, "The Palestine UN Vote: Is There a Duty to Admit?" *Huffington Post*, September 16, 2011, www.huffingtonpost.com/balakrishnan-rajagopal/the-palestine-un-vote-is-_b_964918.html.

argued that Palestine was already a state from the perspective of international law and had been so recognized by well over a hundred governments of other states.[8]

This diplomatic crusade to block Palestinian statehood also further undermines confidence in U.S. claims to serve as a world leader promoting global public goods. This primacy of hard-power geopolitics will also raise serious questions about the capacity of the UN to serve as a vehicle for realizing global justice and upholding the basic rights of peoples. Need we be reminded once again that the inspiring opening words of the UN Charter, "we the peoples," has always given way to "we the governments"—and (more starkly since the end of the Cold War, as this controversy sadly highlights) to "we the hegemon"?

We should by now understand that the U.S. government does whatever Israel wants it to do, but why does Israel seem to mind so much if the Palestinian initiative were to succeed? After all, even the Netanyahu leadership claims it supports Palestinian statehood and the two-state solution. And if the Palestinian critics of the Palestinian Authority are even partially correct, would not the further territorialization of the conflict and its narrowing of the negotiating agenda serve Israeli interests? This interpretation seems reinforced by Mahmoud Abbas's reassurances that the Palestinian Authority security forces will prevent any Palestinian violence targeting Israelis, that the path to direct negotiations is more open than ever, and that this initiative in no way is meant to challenge the legitimacy of the Israeli state. Since the events of the Arab Spring, Israel has shown almost no capacity to act in support of its real interests in the region, as exemplified by its botched relations with Turkey and Egypt, and perhaps this response at the UN is just one more illustration. Such an explanation cannot be ruled out, but there are more sinister interpretations that seem more plausible given Israel's overall pattern of behavior. By insisting that only "direct negotiations" can produce statehood, Israel is providing itself with a gold-plated pretext for refusing to negotiate at all for years to come. Netanyahu almost comically suggested that the delay could last sixty years! And for what reason? Another line of explanation gives the settler leadership its own veto power; it has already vowed to carry out provocative "sovereignty marches" into the West Bank during the UN discussions.

In this conflict, time has never been static or neutral. Each extra day of occupation, refugee status, and involuntary exile in effect lengthens a prison sentence imposed on the entirety of the Palestinian people. This is bad enough, but in addition Israel has taken consistent advantage of the

---

8. John Quigley, *The Statehood of Palestine: International Law in the Middle East Conflict* (New York: Cambridge University Press, 2010).

passage of time to expand its unlawful settlements, alter the demographics of East Jerusalem in its favor, build a separation wall found to be a violation of international law by a vote of 14 to 1 in the World Court, and isolate Gaza from the rest of Palestine and the world. During the Oslo peace process, which gave rise to the mantra of "direct negotiations or nothing," Israel has more than doubled the settlement population and steadfastly refuses to impose even a temporary freeze on expansion in the West Bank during negotiations. It has never been willing even to consider a freeze on settlement construction in East Jerusalem. Israeli leaders talk openly, even boast, about "creating facts on the ground"; Hillary Clinton more discreetly refers to this as "subsequent developments," but it can be more realistically understood as the ratification of massive illegality.[9] Such a political posture exposes the lie beneath an Israeli claim of a commitment to "direct negotiations" as a path to peace. Direct negotiations for almost twenty years have brought the parties no closer to peace and arguably have as their main effect undermined the conditions for a sustainable two-state solution. What direct negotiations have done is to buy time for Israel's unacknowledged ambitions and serve to calm international criticisms of this prolonged and cruel occupation.

Unfortunately, however the diplomatic confrontation unfolds, little is likely to be resolved. The charade of direct negotiations remains on the table. Parties on all sides ignore the revelations of the Palestine Papers, published a few months ago by Al Jazeera English, that showed beyond reasonable doubt that even the supposedly more moderate Olmert government of Israel seemed totally disinterested in a resolution of the conflict, even in the face of repeated Palestinian Authority concessions on fundamental issues made in confidential backroom talks at the highest levels.[10] Add to this the mockery of fairness that arises from allowing the United States to play the role of intermediary, the "honest broker" in such negotiations. Imagine trying to settle a divorce by asking the elder brother of the wealthy husband to arbitrate a fight over assets with the penniless wife. How could such a framework ever hope to achieve peace that is just and sustainable? And what seems deeply flawed in theory has been shown to be even worse in practice. The parties are further from peace than ever. Palestinian rights and expectations have been continuously shrinking as time passes and the occupation serves to consolidate a permanent Israeli presence.

9. CNN Wire Staff, "Clinton and Netanyahu Talk Security and Peace," CNN, November 11, 2010, http://www.cnn.com/2010/WORLD/meast/11/11/israel.us.clinton.

10. The Palestine Papers, along with related news articles and context, can be found at http://www.aljazeera.com/palestinepapers.

In the end, these questions of tactics and principles bearing on the right of self-determination need to be resolved by the Palestinian people. Neither Israel nor the United States nor even the United Nations can displace this fundamental Palestinian responsibility for selecting a road that they believe will lead to peace with justice. But it is a display of gallows humor to expect most Palestinians to look with favor at the resumption of peace talks under the framework that has been used since Oslo was agreed upon in 1993. It has repeatedly demonstrated the futility of direct negotiations. Israel continues to refuse to make even the most minimal gestures of real commitment, such as suspending settlement expansion indefinitely and dropping its deal-breaking insistence on being confirmed as a "Jewish state," a claim that flies in the face of the presence in Israel of a Palestinian minority numbering more than 1.5 million. If Israel is to retain its claim to be a democratic state, it must not insist on such an exclusivist formal identity. There is no way to reconcile claims of ethnic or religious exclusivity with the legal, moral, and political promise of human rights that have become the main signifiers of legitimate government at this time in history.

UNESCO Membership and Palestinian Self-Determination
November 3, 2010[11]

It may not ease the daily pain of occupation and blockade, the endless anguish of refugee status and exile, or the continual humiliations of discrimination and second-class citizenship, but the admission of Palestine to membership in UNESCO is for so many reasons a step forward in the long march of the Palestinian people toward the dignity of sunlight! This notable event in Paris illuminates the path that leads to self-determination, but also brings into the open some of the most formidable obstacles that must be cleared if further progress is to be made.

The simple arithmetic of the UNESCO vote—107 in favor, 14 opposed, 52 abstentions, and 21 absent—fails to tell the story of the vote's one-sidedness. Totting up the for and against votes obscures the wicked arm-twisting, otherwise known as geopolitics, that induced such marginal political entities as Samoa, the Solomon Islands, Palau, and Vanuatu to

---

11. Originally published at http://richardfalk.wordpress.com/2011/11/03/ unesco-membership-and-palestinian-self-determination.

stand against the weight of global opinion and international morality by making a meaningless gesture of opposition to the Palestinian application for UNESCO membership. This is not meant as an insult to such small states, but is intended to lament their vulnerability to powerful American pressures hoping to distort the perception of world public opinion by making the issue seem more contested than it is.

Such a distortion makes a minor mockery of the prevailing pretension that governments are able to offer adequate representation to the peoples of the world. It also illustrates the degree to which formal political independence may obscure a condition of de facto dependence as well as making plain that voting patterns within the United Nations system should never be confused with aspirations to establish at some future time a functioning global democracy in substance as well as procedure. As an aside, geopolitical maneuvers consistently compromise the electoral process within the UN system, especially in the Security Council and, to a lesser extent, in the General Assembly. This actuality of the UN as a political actor demonstrates the urgency and desirability of establishing a global peoples' parliament that could at least provide a second voice whenever a UN policy debate touches on issues of human concern.

What may be the most impressive aspect of the UNESCO vote is that despite a vigorous U.S. diplomacy of threat and intimidation, the Palestinian application for membership easily carried the day. There was enough adherence to principle by enough states to provide the necessary two-thirds vote even in the face of this craven American diplomatic effort to please Israel, an effort bolstered by its threatening punitive action in the form of refusing further financial support for UNESCO, which amounts to some $60 million for the current year and, overall, 22 percent of the organization's annual budget of $643 million in 2010–11. Actually, withholding funds is a U.S. policy embedded in ambiguous legislation that derives from the early 1990s, and so for once a preposterously pro-Israel action cannot be blamed on the present Congress, although it seems obvious that Congress would have taken the same steps—or worse. The leaders of both major U.S. parties have made no secret of their desire to make the most of this new opportunity to draw fresh UN blood. Indeed, rabidly pro-Israel members of Congress are already showboating their readiness to do far more than the law requires so as to manifest the extreme character of devotion to Israel. This unseemly punishment of the UN (and the peoples of the world) for taking a principled stand expresses a more sinister attitude than merely the pique of being a poor loser. The U.S. defunding move, taken without even a few words of regret, amounts to a totally irresponsible willingness to damage the indispensable work of cultural and societal cooperation on international levels just to make the childish point that there is a high price to be paid whenever the wishes of Israel suffer a defeat, with the United States ready always to serve as the dutiful enforcement agent.

Governments of other states have an excellent opportunity to demonstrate their commitment to human well-being and greater independence in global policy arenas by quickly acting to restore confidence in the UN. One way to do this is to offset this unanticipated UNESCO budget deficit with a series of voluntary contributions to the UNESCO budget. What would deliver a most instructive message to Washington and Tel Aviv would be a funding campaign that generates more money than is being withheld. It seems a useful opportunity to show once and for all that such strong-arm fiscal tactics are no longer acceptable and often don't succeed in the postcolonial world. Such an outcome would also confirm that the geopolitical tectonic plates of world order have shifted in such a way as to give increasing prominence to such countries as China, India, Russia, Brazil, and South Africa, all of whom voted to admit Palestine to UNESCO. At least for the moment, in this limited setting, we might get a glimpse of a genuine "new world order"! The Security Council has proved unable and unwilling so far to change its two-tiered structure to accommodate these shifts, but those countries kept on the sidelines can reinvent world politics by becoming more active and autonomous players on the global stage. It is not necessary to wait any longer for France and Britain to read the tea leaves of their decline accurately enough to acknowledge that their role on the global stage has diminished. If these governments want an effective UN, it is past time for them to step aside and let the rising non-Western states run the show for a while, starting with giving up their claim to permanent seats on the Security Council. This is my passing fantasy. It is obvious that most states would rather see world order collapse than defuse a governance crisis by giving way.

Perhaps more enduring than the UNESCO vote is the reinforced image of the wildly inappropriate role given to the United States to act as intermediary and peacemaker in seeking to resolve the underlying conflict and ensure the realization of Palestinian rights that have been so cruelly denied for more than six decades. Observers as diverse as Michel Rocard, the former Socialist Party prime minister of France, and Mouin Rabbani, a widely respected Palestinian analyst of the conflict, share a sense that this discordant American campaign to thwart an elemental Palestinian quest for legal recognition and political participation demonstrates beyond all reasonable doubt—although such a reality should long have been apparent to even the most casual serious observer of the conflict—that the time has come to remove the United States from its presiding role with respect to resolving this conflict. It has always verged on the absurd to expect justice, or even fairness, to flow from a diplomatic framework in which the openly and extremely partisan ally of the dominant party puts itself forward as the "honest broker" in negotiations in a setting where the weaker side is subject to military rule, exile, and the continuous violation of its basic rights. To have given credibility to this tripartite charade for so many years is itself a commentary on the weakness of the Palestinian position and on Palestinians' desperate need to insist henceforth on a balanced international framework if negotiations are ever to have the slightest prospect of producing a sustainable and just peace. Regrettably, the PLO and the Palestinian Authority have yet to take this step, and if Israel were only to announce a temporary and partial freeze on settlement expansion, the Palestinians would gladly return to a negotiating process that has proved to be worse than useless.

Yet to find a new framework does not mean following Rocard's incredibly Orientalist prescription: "The Americans have lost their moral right to leadership in resolving the Israel-Palestine conflict. It is time for Europe to step into the fray."[12] As if Europe had recently demonstrated its capacity for rendering justice because it carried out the NATO intervention in Libya![13] As if the colonial heritage had been suddenly rebranded as a positive credential! As if the Americans ever had a "moral right" to resolve this conflict that was only now lost in the UNESCO voting chamber! It is not clear how a new diplomacy for the conflict that is finally responsive to the situation of the parties, the region, and the world should be structured, but it should reflect at the very least the new realities of an emergent multipolarity skewed toward the non-West. To be provocative for once, maybe Turkey, Brazil, Egypt, and India should now constitute themselves as a more legitimate quartet than that horribly discredited quartet composed of the United States, the EU, Russia, and the UN.

Returning to the UNESCO controversy, it is worth noting the words of denunciation used by Victoria Nuland, the designated State Department spokesperson. She described the vote as "regrettable, premature," contending that it "undermines our shared goal of a comprehensive, just and

---

12. Michel Rocard, "Palestine's Time," *Project Syndicate*, October 27, 2011, http://www.project-syndicate.org/commentary/palestine-s-time.

13. Following UN Security Council authorization of a no fly zone to protect the civilian population of Benghazi against a massacre threatened by Qaddafi's advancing forces, the UN in March 2011 embarked upon its regime-changing intervention of Libya.

lasting peace in the Middle East."[14] Even Orwell might be dazed by such an archly diversionary formulation. Why was the vote regrettable and premature and not the reverse: welcome and overdue? After all, to work for the preservation of religious sacred sites within the halls of UNESCO or to promote safe sanitation and water for the poorest countries is hardly subversive of global stability by any sane reckoning. After enduring occupation for more than forty-four years, it qualifies as comedic to insist that Palestine must not yet come in from the cold because such an entry would be "premature." And how can it be claimed that Palestine's participation within the UN system "undermines" the "shared goal" of regional peace in the Middle East? The only answer that makes any sense of the American position is that whatever Israel says is so is so, and the United States will act accordingly—that is, do whatever Israel wants it to do in the global arena. Such knee-jerk geopolitics is not only contrary to elementary considerations of law and justice, it is also monumentally irrational and self-defeating from the perspective of the national well-being of the United States and of a future peace in the region and beyond.

What in the end may be most troubling about this incident is the degree to which it confirms a growing impression that both the United States and Israel have lost the capacity to serve their own security interests and rationally promote the well-being of their own people. This is serious enough with respect to the damage done to their own societies by such maladroit behavior, but recognizing that these two military heavyweights, both of which possess arsenals of nuclear weaponry, are well on their way to becoming rogue states is frightening to contemplate. These are two of the few governments in the world that continue to rest their future security almost exclusively on an outmoded reliance on hard-power investments in military capabilities and accompanying aggressive ideas about the use of force as an instrument of foreign policy. The effects of this approach are potentially catastrophic for the region and the world. When Israel alienates Turkey, its only surviving friend in the Middle East, and then refuses to take the minimal steps to heal the wounds caused by its recklessly violent behavior, one has to conclude that the Israeli sense of reality has fallen on hard times! And when Israel pushes the United States to lose this much social capital on the global stage by standing up for its defiance of international law, as in relation to rejecting the recommendations of the Goldstone Report, refusing to censure the expansion of its unlawful settlements, or the collective punishment of Gaza, there is no longer much

---

14. Josh Levs, "U.S. Cuts UNESCO Funding after Palestinian Membership Vote," CNN, November 1, 2011, http://www.cnn.com/2011/10/31/world/meast/unesco-palestinian-membership.

doubt that Israeli foreign policy is driven by domestic extremism that then successfully solicits Washington for ill-advised support.

The situation in the United States is parallel. Many excuse, or at least explain, America's unconditionally irrational support for Israel as being produced by the fearsome leverage the American Israel Public Affairs Committee (AIPAC) exerts over electoral politics, as practiced by Congress and rationalized by conservative think tanks. But what this explanation says is that the U.S. government has also lost the capacity to pursue a sensible foreign policy that reflects its own national interests in a crucial region of the world, much less provide leadership based on a wider commitment to a stable and just Middle East. The Arab Spring offered the United States a second chance, so to speak, to overcome its long embrace of vicious autocratic rule in the region, but this opportunity is being senselessly squandered on the altar of subservience to the vindictive whims, expansionist visions, and paranoid fears of the Netanyahu–Lieberman governing coalition in Israel.

Welcoming Palestine to UNESCO is a day of celebration and vindication for the Palestinian people and a political victory for the PLO leadership, but it is also a day when all of us should reflect upon the wider Palestinian tragedy and struggle and seek further steps forward, including membership in such other components of the international system as the World Health Organization, the International Criminal Court, UNICEF, and the International Court of Justice. If the U.S. government were to continue to defund such institutions as Palestine gained recognition, its influence and reputation would take a nosedive. UNESCO has given a momentary respite to those who were completely disillusioned about what to expect from the UN or the system of states when it comes to Palestinian aspirations (remembering all those unimplemented resolutions in the General Assembly) and who instead put their hope and efforts into the initiatives of global civil society, especially the growing BDS campaign and efforts to break open the Gaza blockade by sending more ships carrying humanitarian goods. Now is not the time to shift attention away from such initiatives, but the UNESCO vote does suggest that there are many symbolic battlefields in the ongoing legitimacy war for Palestinian self-determination—and several of these lie within the network of institutions comprising the United Nations.

Khaled Mashaal and Prospects for a Sustainable Israel–Palestine Peace
December 12, 2012[15]

In the aftermath of Khaled Mashaal's emotional visit to Gaza in celebration of Hamas's twenty-fifth anniversary, commentary in Israel and the West has focused on characterizing his remarks at a rally as "defiant" and disclosing "the true face" of Hamas. Media coverage particularly emphasized his dramatic pledge to recover the whole of historic Palestine from the Mediterranean to Jordan, "inch by inch," no matter how long such a process might take. Mashaal also challenged the legitimacy of the Zionist project and justified Palestinian resistance in whatever form it might assume, although he disavowed the intention to attack civilians as such and denied any Hamas complicity in the November 21, 2012, bombing of a Jerusalem bus.

These remarks certainly raise concerns for moderate Israelis who continue to advocate a two-state solution in accordance with UN Security Council Resolution 242, but at the same time, it is important to listen to Hamas fully before reaching any firm conclusions. Mashaal spoke these words at a rally dedicated to reaffirming Gaza's fundamental struggle in the immediate aftermath of the recent eight-day Israeli attack (codenamed Pillar of Defense), as a leader who for the first time in forty-five years had openly dared to set foot in his occupied and oppressed homeland. Mashaal has lived in exile in several countries of the region since he was eleven years old, having been born in the Selwad neighborhood of Ramallah, then under Jordanian control. In 1997 Israel tried to murder him in a notorious incident in Jordan in which only the capture of the Mossad perpetrators induced Israel to supply a life-saving antidote for the poison they had sprayed into Mashaal's ear, in exchange for their release from Jordanian captivity. In Mashaal's imagery, this return to Gaza was his "third birth," the first being in 1956 when he was born, the second when he survived the Israeli assassination attempt, and the third when he was able to kiss the ground upon entering Gaza. These biographical details seem relevant for an assessment of his public remarks.

The context was also given a heightened reality by Hamas's and Gaza's success in enduring the latest Israeli military onslaught, which produced a ceasefire that contained some conditions favoring Gaza, including an

---

15. Originally published as "Hamas, Khaled Mashaal and Prospects for a Sustainable Israel/Palestinian Peace," http://richardfalk.wordpress.com/2012/12/12/hamas-khaled-mashaal-and-prospects-for-a-sustainable-israelpalestine-peace.

Israeli commitment to refrain from targeted assassinations in the future. This context was shaped as well by recent and more distant painful memories that were the main triggers of the upsurge of violence, especially the assassination of the Hamas military leader and diplomat Ahmed al-Jabari and the May 22, 2003, killing of the disabled spiritual founder of Hamas, Sheikh Ahmed Yassin. It was after Sheikh Yassin's death that Mashaal was declared "world leader" of Hamas.

The most important element of context that needs to be taken into account is the seeming inconsistency between the fiery language Mashaal used in Gaza and his far more moderate tone in the course of several interviews with Western journalists in recent weeks. In those interviews Mashaal clearly indicated a readiness for a long-term *hudna,* or truce, provided that Israel ended its occupation of the West Bank, East Jerusalem, and Gaza and agreed to uphold Palestinian rights under international law. He made clear that these rights included the right of return belonging to the four to five million Palestinians living in refugee camps or exile, and contended that such a right was more deserving of recognition than is the Israeli grant of such a right of return to every Jew, even those completely without a prior connection to historic Palestine. This claimed right is potentially a threat to Israel and to Zionism, as it could, at least in theory, threaten the Jewish majority presence in Israel. Whether many Palestinians, if given the choice, would return to live in Israel so as to reinhabit their ancestral homes seems highly questionable, but the right to do so unquestionably belongs to Palestinians, at least to those who previously resided in present Israel.

In these interviews, Mashaal was consistent about Hamas's readiness to pursue these national goals nonviolently, without "weapons and blood," if Israel were to accept such a framework for peace. His words to CNN in a November 21 interview are notable in this respect: "We are ready to resort to a peaceful way, purely peaceful way without blood and weapons, as long as we obtain our Palestinian demands."[16] The extent of "Palestinian demands" was left unspecified, which does create ambiguity as to whether this meant accommodation or some kind of rearticulation of a unified Palestinian entity, as well as whether the peaceful path could precede the end of occupation or must be a sequel to the existence of a state. In the other direction, Mashaal indicated that once Palestinian statehood was fully realized, then the issue of the acceptance of Israeli legitimacy could be placed on the political agenda. His deputy, Mousa Abu Marzook, told me in a conversation in Cairo in a similar vein that the Hamas Charter's

---

16. Video of Mashaal's interview with CNN's Christiane Amanpour is available at http://amanpour.blogs.cnn.com/2012/11/21/hamas-political-leader-speaks-to-amanpour.

pledge to destroy the Zionist state had become "a false issue." This Ph.D. from Louisiana Tech, an intelligent exponent of Hamas thinking, echoed Mashaal's moderate approach, and indicated that as with the U.S. Constitution's treatment of slavery, the Hamas Charter has evolved with changing circumstance and its clauses are subject to modification by interpretation.[17]

Along similar lines, Mashaal has spoken about Hamas as being "realistic" with respect to an appreciation of the balance of forces relative to the conflict. He referred to Arafat's response to those who insisted that Israel would be at mortal risk if a Palestinian state were to be established on the West Bank: the former PLO leader had pointed out that any Palestinian move to threaten Israel militarily in such circumstances was unthinkable. It would be sure to produce a devastating attack that would crush Palestinian hopes forever.

This inconsistency poses a fundamental question: What is the true voice of Hamas? The more hopeful understanding would suggest a gap between the emotional occasion of the speech and the more rational views consistently expressed elsewhere. Such an explanation is the opposite of the Western insistence that only the rally speech gave expression to the authentic outlook of Hamas. In contrast, I would accord greater weight to the moderate formulations, at least for exploratory purposes. Put differently, in Gaza Mashaal was likely expressing a maximalist version of the Palestinian narrative relating to its sense of legitimacy, while in more reflective arenas, ever since Hamas entered electoral politics back in 2006, its dominant emphasis has been on pursuing a political track that envisioned long-term peaceful coexistence with Israel, sidestepping the legitimacy issues, at least once the occupation was definitively ended and the rights of Palestinian refugees were recognized in accordance with international law.

It can be asked, "How can Hamas dare to put forward such a claim in view of the steady rain of rockets that has made life treacherous and miserable for more than a million Israelis living in the southern part of Israel ever since Israel 'disengaged' in 2005?" Such a rhetorical question, repeated over and over again without reference to the siege or Israeli violence, has distorted the Western image of the interaction, suggesting that when Israel massively attacks helpless Gaza it is only exercising its defensive rights, which is the most fundamental entitlement of every sovereign state. Again

---

17. An English translation of the full text of the Hamas Charter (or Covenant), originally published August 18, 1988, is available through the Avalon Project of the Lillian Goldman Law Library at Yale University: http://avalon.law.yale.edu/20th_century/hamas.asp.

the more accurate interpretation depends on a fuller appreciation of the wider context, which would include the American plot to reverse the outcome of Hamas's 2006 electoral victory by arming Fatah with heavy weapons, Israel's punitive blockade since mid-2007, and many instances of provocative Israeli violence, including a steady stream of targeted assassinations and lethal overreactions at the Gaza border. Although not the whole story, the one-sided ratio of deaths as between Israel and Palestine is a good first approximation of comparative responsibility over the period of Hamas ascendancy in Gaza, and it is striking. For instance, between the ceasefire in 2009 and the Israeli attack in November 2012, 271 Palestinians were killed and not a single Israeli. The respected *Haaretz* columnist Gideon Levy has pointed out that since the first rockets were launched against Israel in 2001, fifty-nine Israelis have died as compared to 4,717 Palestinians.[18]

The Western media is stunningly oblivious to these complications of perception, almost never disclosing Israeli provocations in reporting on the timelines of the violence of the parties, and fails to acknowledge that it has been the Israelis, not the Palestinians, who have been mostly responsible for ending periods of prolonged truce. There are further confusing elements in the picture, including the presence of some extremist Palestinian militias that launch rockets in defiance of Hamas policy, which in recent years generally limits rockets to retaliatory roles. Among the ironies of the al-Jabari assassination was that it was evidently his role to restrain these militias on behalf of Hamas, including disciplining those extremists who refused to abide by policies of restricting rocket attacks to retaliatory situations.

There is no doubt that Hamas's reliance on firing rockets in the direction of Israeli civilian population centers violates international humanitarian law and should be condemned as such, but even this condemnation is not without its problematic aspects. The Goldstone Report did condemn the reliance on these rockets in a typically decontextualized manner—that is, without reference to the unlawfulness of the occupation, including its pronounced reliance on collective punishment in the form of the blockade as well as arbitrary violent incursions, frequent military overflights, and a terrifying regime of subjugation that imparts on Palestinians a sense of total vulnerability and helplessness. The Goldstone Report also was silent as to the nature and extent of a Palestinian right of resistance. Such unconditional condemnations of Hamas as a "terrorist organization" are

---

18. Gideon Levy, "An Accounting," *Haaretz*, November 25, 2012, http://www.haaretz.com/opinion/an-accounting.premium-1.480275. B'Tselem keeps updated and detailed statistics of casualties on its website, http://www.btselem.org.

unreasonably one-sided to the extent that they ignore Palestinian moral, political, and legal rights of resistance and fail to consider Israel's unlawful policies. This issue also reveals a serious deficiency in international humanitarian law, especially, as here, in the context of a prolonged occupation that includes many violations of the most fundamental and inalienable rights of an occupied people. The prerogatives of states are upheld while those of peoples are overlooked or treated as nonexistent.

It is also relevant to take note of the absence of alternative means available to the Palestinians to uphold their rights under international law and to challenge the abuses embedded in Israeli occupation policies. Israel, with its drones, Apache helicopters, F-16 fighter aircraft, Iron Dome, and so forth, enjoys the luxury of choosing its targets at will, but Palestinians have no such option. For them the choice is either using the primitive and indiscriminate weaponry at their disposal or essentially giving in to an intolerable status quo. To repeat, this does not make Hamas rockets lawful, but does it make such reliance wrong, given the overall context of violence that includes absolute impunity for Israeli violations of international criminal law? What are we to do with international law when it is invoked only to control the behavior of the weaker party?

It gives perspective to imagine the situation being reversed, as it was during the Nazi occupation of France or the Netherlands during World War II. The liberal West uniformly perceived resistance fighters as unconditional heroes and gave no critical attention to whether the tactics they used unduly imperiled innocent civilian lives. Those who lost their lives in such a resistance were honored as martyrs. Mashaal and other Hamas leaders have made similar arguments on several occasions, in effect asking what Palestinians are supposed to do in the exercise of resistance given their circumstances, which have persisted for so long, and the failures of traditional diplomacy and the UN to secure their rights under international law.

In effect, a sensitive appreciation of context is crucial for a proper understanding, which makes self-satisfied condemnations of the views and tactics of Hamas and Khaled Mashaal misleading and, if heeded, condemns the parties to a destiny of perpetual conflict. The Western mainstream media doesn't help by presenting the rocket attacks as if they take place in a vacuum and without relevant Israeli provocations. Israeli supporters will retort that it is easy to make such assessments from a safe distance, but what is a safe distance? "The risks are ours alone," they will say with a somewhat understandable hostility. But what about the horrible Palestinian circumstances? Are they not also entitled to redress?

Is there a way out of such tragic dilemmas? In my view, only when the stronger side militarily treats "the other" as having grievances and rights and recognizes that the security of the "self" must be based on mutuality will sustainable peace have a chance. In this conflict, the Israelis missed a huge opportunity to move in this direction when the weaker Palestinian side made a historic concession by limiting its political ambition to Occupied Palestine (22 percent of historic Palestine, less than half of what the UN partition plan proposed in 1947) in accord with the consensus image of a solution embodied in Security Council Resolution 242. Instead Israel has sought to encroach further and further on that Palestinian remnant by way of its settlements, separation wall, apartheid roads, and annexationist moves, offering the Palestinians no alternative to oppression than resistance. It is no wonder that even the accommodationist Palestinian Authority supported the recent Hamas anniversary celebrations and joined in proclaiming an intention to reconcile, reuniting Hamas and Fatah under the umbrella of the Palestine Liberation Organization.

It is possible to react to Khaled Mashaal's Gaza speech as the definitive expression of the Hamas creed, but it seems premature and unwise to do so. Instead, it is time to give balanced diplomacy a chance, if indeed there is any political space left for the implementation of the two-state consensus. If there isn't, then it is time to explore alternatives, including a return to a unified Palestine that is governed in accordance with human rights standards and international law. If this diplomatic dead end is the stark reality as of 2012, then it must be concluded that the Zionist leadership's overreaching in Israel, especially its insistence on viewing the West Bank and East Jerusalem as integral to biblical Israel (referencing the former as "Judea and Samaria" and the latter as the eternal Jewish capital), has itself undermined the political, moral, and legal viability of the Zionist project. These alternative options should have been clarified long ago. Now, by taking to heart "the peaceful alternative" depicted by Mashaal, especially in the aftermath of the General Assembly endorsement of Palestinian statehood and signs of an incipient Palestinian unity, there is one last opportunity to do so, should peace-oriented perspectives on the conflict be given a chance, however remote, to guide our thinking, feelings, and actions.

On Political Preconditions for Real Peace Talks
May 15, 2013[19]

To the extent that diplomacy solves international problems, it depends on the satisfaction of the political preconditions that must be met for negotiations between sovereign states to reach sustainable and benevolent results. To clarify the point, in situations where there is a clear winner and loser, political preconditions are irrelevant, as the winner can dictate the terms, either imposing them, as was done after World War II in response to the unconditional surrender of Germany and Japan, or offering proposals on a "take it or leave it" basis. This is what Israel has attempted to do over the course of the twenty years in which the Oslo framework, the Roadmap, and the Quartet have provided the ground rules for diplomacy with respect to Israel–Palestine negotiations. Israel has performed as if the winner and expected Palestine to act as if the loser, but so far this scenario has not produced the desired outcome, a "peace" essentially framed in accordance with Israel's priorities (retaining settlements by critical land swaps, annexing the whole of Jerusalem, maintaining access to West Bank aquifers, ignoring refugees, de-linking Gaza). Palestine, although occupied and without a sympathetic intermediary, and despite many of its people living as refugees or in exile, has not given up the struggle for a fair outcome as defined by international law and international morality.

My point here is conceptual in large part. It applies to various forms of advocacy, including the abolition of nuclear weapons and the establishment of world government. In neither instance are the political conditions present for the realization of such goals, assuming that in some form such outcomes would be desirable. In relation to nuclear weapons, leading state actors are not willing to part with such weaponry, especially as its retention is strongly supported by entrenched bureaucratic and private-sector interests as well as being ideologically grounded in political realism, which continues to shape the worldview of most national elites. With respect to world government, there is no climate of opinion that is strong enough to challenge the nationalist orientation of every government and citizenry that exists in the world. Besides, trying to consolidate governmental authority in the presence of the present degree of radical inequality is more likely to produce global totalitarianism than a benevolent form of centralized, humane global governance.

---

19. Originally published at http://richardfalk.wordpress.com/2013/05/15/
   on-political-precondition.

The reason for addressing this subject at this time is the feverish effort of Secretary of State John Kerry to stimulate the resumption of direct peace negotiations between Israel and Palestine. On neither side are the political preconditions present. The Netanyahu-led government is clearly committed to achieving the political embodiment of Greater Israel and would not settle for anything less. It is seeking as much legitimation as possible for this expansionist objective, hopeful that adroit diplomacy with U.S. help can yield such a result. For Ramallah and the Palestinian Authority there is a lack of representational coherence and political unity, as the elected governing authorities of Gaza are not represented, nor is the wider Palestinian community of refugee communities in neighboring countries. Even if Palestinian negotiators were to accept under pressure some version of Israel's Plan A, it is almost certain that the Palestinian people would not accept it. Given this setting, political preconditions for direct negotiations do not exist, and any resumption of direct negotiations appears to be worth less than nothing.

Why less than nothing? If past efforts are any indication, the side with the weaker standing in the international community and the media is likely to receive most of the blame for the almost certain breakdown at the site of negotiations; this has been Palestine's previous experience. Beyond this, both sides will probably react to diplomatic failure by pursuing with renewed unilateral vigor their respective conception of Plan B. Israel will complain about the absence of a partner for peace and proceed with accelerated expansion of settlements and related road construction, as well as continuing its promotion of unifying the city of Jerusalem; Palestine, on its side, will seek to intensify resistance, possibly emphasizing more its confidence in the global solidarity movement-building around the BDS campaign, highlighted recently by Stephen Hawking's much-heralded boycott of Israeli president Shimon Peres's fifth annual conference of global notables on the theme "Facing Tomorrow."[20]

Time is not neutral in situations of gross disparity. The side with hard-power control can encroach further on the prospects of the weaker side. If we look back at the developments of the past twenty years, we take note of the extraordinary growth in the number of Israeli settlers and the ethnographic and infrastructural changes in the city of Jerusalem, making it difficult to continue to lend credence to the idea that Palestinian self-determination can be realized by a "two-state" solution, which remains the oft-repeated American mantra. What might have seemed like a viable Palestinian state in 1967, when Security Council Resolution 242 was

---

20. Harriet Sherwood and Matthew Kalman, "Stephen Hawking Joins Academic Boycott of Israel," *Guardian,* May 7, 2013, http://www.theguardian.com/world/2013/may/08/stephen-hawking-israel-academic-boycott.

adopted, became less so when the Oslo framework was accepted on the White House lawn in 1993, and by 2013 it is a delusionary goal.

Understanding the relevance of political preconditions is crucial to behaving rationally in seeking solutions to long-festering problems. Where there are gross disparities of power and expectations, a conflict is almost never *ripe* for resolution. The opposite is also true. When political conditions exist for a fair solution, then it is imperative to move forward, flexibly and with an eye on a win-win outcome. Given the perspectives of the two sides, if win-win does not seem realistic, then patience is preferable to a demoralizing charade of false consciousness.

Whose "Two-State" Solution? Endgame or Intermission?
June 6, 2013[21]

From many sources there is a widespread effort to resume a peace process that has in the past led to failure, frustration, and anger—and often to renewed violence. The newly appointed U.S. secretary of state, John Kerry, is about to make his fifth trip to Israel since the beginning of 2013, insisting that the two sides try once more to seek peace and warning that, if this doesn't happen very soon, the prospects for an agreed-upon solution will be postponed not for just a year or two, but for decades. Kerry says if this current effort does not succeed, he will turn his attention elsewhere and the United States will make no further effort. So far, aside from logging the air miles, Kerry seems perversely responsive to Tel Aviv's demands for land swaps to allow settlement blocs to be incorporated into Israel and to promote further Palestinian concessions in relation to security arrangements, and totally unresponsive to Ramallah's demands for some tangible signs from the Israeli government that resumed negotiations will not be another slammed door. In this vein, Kerry's most ardent recent plea was at the Global Forum, an annual event organized under the auspices of the American Jewish Committee. Kerry told this audience that they possessed the influence to make the peace talks happen.

Somewhat surprisingly, even Marwan Barghouti, writing from prison, has seemingly endorsed this Washington activism and seemed to go further, calling upon the U.S. government to use its leverage with Israel to

---

21. Originally published at http://richardfalk.wordpress.com/2013/06/06/
whose-two-state-solution-end-game-or-intermission.

resolve the conflict in a manner that recognizes Palestinian rights and at the same time serves the broader American interest of stability in the Middle East. If Barghouti's response to written questions submitted by Adnan Abu Amer of *Al-Monitor* is read carefully, it reinforces an extremely pessimistic assessment of current prospects for peace.[22] Barghouti is urging the U.S. government to make a 180-degree turn away from its posture of unconditional support for Israel if it wants to be credible with Palestinians in the search for a solution to the conflict that accords with natural justice. The United States would need, above all, to insist that Palestine become a fully sovereign state within the 1967 borders and have East Jerusalem as its capital, while supporting the full implementation of UN Resolution 194, which affirms the right of return of Palestinian refugees, and the removal of the settlements without noting any exceptions. These are all reasonable positions to take, each in furtherance of the relevant standards of international law. Yet it must be observed, and I am sure this is not news to Mr. Barghouti, Palestinian reasonableness in the context of the Israel–Palestine struggle means choosing *not* to be *politically relevant*.

It is from precisely this perspective that Barghouti's words should be carefully and respectfully pondered. He calls the two-state solution "the only possible solution" and adds that it "must not be abandoned." It is a vision of a two-state solution that comes superficially close to what the Israeli peace activist Uri Avnery advocates, but seems light-years away from the kind of "solution" that Israel might consider or Kerry advocate. In other words, there are *two* radically different two-state solutions that are often not being carefully distinguished: what might be called "the American conception," originally detailed in U.S. president Barack Obama's May 19, 2011, speech delivered at the U.S. State Department, which at the time of its utterance seemed to look toward Israel's withdrawal to 1967 borders, with minor border adjustments, but included a general acceptance of Israel's refusal to implement the Palestinian right of return behind the green line and its expectation that the main settlements would be incorporated into Israeli sovereign territory.[23] As so often has happened during the Obama presidency, what seemed initially forthcoming was soon altered by back-pedaling in a manner that has severely damaged American credibility as a

22. Adnan Abu Amer, "Barghouti: Arab Peace Plan Damages Palestinian Cause," *Al-Monitor*, May 28, 2013, http://www.al-monitor.com/pulse/originals/2013/05/marwan-barghouti-fatah-palestine.html.

23. Barack Obama, "Remarks by the President on the Middle East and North Africa," speech delivered at the State Department, Washington, DC, May 19, 2011, http://www.whitehouse.gov/the-press-office/2011/05/19/remarks-president-middle-east-and-north-africa%20.

fair-minded third party. The U.S. government in this instance has gradually come to acquiesce in, even if does not openly avow, Israel's unyielding demands, which makes Washington's approach to the idea of two states for two peoples radically different than the Barghouti–Avnery conception of Palestinian statehood and self-determination. This latter conception is premised on the establishment of a genuinely sovereign and independent Palestine, with East Jerusalem as its capital, and a genuine equality of the two states on matters bearing on security, resources, and refugee identity. There are, to be sure, important differences between Barghouti and Avnery with respect to the right of return, with Avnery opting for a more territorial view of the conflict consistent with his more moderate and humane Zionist views about limiting rights of Palestinian refugees and about the second-class status of the Palestinian minority living in Israel, but still rather far from Barghouti's position on these crucial matters so often ignored by the Western media.

In the background is the persisting unwillingness of the Netanyahu government, despite the overall backing it receives from Washington, to make Kerry's life easier by undertaking some obvious confidence-building gestures: a settlement freeze and the release of some Palestinian political prisoners. Netanyahu insists on no preconditions for resumed negotiations, which means no letup in settlement expansion, no lifting of the Gaza blockade, and the continuing abusive treatment of the West Bank population. Kerry was probably hoping that his remarks at the American Jewish Committee event would generate some pressure on Netanyahu to be somewhat more forthcoming. It is clear that if the Palestinian Authority is to enter direct negotiations while settlement expansion continues unchecked, it would likely be extremely detrimental to Mahmoud Abbas's claim to be the sole legitimate voice of the Palestinian people, a view that Barghouti rejects despite his Fatah affiliation.

If Netanyahu was more adroit, he could yield on these confidence-building prerequisites and put Abbas in a bind. What has the Palestinian Authority to gain by entering into negotiations with an unabashedly expansionist and settler-oriented Israeli government? Perhaps it would win momentary favor in Washington. But for what benefit in relation to the struggle of the Palestinian people for a just solution? There are no signs whatsoever that Israel would even consider an outcome for negotiations that remotely resembled the Barghouti–Avnery two-state conception, even if their differences are set aside for the moment. What would likely happen is that the negotiations would break down, as in the past, with the Palestinians receiving the lion's share of the blame. Israel has much more spin control in the world media, especially if its narrative is backed by the United States, as has been the case in the past and would almost certainly be in the future. The likely *hasbara*[24] assault would put the Palestinians in the position of once more being seen as rejecting what would be put forward to the world as generous Israeli proposals for a two-state solution that, if looked at closely, offer a statelet instead of a state, subject to a humiliating and intrusive Israeli regime of control, all in the name of security. This should recall the disingenuous Israeli claim that its "disengagement" from Gaza in 2005 put an end to the "occupation" of the Gaza Strip.

Barghouti's distance from what Kerry is trying to broker was also underscored by his expression of anger directed at the Arab League's recent acceptance of modifications of its 2002 Arab Peace Initiative made in response to pressures exerted by Kerry. Barghouti's comment on this aspect of Kerry's diplomacy is worth reproducing:

> The Arab peace initiative is the lowest the Arabs have gone in terms of a historical settlement with Israel. The statements of the Arab ministerial delegation to Washington in regards to amending the 1967 borders and accepting the land-swap inflict great damage on the Arab stance and Palestinian rights, and stimulate the appetite of Israel for more concessions. No one is entitled to amend borders or swap land; the Palestinian people insist on Israel's full withdrawal to the 1967 borders, in addition to removing the settlements.[25]

In effect, what Kerry put forward as a diplomatic coup, Barghouti denounced as an Arab betrayal. It all goes to show that there are many contradictory understandings cohabiting within the two-state tent.

It is notable that Barghouti also warns Israel and the United States that reliance on the status quo, which seems so comfortable from Tel Aviv's perspective in recent years, is dangerously shortsighted: "Security cannot be achieved without peace." And further, by implication although not expressed in these words, peace cannot be achieved without justice. In this spirit of defiant nationalism, Barghouti also affirms that a right of resistance belongs to the Palestinian people, but its exercise should be sensitive to the limits of international law—"The tortured and oppressed Palestinian people have the right to defend themselves by all means approved by the UN Charter and international law. Total resistance is the most effective." Barghouti, in his responses, strongly stresses the importance of moving to fulfill the tentative agreement between Fatah and Hamas to achieve Palestinian unity, while restating his awareness that resolving the refugee

---

24. The Hebrew term for Israel's public relations/propaganda effort on the international stage.

25. Abu Amer, "Barghouti: Arab Peace Plan Damages Palestinian Cause."

issue is central to a just solution and reaffirming his faith in an eventual Palestinian victory.

Both Kerry and Barghouti reject a one-state solution as not of any political interest, unfortunately leaving the peace process where it currently belongs—in an unendurable limbo of indefinite extension. Netanyahu and Kerry have a Plan B that might really be their Plan A. It involves what Netanyahu shamelessly calls an "economic peace," a persistence of the occupation and status quo, but in a manner that makes life materially somewhat better for West Bank Palestinians. (Gazans are nowhere to be found on this most dubious "map of conscience.") It cannot be a coincidence that at this time Kerry is peddling a scheme to induce four billion dollars of investment in the West Bank, presumably to convert the occupation and Palestinian statelessness into a new kind of "golden arch." The moment may have arrived to chase the moneychangers from the temple!

In pondering this dismal landscape of peace talk without peace, one wonders what became of the Roadmap and the Quartet. It may be a small blessing that their irrelevance is being tacitly acknowledged. These creations never seemed more than a thin and deceitful veil thrown over a one-sided American control over Israel–Palestine diplomacy.[26] In this sense the boldness of Kerry's statecraft and Barghouti's implicit recognition that the peace ball is in America's court at least moves in the direction of "eyes wide open." For Kerry this means another set of grand gestures; for Netanyahu it means remaining immobile in the comfort zone created by the Palestinian shift away from the tactics of violent resistance; for Barghouti it means a call for resistance, a plea for more solidarity, and a kind of longing for an Israeli, or even an American, De Gaulle or De Klerk to rupture prior expectations dramatically by replacing confrontation with accommodation. Until something as drastic as this occurs, although not necessarily through the work of a charismatic counterhero, we need at least to have the honesty to admit that the end of the tunnel is dark except for occasional flickers of light. I discern such a flicker in the undertakings of those engaged in a legitimacy war against Israel, step by step gaining the high moral and legal ground, which may soon uncover political tipping points that will abruptly alter the relations of forces in support of Palestinian justice claims. The Palestinian legitimacy war combines Palestinian resistance with a global solidarity campaign that is being waged on a global battlefield.

---

26. For compelling documentation, see Rashid Khalidi's *Broker of Deceit* (Boston: Beacon Press, 2013).

Reviving the Israel–Palestine Negotiations: The Indyk Appointment

July 30, 2013[27]

Secretary of State Kerry's appointing Martin Indyk as special envoy to the upcoming peace talks was to be expected. It was signaled in advance. And yet it is revealing and distressing. The only other candidates considered for the job were equally known as Israeli partisans: Daniel Kurtzer, former ambassador to Israel before becoming commissioner of the Israel Baseball League, and Dennis Ross, co-founder in the 1980s (with Indyk) of the AIPAC-backed Washington Institute for Near East Policy, who handled the 2000 Camp David negotiations on behalf of President Clinton.

The winner among these three was Martin Indyk, former ambassador to Israel (from 1995 to 1997 and 2000 to 2001) and onetime AIPAC employee, a British-born, Australian-educated U.S. diplomat with a long list of pro-Israel credentials.

Does it not seem strange for the United States, the convening party and the unconditional supporter of Israel, to rely exclusively for diplomatic guidance in this concerted effort to revive the peace talks on persons with such strong and unmistakable pro-Israel credentials?

What is stranger still is that the media never bothers to observe the peculiarity of a negotiating framework in which the side with massive advantages in hard and soft power, as well as great diplomatic and media leverage, needs to be further strengthened by having the mediating third party so clearly in its corner. Is this numbness or bias? Are we so accustomed to a biased framework that we take it for granted, or do we overlook it because it might spoil the PR effect of reviving the moribund peace process?

John Kerry, whose show this is, dutifully indicated when announcing the Indyk appointment that success in the negotiations would depend on the willingness of the two sides to make "reasonable compromises."[28] But who will decide on what is reasonable? It would be criminally negligent for the Palestinians to risk their future by trusting that Mr. Indyk understands what is reasonable for all parties. But the Palestinians are now potentially entrapped. If they are put in a position where Israel accepts, and the

---

27. Originally published at http://richardfalk.wordpress.com/2013/07/30/
reviving-the-israel-palestine-negotiations-the-indyk-appointment.

28. John Kerry, "Remarks with Ambassador Martin Indyk," press conference,
U.S. Department of State, July 29, 2013, http://www.state.gov/secretary/
remarks/2013/07/212516.htm.

Palestinian Authority rejects, "(un)reasonable compromises," the Israelis will insist they have no "partner" for peace and once more *hasbara* will rule the airwaves.

It is important to take note of the language of "reasonable compromises," which, as in earlier attempts at direct negotiations, excludes any reference to international law or the rights of the parties. Such an exclusion confirms that the essential feature of this diplomacy of negotiations is a bargaining process in which relative power and influence weigh heavily on what is proposed by and acceptable to the two sides. If I were advising the Palestinians, I would never recommend accepting a diplomatic framework that does not explicitly acknowledge the relevance of international law and the rights of the parties. In the relation of Israel and Palestine, international law could be the great equalizer, soft power neutralizing hard power. This is precisely why Israel has worked so hard to keep international law out of the process, which is what I would certainly recommend if I were in Tel Aviv's diplomatic corner.

Can one even begin to contemplate, except in despair, what Benjamin Netanyahu and his pro-settler cabinet consider *reasonable* compromises? On what issues can we expect Israel to give ground: borders, Jerusalem, refugees, settlements, security?

It would have been easy for Kerry to create a more positive format if he had appointed a Palestinian, or at least someone of Middle Eastern background, as co-envoy to the talks. Rashid Khalidi, President Obama's onetime Chicago friend and neighbor, would have been a reassuring choice for the Palestinian side. Admittedly, having published a book a few months ago with the title *Brokers of Deceit: How the U.S. Undermined Peace in the Middle East,* appointing Khalidi, despite his stellar credentials, would have produced a firestorm in Washington. Agreed, Khalidi is beyond serious contemplation, but what about John Esposito, Chas Freeman, Ray Close? None of these alternatives, not even Khalidi, is as close to the Palestinians as Indyk is to the Israelis, yet such a selection would have been seen as a step taken to close the huge credibility deficit. Such credibility, however, remains outside the boundaries of the Beltway's political imagination and thus inhabits the realm of the unthinkable.

It may be that Kerry is sincere in seeking to broker a solution to the conflict, yet this way of proceeding has failure written all over it because the political preconditions for constructive diplomacy do not exist. Perhaps there was no viable alternative. Israel would not come even to negotiate negotiations without being reassured in advance by an Indyk-like appointment. And if Israel had signaled its disapproval, Washington would be paralyzed.

The only remaining question is why the Palestinian Authority goes along so meekly. What is there to gain in such a setting? Having accepted the Washington auspices, why could they not have demanded at least a more neutral or balanced negotiating envoy? I fear the answers to such questions are "blowing in the wind."

And so we can expect to witness yet another charade falsely advertised as "the peace process." Such a diversion is costly for the Palestinians, beneficial for the Israelis. Settlement expansion and associated projects will continue, the occupation with all its rigors and humiliations will continue, and the prospects for a unified Palestinian leadership will be put on indefinite hold. Not a pretty picture.

This picture is made more macabre when we take account of the wider regional scene, especially the horrifying civil war in Syria and the bloody military coup in Egypt. Not to be forgotten, as well, are Israeli threats directed at Iran, backed to the hilt by the U.S. Congress, and the terrible legacy of violent sectarian struggle that is ripping Iraq apart. Naturally, there is speculation that some kind of faux solution to the Israel–Palestine conflict would release political energy in Washington that could be diverted to an anti-Assad intervention in Syria and even an attack on Iran. We cannot rule out such infatuations with morbid geopolitical projects, but neither should we assume that conspiratorial scenarios foretell the future.

The Palestinian National Movement Advances
December 19, 2013[29]

The advocacy of a legitimacy war approach to the Palestinian national movement for self-determination and a just peace is basically committed to Hegelian categories of conflict, shifting its energies away from Marxist forms of encounter based on material assessments of the balance of forces. Put less obscurely, the Palestinian shift toward legitimacy wars is a recognition that, in this kind of conflict, the decisive battles are generally not won by the side with the superior weaponry and technology but rather by the side that prevails in the realm of ideas and symbols of just cause,

---

29. Originally published at http://richardfalk.wordpress.com/2013/12/19/
the-palestinian-national-movement-advances. It was also published as "BDS Campaign: The Palestinian National Movement Advances," *Foreign Policy Journal,* December 19, 2013, http://bit.ly/TkRfRJ.

especially those bearing on nationalist claims of rights based on international law and universal standards of morality. Since the outcome of the colonial wars, the collapse of the Soviet empire, and the failure of Western interventions, the tide of history is flowing favorably for indigenous forces able to win control over these normative heights. This does not imply a renunciation of violence or a guarantee of victory, but it does signify a massive shift in the balance of forces in favor of the side that most successfully uses soft-power instruments in conflict situations.

Such a Hegelian view of historical process intends only to claim an altered emphasis, and does not imply a disregard of material circumstances. When Marx was active, his insights into the political economy of the day were brilliantly conceived, calling attention to the revolutionary vulnerabilities of industrial capitalism to a mobilized working class. Both Hegel and Marx, responsive to the truth claims of science, purported to have discovered the *laws* governing change in the human condition but only truly identified dispositions, and their claims of "determinism" exaggerated what we are able to discern in the present about what will happen in the future. In the context of the Palestinian legitimacy war, there is only a sense that such a victory is likely to produce positive political results, but not a guarantee. The political outcome depends on many unknowable features of context, especially how the side losing a legitimacy war responds.

The battlefields of a legitimacy war are mainly symbolic and nonterritorial. Their relation of forces cannot be measured but should not be understood only as a battle of ideas. It is rather the conversion of ideas into people power in various forms along with a downplaying of relative technological proficiency. In relation to the Palestinian struggle, such soft-power militancy is exhibited by such developments as the growth of the BDS campaign, the decision by the Swarthmore chapter of Hillel to defy the institutional guidelines of its central organization by permitting those critical of Israel to speak under its auspices, the decision of prominent Dutch companies to cut commercial ties with Israeli settlements because such relationships are understood to be problematic under international law, and the decisions by the Association for Asian American Studies and the American Studies Association (ASA) to boycott Israeli academic institutions.[30] In effect, this represents a cascade of societal expressions of solidarity with the Palestinian quest for justice.

---

30. See American Studies Association, "Council Resolution on Boycott of Israeli Academic Institutions," December 4, 2013, http://bit.ly/1kbrWIp. For the text of the Association for Asian American Studies resolution, see Elizabeth Redden, "A First for the Israel Boycott?" *Inside Higher Ed*, April 24, 2013, http://bit.ly/1uHSq9T.

This surge of support for peace with justice has evoked a variety of dysfunctional Israeli responses, including vituperative dismissals and a variety of efforts to change the subject. Nothing is more suggestive of Israel's loss of composure in this new atmosphere than the decision of its leaders, Netanyahu and Peres, to boycott the funeral of the globally sanctified figure of Nelson Mandela, presumably in retaliation for his frequent statements of support for the Palestinian struggle and maybe for fear that Israel's long record of collaboration with apartheid South Africa might finally be scrutinized in a transparent manner if they had showed up. Yet the symbolic impact of this deliberate disaffiliation from such a universal show of reverence for this beloved man has been lodged in the moral consciousness of humanity.

Israel's more calculated responses to these various developments in the legitimacy war are revealing. For instance, a Foreign Ministry representative, Yigal Palmor, complains that the ASA's endorsement of the boycott of Israel's academic institutions is part of a campaign to delegitimize the Jewish state of Israel and that it is morally misdirected, because it fails to target the states with the world's most horrendous human rights records. The first response is significantly deceptive: the ASA boycott, and indeed all related initiatives, have been directed at Israel's *policies* and do not question the legitimacy of the Israeli *state*, although elsewhere there are serious questions raised about Israeli leaders' insistence that others acknowledge Israel as a Jewish state. Such a demand is oblivious to the human rights of the Palestinian minority, which consists of more than 1.6 million persons living in a societal environment that includes numerous discriminatory laws regulating their behavior.

As for the contention that there is no idea of boycotting other states with horrendous human rights records, such an argument incorporates two kinds of misleading contentions. First, it deftly avoids the substantive accusations as to whether Israel's treatment of Palestinians within the academic environment is as prejudicial, as boycott advocates claim, and whether the closeness of Israeli academicians and institutions to the military and political activities of the state is not sufficient grounds for singling out Israel. Add to this Israeli apologists' failure to address the central ASA contention that singling out Israel is justified because of the existence of "significant" American links to Israeli policies long violating fundamental Palestinian rights and contributing to violations of international law.

Israel's ambassador to the United States, Ron Dermer, weighed in with a familiar riposte: "Why Israel?" Dermer advanced the familiar claim that Israel is the only democracy in the region: why should the ASA "as its first ever boycott choose to boycott Israel, the sole democracy in the Middle East, in which academics are free to say what they want, write what they want and research what they want."[31] Such an argument is questionable and unconvincing for many reasons, including Israel's increasingly dubious claim to deserve the mantle of democracy considering its own chosen identity as an "ethnocracy" (to borrow the label recently affixed by the respected Jewish leader Henry Siegman[32]). Also, acknowledging the existence of scholarly freedoms in Israel is beside the point. It does not even attempt to respond to the ASA's main contentions regarding the prejudicial treatment of Palestinians in Israel's educational system and the degree of Israeli academic institutions' collaboration with the state in relation to unlawful occupation policies and activities and the formulation of military strategy.

This harsh Israeli critique is combined with a dismissive attitude claiming that the ASA boycott resolution and, indeed, the wider BDS campaign have had and will have no *practical* impact on Israel's economic well-being and political stability, and that the resolution has no binding effect even on ASA members. What is at stake in such a debate is the meaning of "practical." Similar arguments were made in the context of the comparable campaign against apartheid South Africa and against those of us who favored boycott and sanctions in response to the barbarous policies of Pinochet's Chile. In relation to both South Africa and Chile, the argument was also made that such acts of hostility only hurt the most vulnerable people in the targeted society rather than weaken its regime, although in both instances the most credible representatives of the people were unreservedly supporting maximum pressures deriving from external initiatives of this character.

I remember being told in the late 1970s, in a private meeting of a small group with Robert McNamara, then president of the World Bank, that loans to the Pinochet regime were justifiable as denying funds to Chile would adversely affect the poor without harming the government. McNamara was claiming to be deeply opposed to the behavior of the Pinochet policies and upholding the continuity of the World Bank's relationship to Chile solely on humanitarian grounds. This interpretation did not seem credible at the time. It was directly contrary to what we were being told by several leading diplomats and economists who were prominent in the Allende government and who had led us to arrange this private meeting with the objective of persuading the World Bank to suspend financial assistance to Chile given the horrendous behavior of the Pinochet government.

---

31. Richard Pérez-Peña and Jodi Rudoren, "Boycott by Academic Group Is a Symbolic Sting to Israel," *New York Times,* December 16, 2013, http://www.nytimes.com/2013/12/17/education/scholars-group-endorses-an-academic-boycott-of-israel.html.

32. Henry Siegman, "Netanyahu's Two-State Mask Has Slipped," *Haaretz,* November 12, 2013, http://www.haaretz.com/opinion/.premium-1.557637.

The larger point here is not about the *material* impacts of such moves of disaffiliation and disapproval. We had no illusions that if the World Bank withheld a loan from Chile it would precipitate the collapse of the Pinochet regime. What we did believe, however, that such a step would strengthen the perception of a loss of legitimacy, possibly influencing American foreign policy and certainly encouraging the mounting opposition in Chile but mainly important as a symbolic move. In a similar vein, reflecting on why it is proper to celebrate the endorsement of this ASA resolution takes us back to the essentially Hegelian nature of a legitimacy war. A symbolic victory is not merely symbolic, although symbols should not be underestimated. The ASA outcome is part of a campaign to construct a new subjectivity surrounding the Israel–Palestine conflict. It is the sort of act that lends credibility to claims that a momentum is transforming the climate of opinion surrounding a conflict situation. Such a momentum is capable of breaking down a structure of oppression *at any moment.* Unlike a hard-power encounter between arrayed military forces, the course of a legitimacy war cannot be assessed in advance, partly because the defeats endured by the established order are intangible and will be denied up until an abrupt change of course. As Thoreau observed long ago, "The question is not what you look at, but what you see."[33] Hard-power realists who rule over the peoples of the world, imperiling our destiny, tend to be dangerously shortsighted when it comes to *seeing* the course and effects of legitimacy wars.

Such a concealment of elite reassessment in South Africa seems relevant to notice. The transformative reassessment was kept secret until revealed in the startling announcement to the South African public of Nelson Mandela's totally unexpected release from his Robben Island prison cell. It was a stunning reversal of strategy by the South African leadership. It seems appropriate in this context to recall Gandhi's familiar comment about the cycle of struggle: "First they ignore you, then they laugh at you, then they fight you, and then you win."

This is not a time for optimism about reaching a just end to the Palestinians' long quest for realization of their fundamental rights. It is a time when genuine hope becomes plausible thanks to Palestinian successes in waging a multifront legitimacy war. The eventual political outcome remains obscure and depends heavily on whether and how interests are reassessed in Washington and Tel Aviv. Such a process of reassessment is certain to be shrouded in secrecy until it crosses a threshold of decision; only then will it be revealed. This will occasion

---

33. Henry David Thoreau, *Journal*, August 5, 1851, available at https://www.walden.org/documents/file/Library/Thoreau/writings/Writings1906/08Journal02/Chapter7.pdf.

many expert explanations of why it had to happen! Pundits are far more convincing when operating in a *retrospective* mode than when attempting to *predict* or *prescribe*.

2

Gaza

After the collapse of the Ottoman Empire, the Gaza Strip was treated as part of the mandate of Palestine established by the League of Nations, with Britain playing the quasi-colonial role of mandatory power until 1947. After the 1948 War in Palestine, Gaza was occupied and administered by Egypt, an arrangement that continued until the 1967 War, when Israel became the occupying power. It has long been the eye of the Palestinian storm, with more than 60 percent of its population registered as refugees, a densely compacted and impoverished overall population that in 2013 was estimated at 1.76 million. From the outset, Israel's administration of Gaza has been the object of widespread humanitarian concern.

In 2005 Ariel Sharon, then prime minister of Israel, unilaterally embarked upon a plan of Israeli "disengagement" from Gaza that was strongly opposed at the time by Netanyahu and others in Israel. The Sharon plan included dismantling the twenty-one unlawful Israeli settlements in Gaza along with removing settlers, withdrawing Israeli armed forces, and delegating the internal administration of Gaza to the Palestinians. The plan was hailed at the time in the West as a welcome Israeli peace initiative, but it soon became evident that Israel maintained control of entry to and exit from Gaza, regarded its borders with Gaza itself as subject to its own extensive security demands, and treated primitive rockets fired across the border by Palestinian militia units as "terrorism," a form of resistance that Israel regarded as justifying the claim that it had no partner for peace. Actually, the facts were always complicated, with the West representing the interaction between Gaza and Israel in deeply misleading ways by ignoring Israeli provocations and persisting control, which included targeted assassinations of Palestinian militants, constant military aircraft overflights causing sonic booms, and large-scale periodic military operations that inflicted death and destruction while terrorizing the Gazan population.

In early 2006 legislative elections held within Occupied Palestine produced an unexpected victory for Hamas and considerable popular support in the West Bank and in Gaza. This was followed in mid-2007 by a struggle between Hamas and Fatah, with Hamas victorious. Since 2007 Hamas has administered Gaza. Although Washington had encouraged Hamas to take part in the elections, its victory was treated as validating a set of coercive responses, which intensified after Hamas took over the governing process in Gaza. Israel, the United States, and the European Union formally classified Hamas as a terrorist organization; Israel imposed a comprehensive blockade that exerted a strong downward pressure on the livelihoods of Gazans and virtually destroyed the Gazan economy, which had previously been developing exports of agricultural products. The result of the blockade was extreme hardship and confinement, to some degree alleviated by the construction of an extensive tunnel network that linked Gaza with Egypt and became a supply line for the population, providing a source of revenue for Hamas and partial relief from Israeli travel restrictions. The situation in Gaza was adversely affected by the 2013 counterrevolutionary coup in Egypt, which led to the destruction of nearly all of the estimated one thousand tunnels and a more tightly regulated Rafah crossing that is the only link between Gaza and Egypt.

In response to Israeli allegations of indiscriminate rocket fire from Gaza, which in fact caused little damage and few casualties (although frightening to Israelis living close to the Gaza border), there were several major military incursions by the Israel Defense Forces (IDF) using modern weaponry against an essentially defenseless population. The most dramatic of these military operations took the form of an all-out military assault from land, sea, and air that lasted for twenty-two days, commencing on December 27, 2008, known as Operation Cast Lead. This high-tech military attack on a totally vulnerable Palestinian population was widely condemned around the world and led the UN Human Rights Council to investigate the commission of war crimes by the two sides in the conflict. The widely heralded Goldstone Report did reach findings and offer recommendations that called attention to war crimes charged to both Israel and Hamas. Such charges caused an angry uproar in Israel and were rejected by the United States. As a result of this opposition, the moderate recommendations of the report were never implemented and its chair, Richard Goldstone, actually backed away from the most incriminating finding implicating Israel in the deliberate targeting of Palestinian civilians, a conclusion that the other three members of the UN inquiry commission refused to withdraw.

The selections in this chapter consider the plight of Gaza at various times from 2010 to 2013. This plight would to some extent exist in any event due to poverty, crowdedness, poor water quality and water scarcity, and the insufficiency of agricultural land, but has been greatly worsened by Israel's avowedly punitive approach and reliance on excessive force to impose its will and terrorize the people of Gaza. Contrary to the views disseminated by Western governments and media, the Hamas leadership in Gaza has been willing to negotiate and observe ceasefire arrangements and has offered long-term assurances of peaceful coexistence if Israel lifts the unlawful blockade and withdraws to 1967 borders in accord with Security Council Resolution 242. Israel has on several occasions broken truce arrangements and has consistently ignored Hamas's diplomatic initiatives, arguing that Israel will regard only the Palestinian Authority as representing the Palestinian people.

Whenever the Palestinian Authority enters unity talks with Hamas, Israel warns that it will suffer adverse consequences should Hamas ever be allowed to join in the political leadership of a unified PLO, and so the stalemate persists. It should be noted, as well, that apart from Israel the tensions between Hamas and the Palestinian Authority remain severe, despite the almost unanimous call of Palestinians everywhere for unity. This persisting disunity weakens still further Palestinian leverage in all intergovernmental settings. The latest of several moves toward unity between Fatah and Hamas occurred in April 2014, and it remains to be seen whether it will be implemented. Already the first moves have led Israel to withdraw from direct negotiations with the Palestinian Authority, which were stalled in any event and seemingly at a dead end.

The realities of Gaza remain difficult to discern and, from the perspective of the civilian population, cruel and dehumanizing. Israel, although possessing total military dominance, has not been able to quell the spirit of resistance that persists in Gaza. Also, for outsiders, it is difficult to assess whether mortar and rocket fire originating from Gaza is under the control of Hamas, Islamic Jihad, a more militant group, or some small, breakaway radical independent Palestinian militias. Israel refuses to distinguish between these more militant rivals and treats any violence originating from Gaza as the responsibility of Hamas, then responds accordingly, invariably with disproportionate and excessive force. From the perspective of international law Gaza remains part of occupied Palestine, subject to international humanitarian law, and a site of massive collective punishment of the civilian population, which is unconditionally prohibited by Article 33 of the Fourth Geneva Convention.

The three posts devoted to Gaza focus on the Israeli incursions and underscore the failure of the organized international community, particularly the UN, to protect the civilian population of Gaza. Over a period of more than forty-seven years of occupation, Gazans have endured extreme forms of human insecurity, and the world and even Arab neighbors have not taken action even in response to full-scale military operations and the unlawful blockade. Such a pattern suggests double standards, geopolitical control over the practice of humanitarian intervention, and the application of the supposedly emerging norm of Responsibility to Protect or R2P. This norm was formulated in the aftermath of the Kosovo War of 1999, in which NATO waged war without prior authorization from the UN Security Council. It was seen as expressing the organized international community's responsibility to protect vulnerable civilian populations, and as more appropriate terminology than that of "humanitarian intervention," given the political realities of the postcolonial era. Reliance on R2P within the UN setting was a prominent feature of the Security Council debate that preceded the intervention in Libya in 2011, which was supposedly limited to protecting the endangered population of Benghazi. When the NATO intervention embarked upon regime-changing military operations, its application in the Libyan context became controversial and inhibited a stronger UN response to the brutal actions of the Damascus regime in Syria. The geopolitical character of R2P is also confirmed by its nonapplication in relation to the long ordeal of collective punishment inflicted upon the people of Gaza.

Stop Operation Cast Lead 2:
The Moral Shock and Awe of Global Silence
December 31, 2010[1]

It is dismaying that, during this dark anniversary period two years after the launch of the deadly attacks on the people of Gaza, codenamed Operation Cast Lead by the Israelis, there should be warnings of a massive new attack on the beleaguered people of Gaza. The influential Israeli journalist, Ron Ben-Yishai, writes on December 29, 2010, of the likely prospect of a new IDF major attack, quoting senior Israeli military officers as saying "It's not a question of if, but rather of when," a view that that is shared, according to Ben-Yishai, by "government ministers, Knesset members and municipal heads in the Gaza region."[2] The bloody-minded Israeli chief of staff,

---

1. Originally published as "Stop Operation Cast Lead 2: The Moral Shock and Awe of Global Silence—A New Year's Message for 2011" at http://bit.ly/1prIEXW.

2. Ron Ben-Yishai, "The Great Gaza Debate," *YNet*, December 29, 2010, http://www.ynetnews.com/articles/0,7340,L-4006205,00.html.

Lt. General Gabi Ashkenazi, reinforces this expectation with his recent assertion that "as long as Gilad Shalit is still in captivity, the mission is not complete." He adds, with unconscious irony, "We have not lost our right of self-defense."[3] More accurate would be the assertion, "We have not given up our right to wage aggressive war or to commit crimes against humanity." And what of the more than ten thousand Palestinians, including children under the age of ten, being held in Israeli prisons throughout occupied Palestine?

Against this background, the escalation of violence along the Gaza–Israel border should set off alarm bells around the world and at the United Nations. Israel in recent days has been launching severe air strikes against targets within the Gaza Strip, including near the civilian crowded refugee camp of Khan Younis, killing several Palestinians and wounding others. Supposedly, these attacks are in retaliation for nine mortar shells that fell on open territory, causing neither damage nor injury. Israel has also used lethal force against children from Gaza who were collecting gravel from the buffer zone to repair their homes. As usual, the Israeli security pretext lacks credibility—if ever there was an occasion for firing warning shots in the air, it was here, especially as the border has been essentially quiet in the last couple of years; when harmless rockets or mortar shells have occasionally been fired it has been in defiance of the Hamas effort to prevent providing Israel with any grounds for the use of force. Revealingly, in typical distortion, Ashkenazi portrays the Gaza situation as a prewar scenario: "We will not allow a situation in which they fire rockets at our citizens and towns from 'safe havens' amid [their] civilians."[4] With Orwellian precision, the reality is quite the reverse: Israel, from its safe haven, continuously attacks with intent to kill a defenseless, entrapped Gazan civilian population.

Perhaps worse in some respects than this Israeli warmongering is the stunning silence of the governments of the world and the United Nations. World public opinion was briefly shocked by the spectacle of one-sided war that marked Operation Cast Lead as a massive crime against humanity, but it has taken no notice of this recent unspeakable escalation of threats and provocations seemingly designed to set the stage for a new Israeli attack on the hapless Gazan population. This silence in the face of the accumulating evidence that Israel plans to launch Operation Cast Lead 2 is a devastating form of criminal complicity at the highest governmental levels, especially on the part of countries that have been closely aligned

---

3. Hillel Fendel and Haggai Huberman, "IDF Chief: 'We're Risking Our Men to Bring Home Gilad Shalit,'" *Arutz Sheva*, December 27, 2010, http://www.israelnationalnews.com/News/News.aspx/141364#.U2f9ZvldVeA.

4. Ibid.

with Israel, and also exhibits the moral bankruptcy of the United Nations System. We have witnessed the carnage of "preemptive war" and "preventive war" in Iraq, but we have yet to explore the moral and political imperatives of "preemptive peace" and "preventive peace." How long must the peoples of the world wait?

It is appropriate to recall the incisive words Haidar Eid uttered in reaction to the attacks of two years ago: "While Israeli armed forces were bombing my neighborhood, the UN, the EU, and the Arab League and the international community remained silent in the face of atrocities. Hundreds of corpses of children and women failed to convince them to intervene."[5] International liberal public opinion enthuses about the new global norm of "responsibility to protect," but not a hint that, if such an idea is to have any credibility, it should be applied with a sense of urgency to Gaza, where the population has been living under a cruel blockade for more than three years and is now facing grave new dangers.

Even after the atrocities of 2008 and 2009 have been authenticated over and over—by the Goldstone Report, by an exhaustive report issued by the Arab League,[6] by Amnesty International[7] and Human Rights Watch[8]—there is no expectation of Israeli accountability, and the United States effectively uses its diplomatic muscle to bury the issue, encouraging forgetfulness in collaboration with the media.

Only civil society has offered responses appropriate to the moral, legal, and political situation. Whether these responses can achieve their goals, only the future will tell. The Free Gaza Movement and the Freedom Flotilla have challenged the blockade more effectively than the UN or governments, leading Israel to retreat at least rhetorically, claiming to have lifted the blockade with respect to the entry of humanitarian goods and reconstruction materials. The behavioral truth contradicts the Israeli rhetoric: sufficient supplies of basic necessities are still not being allowed to enter

5. Haidar Eid, "Sharpeville 1960, Gaza 2009," *Electronic Intifada,* January 22, 2009, http://electronicintifada.net/content/sharpeville-1960-gaza-2009/8013.

6. Independent Fact Finding Committee on Gaza to the League of Arab States, *Report of the United Nations Fact-Finding Mission on the Gaza Conflict,* September 25, 2009, http://www2.ohchr.org/english/bodies/hrcouncil/docs/12session/A-HRC-12-48.pdf.

7. Amnesty International, *Operation Cast Lead: 22 Days of Death and Destruction,* 2009, http://bit.ly/1numbYY.

8. Human Rights Watch, "Israel/Occupied Palestinian Territories (OPT): Events of 2009," updated 2014, http://www.hrw.org/world-report-2010/israel-occupied-palestinian-territories-opt.

Gaza, the water and sewage systems are seriously crippled, there is not enough fuel available to maintain adequate electric power, and the damage from Operation Cast Lead remains, causing a desperate housing crisis (more than a hundred thousand units are needed just to move people from tents). Also, most students are not allowed to leave Gaza to take advantage of foreign educational opportunities, and the population lives in a locked-in space constantly threatened with violence, night and day.

This portrayal of Gaza is hardly a welcoming prospect for the year 2011. At the same time, the spirit of the people living in Gaza should not be underestimated. I have met Gazans, especially young people, who could be weighed down by the suffering their lives have brought them and their families since their birth, yet possess a positive sense of life and its potential and make every use of any opportunity that comes their way, minimizing their problems and expressing warmth toward more fortunate others and enthusiasm about their hopes for their future. I have found such contact inspirational, and it strengthens my resolve and sense of responsibility: these proud people must be liberated from the oppressive circumstances that constantly imprison, threaten, impoverish, sicken, traumatize, maim, kill. Until this happens, none of us should sleep too comfortably!

Yet Another Gaza Catastrophe: Will They Ever Learn?
November 18, 2012[9]

The Western media's double standards on the new and tragic Israeli escalation of violence directed at Gaza were epitomized by an absurdly partisan *New York Times* front-page headline: "Rockets Target Jerusalem; Israel Girds for Gaza Invasion."[10] Decoded somewhat, the message is this: Hamas is the aggressor, and Israel—when and if it launches a ground attack on Gaza—must expect itself to be further attacked by rockets. This is a stunningly Orwellian rephrasing of reality. The true situation is quite the opposite: namely, that the defenseless population of Gaza can be assumed now to be acutely fearful of an all-out imminent Israeli assault—while it is also true, without minimizing the reality of a threat, that some rockets fired from Gaza fell harmlessly (although with admittedly menacing

---

9. Originally published at http://richardfalk.wordpress.com/2012/11/18/
   the-latest-gaza-catastrophe-will-they-ever-learn.

10. Slideshow, November 16, 2012, http://www.nytimes.com/interactive/2012/11/16/
   world/middleeast/20121116-Gaza-POD.html?_r=0.

implications) on the outskirts of Jerusalem and Tel Aviv. There is such a gross disproportion in the capacity of the two sides to inflict damage and suffering, due to Israel's total military dominance, as to make perverse this reversal of concerns as to what might befall Israeli society if the attack on Gaza further intensifies.

The reliance of Hamas and the various Gaza militias on indiscriminate, even if wildly inaccurate and generally harmless, rockets is a criminal violation of international humanitarian law, but the low number of casualties and the minor damage caused need to be assessed in the overall context of massive violence inflicted on the Palestinians. The widespread non-Western perception of the new cycle of violence involving Gaza is that it looks like a repetition of Israeli aggression against Gaza in late 2008 and early 2009, which similarly fell between the end of American presidential elections and scheduled Israeli parliamentary elections.

There is the usual discussion over where to locate responsibility for the initial act in this renewed upsurge of violence. Was it some shots fired from Gaza across the border and aimed at an armored Israeli jeep, or was it the targeted killing by an Israeli missile of Ahmed al-Jabari, leader of the military wing of Hamas, a few days later? Was it some other act by one side or the other? Or is it the continuous violence against the people of Gaza arising from the blockade that has been imposed since mid-2007? The assassination of al-Jabari came a few days after an informal truce negotiated through the good offices of Egypt and quite ironically agreed to by none other than al-Jabari, acting on behalf of Hamas. Killing him was clearly intended as a major provocation, disrupting a carefully negotiated effort to avoid another tit-for-tat sequence of violence of the sort that has periodically taken place during the last several years. An assassination of such a high-profile Palestinian political figure as al-Jabari is not a spontaneous act. It is based on elaborate surveillance over a long period and is obviously planned well in advance, partly with the hope of avoiding collateral damage and thus limiting unfavorable publicity. Such an extra-judicial killing, though part and parcel of the new American ethos of drone warfare, remains an unlawful tactic of conflict, denying adversary political leaders separated from combat any opportunity to defend themselves against accusations, and implies a rejection of any disposition to seek a peaceful resolution of a political conflict. It amounts to imposing capital punishment without due process, denying elementary rights to confront an accuser.

Putting aside the niceties of law, the Israeli leadership knew exactly what it was doing when it broke the truce and assassinated such a prominent Hamas leader, someone generally thought to be second only to the Gaza prime minister, Ismail Haniyeh. There have been rumors—and veiled threats—for months that the Netanyahu government plans a major assault of Gaza; the timing of the ongoing attacks seems to coincide with the dynamics of Israeli internal politics, especially the traditional Israeli practice of shoring up the image of toughness of the existing leadership in Tel Aviv as a way of inducing Israeli citizens to feel fearful, yet protected, before casting their ballots.

Beneath the horrific violence, which exposes the utter vulnerability of all those living as captives in Gaza, one of the most crowded and impoverished communities on the planet, is a frightful structure of human abuse upon which the international community continues to turn its back while elsewhere preaching adherence to the norm of "responsibility to protect" whenever it suits NATO. More than half of the 1.6 million Gazans are refugees living in a total area of just over twice the size of the city of Washington, DC. The population has endured a punitive blockade since mid-2007 that makes daily life intolerable, and Gaza has been harshly occupied ever since 1967.

Israel has tried to fool the world by setting forth its narrative of a good-faith withdrawal from Gaza in 2005, which it claims was exploited by Palestinian militants at the time as an opportunity to launch deadly rocket attacks. The counternarrative accepted by most independent observers is that Israel's removal of troops and settlements was little more than a mere redeployment to the borders of Gaza, with absolute control over what goes in and what leaves, maintaining open season, a license to kill at will with no accountability and no adverse consequences, backed without question by the U.S. government. From an international law point of view, Israel's "disengagement" from Gaza didn't end its responsibility as an occupying power under the Geneva Conventions; thus, its master plan of subjecting the entire population of Gaza to severe forms of collective punishment amounts to a continuing crime against humanity, as well as a flagrant violation of Article 33 of Geneva IV. It is not surprising that so many who have observed the plight of Gaza at close range describe it as the largest open-air prison in the world.

The Netanyahu government pursues a policy that is best understood from the perspective of settler colonialism. What distinguishes settler colonialism from other forms of colonialism is the colonists' resolve not only to exploit and dominate, but to make the land their own and superimpose their own culture on the indigenous population. In this respect, Israel is well served by the Hamas–Fatah split and seeks to induce the oppressed Palestinians to give up their identity along with their resistance struggle, even to the extent of asking Palestinians in Israel to take an oath of loyalty to Israel as a "Jewish state." Actually, unlike the West Bank and East Jerusalem, Israel has no long-term territorial ambition in Gaza.

Its short-term solution to its so-called "demographic problem" (that is, worries about the increase in the population of Palestinians relative to Jews) could be greatly eased if Egypt would absorb Gaza or if Gaza would become a permanently separate entity, provided it could be reliably demilitarized. What makes Gaza presently useful to the Israelis is their capacity to manage the level of violence, both as a distraction from other concerns (e.g., backing down in relation to Iran, accelerated expansion of the settlements) and as a way of convincing their own people that dangerous enemies remain and must be dealt with by the iron fist of Israeli militarism.

In the background, but not very far removed from observers' understanding, are two closely related developments. The first is the degree to which the continuing expansion of Israeli settlements has made it unrealistic to suppose that a viable Palestinian state will ever emerge from direct negotiations. The second, underscored by the recent merger of Netanyahu and Lieberman forces, is the extent to which the Israeli governing process has indirectly itself irreversibly embraced the vision of "Greater Israel" encompassing all of Jerusalem and most of the West Bank. The fact that world leaders in the West keep repeating the mantra of "peace through direct negotiations" is either an expression of the grossest incompetence or totally bad faith. At minimum, Washington and the others calling for the resumption of direct negotiations owe it to all of us to explain how it will be possible to establish a Palestinian state within 1967 borders when this means the displacement of most of the six hundred thousand armed settlers now defended by the IDF and spread throughout occupied Palestine. Such an explanation would also have to show why Israel is being allowed to quietly legalize its hundred or so "outposts," settlements spread around the West Bank that were previously unlawful even under Israeli law. Such moves toward legalization deserve the urgent attention of all those who continue to proclaim their faith in a two-state solution, but instead are ignored.

This brings us back to Gaza and Hamas. The top Hamas leaders have made it abundantly clear over and over again that they are open to permanent peace with Israel if there is a total withdrawal to the 1967 borders (22 percent of historic Palestine) and the arrangement is supported by a referendum of all Palestinians living under occupation. Israel, with Washington's backing, takes the position that Hamas is a "terrorist organization" that must be permanently excluded from the procedures of diplomacy, except of course when it serves Israel's purposes to negotiate with Hamas. It has done this, for example in 2011 when it negotiated the prisoner exchange in which several hundred Palestinians were released from Israeli prisons in exchange for the release of the captive Israel soldier Gilad Shalit, and when it seems convenient to take advantage of Egyptian mediation to establish temporary ceasefires. As the celebrated Israeli peace activist and former Knesset member Uri Avnery reminds us, Muslims consider a ceasefire, or *hudna* in Arabic, to be sanctified by Allah; this has been used and faithfully observed ever since the time of the Crusades. Avnery also reports that, up to the time he was assassinated, al-Jabari was in contact with Gershon Baskin of Israel, seeking to explore prospects for a long-term ceasefire; Israeli leaders, unsurprisingly, showed no interest.

There is a further feature of this renewal of conflict involving attacks on Gaza. Israel sometimes insists that since it is no longer, according to its claims, an occupying power, it is in a state of war with a Hamas-governed Gaza. But if this were to be taken as the proper legal description of the relationship between the two sides, then Gaza would have the rights of a combatant, including the option to use proportionate force against Israeli military targets. As earlier argued, such a legal description of the relationship between Israel and Gaza is unacceptable. Gaza remains occupied and essentially helpless, and Israel as occupier has no legal or ethical right to engage in war against its people and government—which, incidentally, was elected in internationally monitored free elections in early 2006. On the contrary, Israel's overriding obligation as occupier is to protect the civilian population of Gaza. Even if casualty figures in the present violence are low compared with Operation Cast Lead, the intensity of air and sea strikes against the helpless people of Gaza strikes terror in the hearts and minds of every person living in the Strip, a form of indiscriminate violence against the spirits and mental health of an entire people that cannot be measured in blood and flesh, but by reference to the traumatizing fear it has generated.

We hear many claims in the West as to a supposed decline in international warfare since the collapse of the Soviet Union twenty years ago. This trend is to some extent a welcome development, but the people of the Middle East have yet to benefit from it, least of all the people of occupied Palestine. Of these, the people of Gaza are suffering the most acutely. This spectacle of one-sided war, in which Israel decides how much violence to unleash and Gaza waits to be struck, firing off militarily meaningless salvos of rockets as a gesture of resistance, represents a shameful breakdown of civilizational values. These rockets do spread fear and cause trauma among Israeli civilians, even when they strike no targets, and represent an unacceptable tactic. Yet such unacceptability must be weighed against the unacceptable tactics of Israel, which holds all the cards in the conflict. It is truly alarming that now even the holiest of cities, Jerusalem, is threatened with attacks, but the continuation of oppressive conditions for the people of Gaza inevitably leads to increasing levels of frustration—in effect, cries for help—that the world has ignored at its peril for decades. These are survival screams. To realize this is not to exaggerate. To gain perspective, it is only necessary to read a recent UN report that concludes that the deterioration of services and conditions will make Gaza uninhabitable by 2020.[11]

That means, completely aside from the merits of the grievances on the two sides, that one side is militarily omnipotent while the other side is crouching helplessly in fear. Such a grotesque reality passes under the radar screens of world conscience because of the geopolitical shield behind which Israel is given a free pass to do whatever it wishes. Such a circumstance is morally unendurable and should be politically unacceptable. It needs to be actively opposed globally by every person, government, and institution of good will.

The Gaza Ceasefire: An Early Assessment
November 24, 2012[12]

The Gaza ceasefire, unlike a similar ceasefire achieved after Operation Cast Lead four years ago, has a likely significance far beyond ending the violence after eight days of murderous attacks. It is just possible that it will be looked back upon as a turning point in the long struggle between Israel and Palestine. Many have talked about the "fog of war," but it pales beside the "fog of truce-making," and in our media-infected air the outcomes are already being spun in all possible directions. Supporters of each side give their own spin, allowing both to proclaim "victory." But as with the violent phases of the conflict, it is clarifying to distinguish the more persuasive claims and interpretations from those that are less persuasive. What follows is one such attempt at such clarification.

It remains too soon to tell whether the ceasefire will hold for very long and, if it does, whether its central provisions will be implemented in good faith. At this early moment, the prospects are not promising. Israel has already used excessive violence to disperse Palestinians who gathered on the Gaza side of the border to celebrate what they thought was their new freedom to venture close to the border. Israeli security forces, after firing warning shots, killed one Palestinian civilian and

---

11. United Nations Country Team in the Occupied Palestinian Territories, *Gaza in 2020: A Liveable Place?* (New York: United Nations, 2012), http://www.unrwa.org/userfiles/file/publications/gaza/Gaza%20in%202020.pdf.

12. Originally published at http://richardfalk.wordpress.com/2012/11/24/the-gaza-ceasefire-an-early-assessment.

wounded another twenty with live ammunition. Israel's explanation was that the soldiers had given warnings and, since there had been no agreement implementing the ceasefire, the old regime of control was still in place. It is notable that Hamas protested but made no moves to cancel the ceasefire or to retaliate violently; however, the situation remains tense and fragile.

Putting aside the precariousness of the current situation and the accompanying uncertainties, it still seems useful to look at the process by which the ceasefire was brought about and how this sheds light on the changing dynamics of the conflict itself, as well as on some underlying shifts in the regional and global balances of forces.

First of all, the role and outlook of the Arab governments was far more proactive than in past instances of intensified Israel–Palestine violence. During the just-concluded attacks, several foreign ministers from the region visited Gaza on November 20, 2012, and were received by the Hamas governing authorities, thus undermining Israel's longstanding effort to isolate Hamas and exclude it from diplomatic channels. Egypt played the critical role in brokering the agreement, despite the Muslim Brotherhood affiliation of its leaders. Mohamed Morsi, the Egyptian president, emerged as the key diplomatic figure, widely praised at the time by the West for his "pragmatism," which can be understood as meaning his capacity to address the concerns of both sides without intruding his own pro-Palestinian outlook.[13] Indeed, such a brokered agreement inverted what American diplomacy brought to the table in past negotiations: a pretension of balance, a reality of partisanship.

Second, the text of the agreement implicitly acknowledged Hamas as the governing authority of Gaza and thereby gives it, at least temporarily, a greatly enhanced status among Palestinians, regionally and internationally. Its claim to be a legitimate representative of the Palestinian people has now become plausible, making Hamas a political actor that has, for the moment, been brought in from the terrorist cold. While Hamas remains formally a "terrorist organization" in the eyes of Israel, the United States, and Europe, throughout this just-concluded feverish effort to impose a ceasefire on the conflict it was treated as "a political actor" with sovereign authority to speak for the people in Gaza. Such a move represents a potential sea change, depending on whether there is an effort to build on the momentum achieved or a return to the futile Israeli–U.S. policy of excluding Hamas from diplomatic channels by insisting that it be classified as a terrorist organization. Correspondingly, the Palestinian Authority and its

---

13. Morsi was deposed during the July 2013 military coup and, as this book went to press, was being tried by Egyptian courts on a variety of charges.

leader, Mahmoud Abbas, have been awkwardly sidelined, overshadowed, and made to appear irrelevant in the midst of this latest terrible ordeal affecting the Palestinian people.

Third, Israel accepted as integral conditions of the ceasefire two sets of obligations toward the people of Gaza to which it would never have agreed before it launched its Operation Pillar of Cloud[14]: (1) agreeing not to engage in "incursions and targeting of individuals"; and (2) agreeing to meet so as to arrange for "opening the crossings and facilitating the movements of people and the transfer of goods and refraining from restricting residents' free movement and targeting residents in border areas."[15] If implemented by Israel, this means the end of targeted assassinations and the lifting of the blockade that has tormented Gaza for more than five years. These are major setbacks for the Israeli policy. Tel Aviv's political acceptance of a prohibition on targeted assassinations, if respected, renounces a favorite tactic of Israeli governments for many years which, although generally regarded as illegal, Israel still practiced with impunity. Indeed, the most dramatic precipitating event in the recent controversial unfolding crisis timeline was the November 14 killing of Ahmed al-Jabari, a military–political leader of Hamas who at the very time was negotiating a truce relating to cross-border violence.

Fourth, the role of the United States, while still significant, was considerably downsized by these other factors, especially the need to allow Egypt to play the main role as arbiter. This suggests a regionalization of diplomacy that diminishes the importance and seriously erodes the legitimacy of extraregional interference. This is bad news for the Israelis. Turkey, also now a sharp critic of Israel, played a significant role in defusing the escalating crisis as did Egypt. There exists a revealing gap between the United States's insistence all along that Israel's use of force was fully justified because every country has the right to defend itself and the ceasefire text, which placed restrictions on future violence applicable to both sides. After the ceasefire, the United States must make a defining choice: either continue its role as Israel's unconditional enabler or adopt a more "pragmatic" approach to the conflict, in the manner of Morsi. If it remains primarily an enabler, its diplomatic role is likely to diminish rapidly, but if it should adopt a balanced approach, it might still be able to take the lead in establishing a real peace process that considers

---

14. Operation Pillar of Cloud was an eight-day Israeli military operation initiated on November 14, 2012; it ended with the signing of a ceasefire agreement.

15. Anup Kahle, "Full Text: Terms of Israel-Palestinian Cease-Fire," *Washington Post*, November 21, 2012, http://www.washingtonpost.com/blogs/worldviews/wp/2012/11/21/full-text-terms-of-israel-palestinian-cease-fire.

the rights of both sides under international law. To make such a shift credible, President Obama would have to make a major speech to the American people explaining why it is necessary for the United States to choose between partisanship and diplomacy in reshaping its future relationship to the conflict. However sensible such a shift would be both for U.S. foreign policy and for the stability of the region, it is highly unlikely to happen. There is nothing in Obama's resume that suggests a willingness to go to the people to circumvent a dysfunctional outlook in the U.S. Congress.

Fifth, the United Nations was made to seem almost irrelevant, despite Secretary-General Ban Ki-moon's presence in the region during the diplomatic endgame. He did not help matters by seeming to echo the sentiments coming from Washington, calling attention almost exclusively to Israel's defensive rights. The UN could provide more neutral auspices for future negotiations if it were to disentangle itself from Western geopolitics. To do this would require withdrawing from participation in the Quartet and pledging a commitment to a sustaining and just peace for both peoples. As with the United States, it is highly unlikely that the UN would make such a move, at least not without permission from Washington. As with Obama, there is nothing in Ban Ki-moon's performance as Secretary-General that suggests the willingness and capacity to act independently when the stakes are high.

Sixth, the immediate aftermath of the ceasefire was a call from the Gaza streets for Palestinian unity, symbolized by the presence of Palestinian Authority, Hamas, Islamic Jihad, and Popular Front for the Liberation of Palestine flags all flying in harmonious coexistence. As the *New York Times* commented, it was "a rainbow not visible here in years."[16] If Palestinian unity holds and becomes a practical reality, including elections throughout Occupied Palestine, it may turn out that the ceasefire is more than a temporary tense truce but is a new beginning in the long march toward Palestinian justice.

All in all, the outcome of Operation Pillar of Cloud was a resounding defeat for Israel in at least three respects: despite Israel's pounding Gaza for eight days and threatening a ground invasion, Hamas did not give in to its demands for a unilateral ceasefire; the military capabilities of Gaza rockets exhibited a far greater capacity than in the past to inflict damage throughout the whole of Israel, including Tel Aviv and Jerusalem, which suggests that in any future recurrence of major violence the destructive capabilities at Gaza's disposal will become even greater; and the Israeli politics of

---

16. Jodi Rudoren and Isabel Kershner, "Factions in Gaza Make Unity Vow after Cease-Fire," *New York Times,* November 22, 2012, http://nyti.ms/V2fVQA.

promoting the Palestinian Authority as the only legitimate representative of the Palestinian people while refusing to deal with Hamas was dealt a heavy, perhaps fatal, blow.

Israeli officials are giving a chilling slant to this attack on Gaza, brazenly describing it as "a war game" designed to rehearse for an impending attack on Iran. In the words of Israel's ambassador to the United States, Michael Oren, "Israel was not confronting Gaza, but Iran."[17] Considering that at least 160 Gazans were killed, a thousand wounded, and many more traumatized, this is, or should be, a shocking admission of intent to commit crimes against humanity. It should at least prompt the UN Human Rights Council to appoint a fact-finding mission to assess the allegations of criminal conduct during the military attack. In effect, the situation demands a second Goldstone Report—this time with the political will to follow through once the incriminating findings are reported.

These developments will themselves be affected by the pervasive uncertainties that make it likely that the ceasefire will be a short truce rather than a definitive turn from violence to diplomacy. Will the parties respect the ceasefire? Israel has often made international commitments it later completely abandons, as has been the case with dismantling the numerous "outposts" (that is, "settlements" unlawful even under Israeli law) or in relation to its commitment to settle the "final status" issues associated with the Oslo framework within five years. It is not encouraging that Israeli officials are already cynically telling the media that they agreed to nothing beyond the immediate cessation of hostilities.[18] The undertakings of the text are thus minimized as "talking points" rather than agreed commitments that lack only mechanisms for implementation. If Israel refuses to give effect to the agreed stoppage of targeted assassinations and does not move to end the blockade in good faith, it will not be surprising to see the rockets flying again.

The Palestinian Authority is now poised to regain some of its lost ground by seeking UN General Assembly recognition of its status as "a non-member state" on November 29, 2013, a move Tel Aviv and Washington are resisting fiercely. It is probably too much to expect a softening of this diplomacy. Any claim of Palestinian statehood, even if only of symbolic significance, seems to threaten deeply Israel's posture of agreeing to the creation of a Palestinian state in the abstract as an outcome of

---

17. David E. Sanger and Thom Shanker, "For Israel, Gaza Conflict Is Test for an Iran Confrontation," *New York Times*, November 22, 2012, http://nyti.ms/1pzM5xO.

18. For example: Fares Akram and Jodi Rudoren, "Israel Seizes 2 Gaza Boats Near New Offshore Limit," *New York Times*, November 29, 2012, http://nyti.ms/1uTeQoJ.

negotiations while doing everything in its power to oppose all Palestinian efforts to claim statehood.

Such speculations must be conditioned by the realization that, as the clock ticks, the international consensus solution to the conflict, an independent sovereign Palestine, is slipping out of the realm of the feasible. The situation of prolonged occupation has altered the demography and the expectations of the Israelis. With as many as 600,000 unlawful settlers in the West Bank and Jerusalem, no foreseeable Israeli government would survive if it agreed to any arrangement that required even a small percentage of those settlers to leave. On the Palestinian side, no arrangement would be sustainable without the substantial reversal of the settlement phenomenon. So long as this eight-hundred-pound gorilla strides freely, attaining a genuine peace based on the international consensus of two states for two peoples seems an exercise in wishful thinking.

At the same time, history has shown us over and over again that "the impossible" happens: impossible in the sense that it is an outcome informed observers rejected as "possible." It happened when European colonialism was defeated, and again when the Soviet internal and external empire suddenly disintegrated, and then when the South African apartheid regime was removed. The Palestinian destiny continues to seem entrapped in such a foreclosed imaginary, yet we have learned from history that the struggles of oppressed peoples can on occasion achieve the unforeseeable. It is just barely possible that this latest display of Palestinian steadfastness in the face of Operation Pillar of Cloud, together with the post-2011 increased responsiveness of the governments of Israel's neighbors to the wishes of their own citizenry, will give rise to a sequence of events that alters the equations of regional and global power just enough to finally give peace a chance.

3

Prison Resistance

In the course of the Palestinian turn toward nonviolent forms of struggle and resistance, one focus has been on Palestinian prisoners' recourse to prolonged hunger strikes. They have undertaken such strikes to protest abusive conditions of arrest and imprisonment, especially the practice of "administrative detention" that allows Israelis to keep individuals imprisoned for long periods without disclosing charges or preparing an indictment. There are several instances of Palestinians being released as part of the Gilad Shalit prisoner exchange, then soon rearrested without any indication of wrongdoing. Such experiences are extremely unsettling and have led to demonstrations and protests. Palestinian prisoners have also relied upon hunger strikes to express their continuing engagement with the broader Palestinian struggle and to induce those on the outside to join in their protest against prison conditions and, more generally, the oppressiveness of continued Israeli occupation.

The selections presented here emphasize the bravery and fortitude of Palestinian hunger strikers, how their protest activity was initiated, and how it spread among Palestinians. Another persistent theme is the failure of Western media to report on these hunger strikes in a manner remotely similar to the high-profile media coverage it accorded to the Irish hunger strikers of the early 1980s, a protest activity that led to political developments that produced a partial settlement of the underlying conflict between Catholic and Protestant communities in Northern Ireland. Particularly shameful are those liberal columnists in the United States who have been urging the Palestinians to adopt nonviolent tactics of resistance. Such liberals argue that, since Israel is a democratic society with humane values, it would respond to such nonviolent tactics in a manner that would be more responsive to Palestinian grievances. It is less surprising that Israel was unresponsive than that these liberal voices of reason, perhaps most notably Thomas Friedman, were silent, not even noticing this shift away from armed struggle and violence both within prisons and in the wider Palestinian national movement.

Israel has acted callously and pragmatically in response to the challenges posed by hunger strikers. Obviously, there was anxiety on Israel's side that if hunger strikers died, it would lead to a resistance surge, perhaps even a third intifada, and greater worldwide attention. To avoid such unwelcome developments, Israel made concessions when hunger strikers were at the edge of death.

It has been observed recently that hunger strikes as a form of political protest have spread around the world in recent years, partly inspired by the Palestinian example.[1] For Americans, the most notable recourse to such forms of protest has been among the prisoners detained for years at Guantánamo without charges, under abusive conditions. Hunger strikes have also taken place in overcrowded California prisons where prisoners are denied even minimal rights. These hunger strikes have received media coverage far greater than what was accorded to the Palestinians, but only minimal steps have been taken so far to overcome grievances.

I believe that the Palestinian hunger strikes are of great significance to the unendurable character of an occupation of Palestine that gives many indications of becoming permanent, at least in some of its salient characteristics, such as the settlements, the wall, and the Jews-only transportation infrastructure. It should be understood that a strong spirit of resistance continues to animate the Palestinian people, despite so many setbacks and disappointments. Unfortunately, this spirit is not evident in most of the activities of the Palestinian governmental leadership, which seems ready to resolve the conflict on a basis that concedes most of what is left of Palestine to direct and indirect Israeli control. Such "peace" would be a humiliating outcome for decades of Palestinian sacrifice and humiliation, amounting to an acceptance of the Zionist dream of "Greater Israel." So far, even such a readiness falls short of continuous expanding Israeli ambitions, and thus the struggle goes on. In this setting, hunger strikes have become a potent weapon of resistance for the Palestinian people, even if their leaders take little or no notice of such acts of self-sacrifice. Not only have Palestinian tactics shifted in the direction of nonviolence, but there has been a transfer of initiative from the political leaders and diplomatic representatives to the people.

I devoted a large number of posts to this surge of hunger strikes that began with Khader Adnan, who struck in early 2011 as a protest against

---

1. See for example, David Mizner, "Starving for Justice: From California to Israel, Hunger Strikes Are Erupting All Over the World," *Nation*, December 4, 2013, http://www.thenation.com/article/177464/starving-justice.

his traumatic and brutal nighttime arrest in the presence of his wife and children, followed by a return to prison without charges or any prospect of a trial. The post are arranged sequentially to express the manner in which Adnan's example inspired others, who were subsequently abused at the time of arrest and imprisoned under administrative detention procedures. These posts also indicate the spread of such defiant acts in the isolation of prisons from brave individuals to Palestinian prison populations en masse. As well, the posts take note of Israeli attempts to suppress such activity by resorting to punitive measures such as consigning hunger strikers to solitary confinement and threatening force-feeding in violation of international medical standards. In the case of Hana Shalabi, Israeli authorities agreed to an early release of a prisoner whose life was in jeopardy, but imposed conditions on release: in her case, being banished from her West Bank village of residence and family home for a period of three years.

A post toward the end of this cluster takes note of the increased incidence of suicide among young Americans who have taken part in the occupations of Iraq and Afghanistan, and ventures the view that there are affinities between the desperate acts of those Americans who take their own lives after carrying out such abusive military roles and those Palestinians who carry their hunger strikes to the very precipice of death.

Saving Khader Adnan's Life Saves Our Own Soul
February 18, 2012[2]

The world watches as tragedy unfolds beneath its gaze: Khader Adnan is entering his sixty-third day as a hunger striker in an Israeli prison being held under an administrative detention order without trial, without charges, and without any indication of the evidence against him. From the outset of his brutal arrest by scores of soldiers—featuring blindfolding, cuffing, and physical roughness in the middle of the night, a gratuitous ritual enacted the presence of his wife and young daughters—Mr. Adnan has been subject to inhumane and degrading treatment that is totally unlawful, inexcusable, and an assault on our moral justification. At present, approximately three hundred other Palestinians are being held in administrative detention, and Mr. Adnan has indicated that his protest is also on their behalf, and indeed against the practice of administrative detention itself.

---

2. Originally published at http://richardfalk.wordpress.com/2012/02/18/795.

The only plausible explanation of such Israeli behavior is to intimidate by terrifying all Palestinians, who have lived for almost forty-five years under the yoke of an oppressive occupation that continuously whittles away at their rights under international humanitarian law, especially their right to self-determination, which is encroached upon every time a new housing unit is added to the colonizing settlements that dot the hilltops surrounding Jerusalem and throughout the West Bank. While prospects of a viable Palestinian political future are continuously diminished by Israeli expansionism, the world politely watches in stunned silence. Only resistance from within and solidarity worldwide can provide the Palestinians with hope about their future. They have been failed over and over again by the UN, by the EU, by their Arab neighbors, and above all by that global leader beholden to Israel whose capital is in Washington, DC. It is only against this broader background that the importance of Khader Adnan's resistance to the continuing struggle of Palestinians everywhere can begin to be appreciated as a political act as well as an insistence on the sacred dignity of the human person.

The case of Khader Adnan is a revealing microcosm of the unbearable cruelty of prolonged occupation and of the contrast drawn in the West between the dignity of a single Israeli prisoner held in captivity and the steadfast refusal to be attentive to the abuse of thousands of Palestinians languishing in Israeli jails. Mr. Adnan's father poignantly highlighted this contrast a few days ago by referring to Gilad Shalit, the Israeli soldier Hamas held in captivity for several years and recently released in good health: "Where are the mother and father of Gilad Shalit? Do they not feel for me in this humanitarian case? Where are they?" The comparison pointedly suggests that it is Mr. Adnan who is the more deserving of such a global outpouring of concern: "My son was arrested from his house, from among his wife and children, was taken prisoner. He was not carrying any weapon. Whereas Shalit was fighting against the people of Gaza, and destroying their homes, and firing upon, and Shalit was released."[3] In fact, Shalit has not been personally associated with violence against the Palestinians and their property, but he was operating as a member of the IDF, which has been consistently engaged in such activity, frequently in stark violation of international humanitarian law. While Shalit was being held, foreign authority figures from the UN Secretary-General on down displayed their empathy not only for Shalit but for the intense anxiety experienced by Israelis concerned for his well-being—but these same

3. Ali Abunimah, "VIDEO: Hunger Striker Khader Adnan's Father Says Son's Morale Is 'High' and Appeals to Parents of Gilad Shalit," *Electronic Intifada*, February 15, 2012, http://bit.ly/1prsLkp.

personalities are notably silent in the much more compelling ordeal taking place before our eyes in the form of Mr. Adnan's captivity seemingly unto death. It should not be surprising that surviving family members of Irish Republican Army (IRA) hunger strikers should step forward to express solidarity with Mr. Adnan and compare the transforming acts of Irish resistance in 1981 (in which ten hunger strikers died, and Britain shifted from counterterrorism to a politics of reconciliation) to that of the Palestinians, increasingly referring to Khader Adnan as the "West Bank Bobby Sands."

And who is Khader Adnan? We do not know very much about him except that he is a member of the Islamic Jihad party, a thirty-three-year-old father of two young daughters, a baker by profession, and viewed with respect and affection by his neighbors. There are no accusations that implicate him in violence against civilians, although he has a history of imprisonment associated with his past activism. A fellow prisoner from an earlier period of confinement in Ashkelon Prison, Abu Maria, recalls Mr. Adnan's normalcy, humanity, and academic demeanor while sharing a cell, emphasizing his passionate dedication to informing other imprisoned Palestinians about the history and nature of the conflict: "Prison was like a university in those times and he was one of the professors." Commenting on his hunger strike that has brought him extreme pain, Abu Maria says he is convinced that Khader Adnan wants to live, but not at the price of enduring humiliation for himself and others held in administrative detention: "He is showing his commitment and resistance in the only way he can right now, with his body."

Addameer, the respected Palestinian NGO concerned with prisoner issues, "holds Israel accountable for the life of Khader Adnan, whose health has entered an alarmingly critical stage that will now have irreversible consequences and could lead to his fatal collapse at any moment."[4] Physicians who have observed his current condition conclude that, at most, Mr. Adnan could live a few more days, saying that such a hunger strike cannot be sustained beyond seventy days in any event. Any attempt at this stage to keep Mr. Adnan alive by forced feeding would be widely viewed as a violation of his right to life and is generally regarded as torture.

Finally, Israel's reliance on administrative detention in cases of this sort is totally unacceptable from the perspective of international law, including the Geneva Conventions, especially with no disclosure of the exceptional circumstances or evidence that might warrant for reasons of imminent

---

4. Addameer, "Khader Adnan's Life in Grave Danger as He Continues His Struggle against Israel's Human Rights Violations," press release, February 13, 2012, http://www.addameer.org/etemplate.php?id=438.

security the use of such an extralegal form of imprisonment for a few days. Given the number of Palestinians being held in a similar manner, it is no wonder that sympathy hunger strikes among many Palestinians in and out of Israeli jails are under way as expressions of solidarity. Have we not reached a stage in our appreciation of human rights where we should outlaw such barbarism by state authorities, which is cunningly shielded from critical scrutiny by the anonymity and bureaucratic neutrality of the term "administrative detention"? Let us hope and make sure that the awful experience of Khader Adnan does not end with his death, and let us hope and do everything in our power to encourage a worldwide protest against both administrative detention and prisoner abuse by the government of Israel, and in due course elsewhere. The Palestinian people have suffered more than enough already; passivity in the face of such state crimes is an appalling form of complicity. We should expect more from our governments, the UN, human rights NGOs, and ourselves.

Saving Khader Adnan's Life and Legacy
February 21, 2012[5]

It is a great relief to those millions around the world who were moved to prayer and action by Khader Adnan's extraordinary sixty-six-day hunger strike, which has ended due to Israel's agreement to release him on April 17. We who were inspired by such a heroic refusal to accept humiliation and arbitrary arrest can only hope that for the sake of his family, for the cause of Palestinian resistance, and for the struggle to achieve a just peace Mr. Adnan will fully recover to resume his personal and political life. We cannot take for granted that there will be a full recovery given Mr. Adnan's critical condition, confirmed by examining doctors just prior to his decision on February 21 to resume eating in a normal manner.

While it is appropriate to celebrate this ending of the strike as a "victory," there are several disturbing features that deserve comment. To call an arrangement that saved someone's life a "deal," as the media consistently put it, is itself demeaning and reveals at the very least a failure to appreciate the gravity and deep dedication of purpose bound up with such a nonviolent form of resistance. Similarly, the carelessness of the initial reactions was notable, with media sources often referring to Mr. Adnan's

---

5. Originally published at http://richardfalk.wordpress.com/2012/02/21/
   saving-khader-adnans-life-and-legacy/.

"release"—when in fact he will still be held in administrative detention for several more weeks, and could conceivably be confined much longer, should Israeli military authorities unilaterally decide that "substantial evidence" against him emerges in the period immediately ahead.

It should also be noted that on matters of policy and principle Israel did not retreat even an inch: Mr. Adnan will remain in captivity and be subject to the "legal" possibility that his period of imprisonment could still be extended indefinitely; beyond this, Israeli authorities express no willingness whatsoever to review the cases of the 309 other Palestinians who are presently being held under the administrative detention procedure.

These Palestinians being held include one prisoner detained for more than five years and seventeen others detained for periods of two to four years. Israel did not even agree to review its misapplications of this administrative procedure within its own framework of claims about addressing imminent security threats. The general justification of administrative procedures by governments that rely upon it is to insist that its use is reserved for true and credible emergency situations. But as Mustafa Barghouthi points out in the *New York Times*, such a claim strains credulity past the breaking point in the Israeli case. Barghouthi writes tellingly that it is worth observing that

> among . . . [those] Palestinians now held in "administrative detention" are 21 of the 120 elected members of the Palestinian Legislative Council, most of whom have been held for years for no apparent crime other than being democratically elected in 2006 in an election universally regarded as free and fair, as candidates of the party which won a clear majority of seats but which Israel does not like.[6]

In other words, Israel's claims that exceptional circumstances take precedence over due process protections do not exist in many of the evident political uses of administrative detention as a means of weakening all forms of Palestinian resistance, including nonviolent opposition politics.

It should also be noted that Israeli commentary treated the arrangement ending the standoff produced by the hunger strike with measured cynicism, if not disdain. Even those Israelis who supported the agreement justified it as a practical way of avoiding trouble down the road should Khader Adnan have died while held by Israelis, given the breadth and depth of support his extended hunger strike was receiving among

6. Mustafa Barghouthi, "Peaceful Protest Can Free Palestine," *New York Times*, February 21, 2012, http://www.nytimes.com/2012/02/22/opinion/peaceful-protest-can-free-palestine.html.

Palestinians and sympathizers from around the world. Keeping Mr. Adnan alive was also seen by Israelis as a means to avoid a wider scrutiny of the institution and practice of administrative detention as it has been used by the Israeli military "justice" system.

The timing of the announcement of the arrangement is also significant. It was made an hour before an emergency session of the Israel Supreme Court that was scheduled to hear Mr. Adnan's petition for release; there is speculation that, although this highest judicial body in Israel has in the past consistently supported the military position in such instances, the situation was so extreme that it might prove embarrassing for Israeli military authorities. There were even some worries on the Israeli side that the extremities of this case could produce an adverse result and even a repudiation of the manner in which Israeli authorities used administrative detention as a procedure allegedly for security, but seemingly for the harassment and intimidation of militant opponents of an oppressive forty-five-year occupation aggravated by continuously appropriating Palestinian land and water for the benefit of settlement expansion while disrupting and "cleansing" long-term Palestinian residency.

What was entirely absent from the Israeli public discourse was some expression of compassion, even if only for the Adnan family, which consists of two daughters of four years or less and his articulate pregnant wife, Randa. There was not even the slightest show of respect for the dignity of Mr. Adnan's long hunger strike or sympathy for the acute suffering that accompanies such a determined forgoing of food and speech for an extended period. Instead, the Israeli commentary that was supportive of the arrangement stressed only pragmatic considerations from the perspective of Israel's interests. It was one more lost opportunity for Israelis of all shades of opinion to reach across the abyss of political conflict to affirm a common humanity.

But in a contrary spirit, the spokesperson for the Netanyahu government, Mark Regev, seemed only interested in deflecting criticism directed at Israel. He parried by cynically observing that other governments rely on administrative detention in the name of security, including the United States, so why shouldn't Israel? He also added that the legality of Israel's use of administrative detention should not be questioned since it depended not on Israeli law, but on a 1946 law enacted when Britain was controlling Palestine—unintentionally conceding that Israel is the "colonial" successor to the British! If the legal veil is lifted from administrative detention, its character is one of "internment," a standard practice of colonial powers in dealing with unruly natives.

Israeli ultra-hardliners went further in this direction, referring to Mr. Adnan as a "terrorist" despite the vagueness of official allegations, which never made such a claim but only mysteriously contended that he constituted what an official in Tel Aviv described as "a threat to regional security," whatever that might mean. As might be expected, the notorious Israeli foreign minister Avigdor Lieberman was characteristically forthright, calling his "release" "a wrong decision" yet accepting the outcome because it is "our duty to honor and respect every Supreme Court decision even when we don't agree with it."[7] As we know, Mr. Adnan was not released, nor did the Israel Supreme Court make a decision. This comedy of errors by a leading government official should raise questions about Lieberman's competence, not to mention his questionable political judgment as to policy. Lieberman's mean-spiritedness extended to attacks on Arab members of the Knesset who visited Mr. Adnan, representing their visit as somehow an indication that they were "representing terrorists." Similarly, Knesset minister Danny Danon ignored the context and scorned the agreement ending the hunger strike by calling it reprehensible and claiming that Israel had "capitulated to terrorism."[8]

The issues directly raised by this hunger strike are ones of human rights and humane treatment, as well as reliance on administrative detention, and are quite independent of whether or not we endorse Mr. Adnan's past and present tactics of resistance, which are not at all clear. Some apologists for Israel have tried to deflect these ethical and legal concerns by emphasizing Mr. Adnan's association with Islamic Jihad and its record of violent attacks and extremist politics. Israelis casually refer to Mr. Adnan as a "terrorist" without charges or proof. He has, in fact, been most often described more neutrally in recent years by those knowledgeable about his role and activities as a spokesperson for Islamic Jihad, but not engaged beyond this. There is no indication in his past or present that he was directly involved in violence, although an undated and unverified YouTube video has surfaced somewhat suspiciously in which Mr. Adnan is depicted as advocating violent resistance and an active recruiter of suicide bombers. Although Islamic Jihad has been responsible in the past for suicide bombings, it has seemingly abandoned the practice, which is in line with Hamas's repudiation of such forms of violent resistance more than ten years ago. Mr. Adnan's prior arrests stemmed from militant peaceful demonstrations that landed him in Israeli jails seven times and a Palestinian Authority prison

7. Associated Press, "Israel to Free Palestinian Hunger Striker Khader Adnan," Fox News, February 21, 2012, http://www.foxnews.com/world/2012/02/21/israel-to-free-palestinian-hunger-striker-khader-adnan.

8. Joanna Paraszczuk and Ben Hartman, "Palestinian Prisoner Ends 66-Day Hunger Strike," *Jerusalem Post*, February 21, 2012, http://www.jpost.com/National-News/Palestinian-prisoner-ends-66-day-hunger-strike.

once, and induced him to undertake shorter hunger strikes on three previous occasions, one as recently as 2010. From what is known, Mr. Adnan is definitely a committed activist who has associated himself with Islamic Jihad, but works on a daily basis as a village baker and maintains a strong family role and popular community presence in his small West Bank town of Arraba.

It is important to pause long enough to take account of Khader Adnan's achievement symbolically, substantively, and with respect to future possibilities. We should note that his hunger strike of sixty-six days is the exact length of Bobby Sands's hunger strike in 1981, strengthening the bond between the two men, a bond that has been movingly confirmed by a number of family members of Irish strikers. What is more, the date of Bobby Sands's death, May 5, 1981, is generally viewed as the turning point in the Irish struggle, the time when the British government finally started treating the IRA as a political actor with genuine grievances rather than as a terrorist organization that must be run into the ground and exterminated. We can only hope that February 21, 2012, will live in history as a turning point in the Palestinian struggle. Only the future will reveal whether this is a pious wish on my part or becomes over time a reality.

Substantively, it is crucial to support a campaign to free the other several hundred Palestinians currently being held in administrative detention and to exert enough pressure to end reliance on the practice altogether. Mr. Adnan's brave stand will have been mostly without effect if his compelling exposure of the cruelty and arbitrariness of Israeli reliance on administrative detention is allowed to slip from view now that his strike is over. Instead, knowing what we have come to know, it is the responsibility of all of us to do all we can to discredit and force Israel to abandon administrative detention and challenge its role in the United States and elsewhere. A fitting tribute to Mr. Adnan's hunger strike would be to put opposition to administrative detention on the top of the human rights agenda throughout the world. We should begin by refusing to use the phrase "administrative detention," rechristening it as "administrative torture" or "lawless captivity," and associate it with the past colonial and present authoritarian tendencies of "democratic" governments.

We will know the enduring significance of Mr. Adnan's self-sacrifice by what takes place in the future. Will this event, possibly along with other influences, inspire a greater commitment to the Palestinian struggle for peace, justice, and liberation in occupied Palestine and throughout the world? Maybe the "regional threat" referred to by the Israeli official justifying Mr. Adnan's detention was an indirect and, I hope, accurate reference to the growing impact of the positive sides of the Arab Spring: that is, as an occasion prompting a further awakening of self-empowerment among

Palestinians both in relation to their struggle and in their renewed quest for unity among themselves. Let us hope that Khader Adnan's bravery becomes contagious and will be remembered as a charismatic event in the long narrative of the Palestinian struggle for self-determination.

Hana Shalabi:
A Brave Act of Palestinian Nonviolence
March 10, 2012[9]

No sooner had Khader Adnan ended his life-threatening sixty-six-day hunger strike than new, urgent concerns were voiced for Hana Shalabi, another West Bank hunger striker now without food for more than twenty-four days. Both strikes were directed by Palestinian activists against the abusive use of administrative detention by Israeli West Bank occupying military forces, protesting both the practice of internment without charges or trial and the degrading and physically harsh treatment administered during the arrest, interrogation, and detention process.

The case of Hana Shalabi should move even the most hardhearted. She seems a young, tender, and normal woman who is a member of Islamic Jihad, is dedicated to her family, hopes for marriage, and enjoys simple pleasures like shopping. She was previously held in administrative detention at the HaSharon Prison in Israel for a thirty-month period between 2009 and 2011, and was released in the prisoner exchange four months ago that freed 1027 Palestinians and the lone captive Israeli soldier, Gilad Shalit. Since her release she has been trying to recover from the deep sense of estrangement she experienced in prison; she has rarely left her home or the company of her family. As she was returning to normalcy she was rearrested in an abusive manner, which allegedly included a strip search by a male soldier. On February 16, 2012, the day her administrative detention was renewed, Hana Shalabi indicated her resolve to start a hunger strike to protest her own treatment and to demand an end to administrative detention, on which Israel now relies to hold at least 309 Palestinians in prison. Her parents have been denied visitation rights, Shalabi has been placed in solitary confinement, and her health has deteriorated to the point of concern for her life. Impressively, her parents have committed themselves to a hunger strike for as long as their daughter remains under administrative detention. Her mother, Badia Shalabi, has made a video in which she

---

9. Originally published at http://richardfalk.wordpress.com/2012/03/10/821.

says that even to see food makes her cry considering the suffering of her daughter.

These extraordinary hunger strikes have met with silence or indifference in both Israel and the West. Israeli authorities declare that such a posture is a voluntary action for which they have no responsibility. The UN has not raised its voice, as well. I share the view of Khitam Saafin, chairwoman of the Union of Palestinian Women's Committees: "The United Nations must be responsible for the whole violations that are going on against our people. These prisoners are war prisoners, not security prisoners, not criminals; they are freedom fighters for their rights."[10] The plight of Hana Shalabi is also well expressed by Yael Maron, a spokesperson for the Israeli NGO Physicians for Human Rights–Israel: "The story of Hana Shalabi, like that of Khader Adnan, before is in my opinion a remarkable example of a struggle that's completely nonviolent towards one's surroundings. It is the last protest a prisoner can make, and I find it brave and inspiring."[11]

To engage in an open-ended hunger strike, especially as a person who is not in a leadership role, requires a deep and abiding dedication to right a perceived wrong of the greatest gravity. It is physically painful and dangerous to bodily health, as well as being psychologically demanding in the extreme. It presupposes the strongest of wills and usually arises, as in these instances, from a sense that any lesser form of resistance is futile and has a long record of failure. In the end, it is an appeal to the conscience and humanity of the other and a desperate call to all of us to understand better the cartography of abuse that abusive imprisonment entails, which I would imagine is pervasively humiliating for a religiously oriented young Muslim woman. To risk life this way without harming or even threatening the oppressor is to turn terrorism against the innocent on its head. It is potentially to sacrifice one's life to make an appeal of last resort, an appeal that transcends normal law and politics.

We can only fervently hope and pray that Hana Shalabi's heroic path of resistance will end with her release and the restoration of her health. For Israel's own moral well-being it is time, really long past time, to renounce reliance on administrative detention and to do more than this, to end forthwith its varied crimes of occupation. At this point the only possible way to do this is to withdraw unconditionally behind the 1967 borders and to start peace negotiations from that altered position. It is politically

10. Jillian Kestler D'Amours, "Interview: Why Hana al-Shalabi's Hunger Strike Is the Focus of Women's Day in Palestine," *Electronic Intifada,* March 7, 2012, http://bit.ly/1qk4gJB.

11. Sandy Boyer, "On Hunger Strike against her Israeli Jailers," *Socialist Worker,* March 21, 2012, http://socialistworker.org/2012/03/21/on-hunger-strike-in-palestine.

unimaginable that Israeli leaders will heed such a call, but it is morally unimaginable that Israel will survive its impending spiritual collapse if it does not do so.

In the meantime, we who are beyond these zones of occupation, abuse, and imprisonment must not only stand and watch as this tragic drama plays itself out. Wherever we are, whatever we can do, we need to act, to appeal, to shout, and to denounce the inhumanity of allowing such cruelty to be enacted before our watching eyes.

Hana Shalabi's Hunger Strike Has Ended, But Not Her Punishment
March 30, 2012[12]

As it did with Khader Adnan, Israel "compromised" with Hana Shalabi on the forty-third day of her hunger strike in protest against administrative detention and her abysmal treatment. But Israel's concept of "compromise," if considered, becomes indistinguishable from the imposition of a further "vindictive punishment." How else to interpret Israel's unlawful order to coercively exile (not technically deport, because she is being sent to a location within occupied Palestine) Ms. Shalabi for three years to the Gaza Strip, far from her home village of Burqin in the northern part of the West Bank and, more significantly, far from her grief-struck family? As journalist Linah Alsaafin put it a few days ago after interviewing Hana's sister Zahra, "I don't want to immortalize her, I just want her to live." We can join her in being relieved that Hana Shalabi did not join the Palestinian honor roll of martyrs, yet Israel has transferred someone who is in critical medical condition to a slightly more open prison than what detainees experience, which is how Gaza has been described during its years of isolation and blockade. To call this release "freedom" is to make a mockery of the word; even to call it "release" is misleading.

Hana Shalabi is now being compared to Winnie Mandela, who was exiled to the remote town of Branford in South Africa and forbidden to leave as a punishment for her nonviolent and militant resistance to the apartheid regime that had imprisoned her then-husband, Nelson Mandela. When I had the opportunity to meet and spend time with Winnie Mandela in 1968, a couple of years prior to her exile, she was a wonderfully radiant

---

12. Originally published at http://richardfalk.wordpress.com/2012/03/30/
hana-shalabis-hunger-strike-has-ended-but-not-her-punishment.

and magnetic personality with a deep political commitment to justice and emancipation from racism, yet also a joyful presence who, despite living under apartheid, was life-affirming and inspiring. When she returned from exile, she was radicalized and embittered. She joined in some violent oppositional tactics, seemingly exhibiting the alienating impact of the South African government's punitive effort to diminish and marginalize her. This part of Mandela's postexile story should not be forgotten, nor should it be ignored that she was not confronting the sort of life-threatening situation that Hana Shalabi faces as she seeks to recover from this long hunger strike. Also, Winnie Mandela's youngest daughter, Zindzi, was at least allowed to accompany her, unlike the total separation from loved ones that has been decreed for Ms. Shalabi, who in her current condition cannot even be considered a "political" threat, much less a "security" threat. Israel has compounded the crime of administrative detention with this shamefully gratuitous act of vindictiveness.

Article 49(1) of the Fourth Geneva Convention reads as follows: "Individual or mass forcible transfers, as well as deportations of protected persons from occupied territory to the territory of the Occupying Power or to that of any other country, occupied or not, are prohibited, regardless of their motive." The intent here is clear, even though the language leaves room for lawyers' quibbles: Is the Gaza Strip another country? Israel itself claims that its 2005 disengagement from Gaza relieves it of responsibility. In any event, Israel's order of banishment will be doubly enforced, neither allowing Hana Shalabi to leave Gaza nor to enter the West Bank, where her family lives. Given mobility restrictions her family will not be able to visit her in Gaza. Finally, it should be appreciated that this form of "collective punishment" also adds to the pain and grief of Ms. Shalabi's family, who will be denied even the opportunity to provide the help and love that are obviously needed during what will be at best a long and difficult recovery period. In this sense, the spirit and letter of Article 27 of Geneva IV has also been violated in her arrest, detention, and now in this release: "Protected persons are entitled, in all circumstances, to respect for their persons, their honour, their family rights, their religious conviction and practices, and their manners and customs. They shall at all times be humanely treated, and shall be protected especially against all acts of violence or threats thereof and against insults and public curiosity." Denying Ms. Shalabi any visitation rights while confined to an Israeli prison hospital prior to the implementation of her order of "deportation," as well as denying Physicians for Human Rights–Israel or Addameer the opportunity to examine and talk with her underscores the stone-coldness of the Israeli prison administration.

It is up to the Palestinian solidarity movement not to let this Palestinian hunger strike be in vain. At best, it might be seen later as one of the earlier expressions of a Palestinian Spring. At the very least, it should become a key moment in an intensifying campaign against the practice of administrative detention in occupied Palestine, as well as against abusive arrest procedures and general prison conditions.

This ambiguous, punitive "release" was apparently agreed upon not only on the forty-third day of Ms. Shalabi's hunger strike, but on the eve of the thirty-sixth commemoration of Land Day by Palestinian activists within Israel and in occupied Palestine. It is important for all of us to recall that it was on this day in 1976 that Israel killed six Palestinian citizens of Israel who were protesting, in violation of a curfew then in effect, Israel's expropriation of their land. The protests on Land Day 2012, especially near the Qalandia checkpoint, have been met with tear gas, rubber bullets, and water cannons, apparently with some Palestinian injuries. As Palestinian activists have pointed out, the Arab Spring has frightened the Israeli government.

It does appear that these hunger strikes, augmented by sympathetic and symbolic strikes within Israeli jails, in Palestine, and around the world as well as vibrant protests on Land Day and a worldwide BDS movement, are all signs of a Palestinian reawakening that will gather political leverage as its momentum builds. This is my hope for the year ahead.

Is the Massive Palestinian Hunger Strike the Beginning of the Palestinian Spring?
May 8, 2012[13]

There is ongoing militant expression of Palestinian resistance to the abuses of Israel's forty-five years of occupation and de facto annexation of the West Bank and East Jerusalem and its five-year blockade of Gaza, taking the form of a series of hunger strikes. Recourse to this desperate tactic of courageous self-sacrifice is an extreme form of nonviolence and should, whenever and wherever it occurs, be given close attention. Palestinians have protested by hunger strikes in the past but failed to inspire the imagination of the wider Palestinian community or shake the confidence of

---

13. Originally published as "Historic Hunger Strikes: Lightning in the Skies of Palestine," http://richardfalk.wordpress.com/2012/05/08/ historic-hunger-strikes-lightning-in-the-skies-of-palestine.

Israeli officialdom. Despite the averted gaze of the West, especially here in North America, there are some signs that this time the hunger strikes have crossed a historic threshold of no return.

The strikes started with the individual action of a single person, Khader Adnan, at the end of 2011. Dragged from his home during a night raid by dozens of Israeli soldiers, humiliated and roughed up in the presence of his two- and four-year-old daughters, carried away shackled and blindfolded, roughly interrogated, and then made subject to an administrative decree for the eighth time in his young life, Mr. Adnan's inner conscience must have screamed "Enough!": he embarked on an open-ended hunger strike. He continued it for sixty-six days, and agreed to take food again only after the Israeli authorities relented somewhat, including a pledge not to subject him to a further period of administrative detention unless further incriminating evidence came to the surface. Upon release, Mr. Adnan, to depersonalize his ordeal, insisted on visiting the families of other Palestinians currently under administrative detention before returning to his own home. He has spoken out with firm gentleness and invited persons of conscience everywhere to join in the struggle to induce Israel to abandon administrative detention and the accompanying violations of Palestinian human rights. In an open letter, Mr. Adnan wrote:

> I call on you to stand for justice, pride, and dignity in the face of occupation. The assault on the freedom and dignity of the Palestinian people is an assault on free people of the world by a criminal occupation that threatens the security, freedom, and dignity of all, no matter where.
>
> Please, continue in exposing this occupation, boycotting and isolating it internationally.[14]

Following Adnan, and inspired by him, was Hana Shalabi, a young Palestinian woman subject to a similar abusive arrest, accompanied by humiliations associated with her dress and sexual identity. Shalabi had been released a few months earlier in October 2011 as part of the prisoner exchange that was negotiated to obtain the release of the sole Israeli captive, Gilad Shalit. She had seldom strayed from her family home prior to the re-arrest on February 16, 2012. Shalabi was released after she was in critical condition, but in a vindictive manner, being sent to live in Gaza for three years, separated from her family and village. She also made it clear that her experience of resistance was not meant for herself alone, but was intended to contribute to the struggle against prison abuse and the practice

---

14. The entire letter is reproduced in my blog post.

of administrative detention, and even more generally to the struggle for Palestinian rights.

The example Adnan and Shalabi set inspired others. Several Palestinians detained by administrative detention decrees commenced hunger strikes at the end of February, and as many as 1,650 others, possibly more, initiated a massive hunger strike on Palestinian Prisoners' Day, April 17. Their struggle has been named "the battle of empty stomachs." The main battlefield is the mind of the oppressor: whether to give in and seem weak or remain firm and invite escalating censure, as well as Palestinian militancy, should any of those now in grave condition die.

The latest news suggests that Bilal Diab and Thaer Halahleh, continuing their hunger strike that started on February 28, are clinging to life by a thread. A few days ago they were both finally transferred to civilian hospitals. Mr. Halahleh, after his seventieth day without food, announced that he was no longer willing even to drink water or accept further medication.

As might be expected, the voices of concern from the international community have been muted and belated. The International Committee of the Red Cross has finally expressed in public its concern for the lives of these strikers. The UN envoy to the Middle East, Robert Serry, never outspoken, acknowledged a few days ago in a brief and perfunctory statement that he was "deeply troubled" by the danger to these hunger strikers, as if such a sentiment was somehow sufficient to the outrages being inflicted. More persuasively, several human rights NGOs, including Physicians for Human Rights–Israel, have been reminding Israel of its obligation to allow family visits, which prison authorities have repeatedly denied although it is an accepted tenet of medical ethics affirmed in Israel's Patient's Rights Law.

On May 7, 2012, Israel's High Court of Justice denied urgent petitions for release from administrative detention filed on behalf of Mr. Diab and Mr. Halahleh. The court, in a classic example of the twisted way judges choose to serve the state rather than the cause of justice, declared: "Hunger strikes cannot serve as an element in a decision on the very validity of administrative detention, since that would be confusing the issue." Would it be so confusing to say that without some demonstration of evidence of criminality, rejecting such a petition amounts to imposing a death sentence without even the pretensions of "a show trial" that relies on coerced confessions? Israel's highest judicial body leaves no doubt about their priorities by invoking anti-terrorism as a blanket justification, saying that Israel "should not have to apologize for securing its own safety."[15]

---

15. Jack Khoury, "Israel High Court Rejects Hunger Strikers' Appeal, But Advises Caution in Administrative Detentions," *Haaretz*, May 7, 2012, http://bit.ly/1lh5dzs.

On a wider canvas, the hunger strikes are clearly having some effect on Israeli prison policy, although it is not clearly discernible as yet. The Israeli internal security minister, Yitzhak Aharonovitch, convened a meeting in which he voiced the opinion that Israeli reliance on administrative detention was excessive and should be reduced.[16]

The following demands have been articulated by the April 17 hunger strikers, under the banner of the "Prisoners' Revolution":

- Ending the Israeli administrative detention and solitary confinement in which Palestinians have been imprisoned for more than ten consecutive years in solitary cells that lack basic human necessities of life.
- Allowing family visits to those from the Gaza Strip due to political decisions and unjust laws.
- Improving the livelihood of prisoners inside Israeli jails and allowing basic needs such as proper health treatment, education, TV, and newspapers.
- Putting an end to the humiliation policy carried out by the Israel Prison Service against Palestinian prisoners and their families through humiliating naked inspection, group punishment, and night raids.

Having followed these hunger strikes for several months, I am convinced that these individuals subject to administrative detention are ordinary people living normal lives, although chafing under the daily rigors and indignities of prolonged occupation. Israeli commentary tends to divert humanitarian concerns by branding them as "terrorists," taking note of their alleged affiliation with Islamic Jihad. Adnan, who is obviously preoccupied with his loving family and is a baker by profession, working in his village, does not seem to be a particularly political person beyond the unavoidable political response to a structure of domination that is violent, cruel, and abusive. The language of his open letter exhibits moral intensity and seeks support for the Palestinian struggle for a sustainable peace with justice. It has none of the violent imagery or murderous declarations found in al-Qaeda's characteristic calls for holy warfare against the infidels.

I was impressed by Zahra Shalabi's response when asked about the alleged connection with Islamic Jihad. She smiled and said, "She's not really Islamic Jihad. She doesn't belong to any faction. When Israel imprisons you, their security forces ask which political faction you belong to.

---

16. Barak Ravid, "Israel Should Reduce Use of Administrative Detentions for Palestinians, Top Official Says," *Haaretz*, May 3, 2012, http://bit.ly/1qrNben.

Hana chose Islamic Jihad on a whim." Even if it was more than a whim, for a religious person to identify with Islamic Jihad does not at all imply a commitment to or support for terrorist tactics of resistance. Zahra asks rhetorically, "Does she have missiles or rockets? Where is the threat to Israel? . . . Why can't we visit her? She has done nothing." And finally, "I would never place my enemy in my sister's position. . . . I would not wish this on anyone."[17]

Israel has, by vague allegations of links to terrorist activities, tried its best to dehumanize these hunger strikers and to dismiss such actions as the foolish or vain bravado of people ready to renounce their lives by their own free will. But their acts and words, if heeded with empathy, their show of spiritual stamina and sense of mission convey an altogether different message, one that exhibits the finest qualities that human beings can ever hope to achieve. Those of us who watch such heroic dramas unfold should at least do our best to honor these hunger strikers and not avert our eyes, and do our utmost to act in solidarity with their struggles in whatever way we can.

We cannot now know whether these hunger strikes will spark Palestinian resistance in new and creative ways. What we can already say with confidence is that these hunger strikers are writing a new chapter in the storyline of resistance *sumud*; their steadfastness is, for me, a Gandhian moment in the Palestinian struggle.

Media Missing in Action
May 12, 2012[18]

Can anyone doubt that if there were more than 1,500 prisoners engaged in a hunger strike in any country in the world other than Palestine, the Western media would be obsessed with the story? Such an obsession would be greatest if such a phenomenon were to occur in an adversary state such as Iran or China, but almost anywhere it would be featured news—that is, anywhere but Palestine. It would be highlighted day after

---

17. Linah Alsaafin, "Palestine: Inside the Home of Hana Shalabi," *Al-Akhbar English*, March 26, 2012, http://english.al-akhbar.com/content/palestine-inside-home-hana-shalabi.

18. A version of this post was published as "Palestinian Hunger Strikes: Media Missing in Action" on *Al Jazeera English*, www.aljazeera.com/indepth/opinion/2012/05/2012551069467110.html.

day and reported on from all angles, including the severe medical risks associated with such a lengthy refusal to take food, with respected doctors and human rights experts sharing their opinions.

At this time there are two Palestinians enduring their sixty-sixth day without food, Thaer Halahleh and Bilal Diab. Both men are reported by respected prisoner-protection association Addameer and Physicians for Human Rights–Israel to be in critical condition, with their lives hanging in the balance. Examining doctors indicated two days ago that both detainees were reported to "suffer from acute muscle weakness in their limbs that prevents them from standing" and are under the "dual threat" of "muscle atrophy and thrombophilia, which can lead to a fatal blood clot."[19] Despite this dramatic state of affairs, until today Western governments, media, and even the United Nations have taken scant notice of the life-threatening circumstances confronting Halahleh and Diab, let alone the massive solidarity strike that is of shorter duration, but still notable as a powerful expression of nonviolent defiance.

In contrast, consider the attention that the Western media has been devoting in recent days to a blind Chinese human rights lawyer, Chen Guangcheng, who managed to escape from house arrest in Beijing a few days ago, find a safe haven at the U.S. embassy, arrange a release, and then seek an exit from China. This is an important and disturbing international incident, to be sure, but is it truly so much more significant than the Palestinian story as to explain the total neglect of the extraordinary exploits of thousands of Palestinians who are sacrificing their bodies and quite possibly their lives to protest, nonviolently, severe mistreatment in the Israeli prison system, and by extension, the oppressiveness of an occupation that has gone on for forty-five years? Except among their countrymen and to some extent the region, these many thousand Palestinian prisoners have been languishing within an opaque black box for over four decades, are denied international protection, exist without rights of their own, and cope as best they can without even a proper acknowledgement of their plight.

There is another comparison that comes to mind. Recall the outpouring of concern, grief, and sympathy throughout the West for Gilad Shalit, the Israeli soldier who was captured on the Gaza border and held captive by Palestinians for five years. A powerful global campaign for his release on humanitarian grounds was organized and received constant reinforcement in the media. World leaders pleaded for his release, the UN Secretary-General exhibited concern, and Israeli commanding officers even told

---

19. Saed Bannoura, "PHR-Israel Warns of Deteriorating Condition of Two Striking Detainees," *International Middle East Media Center*, May 1, 2012, http://www.imemc.org/article/63392.

IDF fighting forces during the massive attacks on Gaza at the end of 2008, which killed more than 1,450 Palestinians, that the real mission of Operation Cast Lead was to free Shalit or at least inflict pain on the entire civilian population of Gaza for his capture, a grotesque instance of unlawful collective punishment. When Shalit was finally released in a prisoner exchange a few months ago, there was a joyful homecoming celebration in Israel that abruptly ended when, much to the disappointment of the Israeli establishment, Shalit reported good treatment during captivity. Shalit's father went further, saying that if he was a Palestinian he would have tried to capture Israeli soldiers.

This current wave of hunger strikes started on April 17, Palestinian Prisoners' Day, and was directly inspired by the earlier recently completed long and heroic hunger strikes of Khader Adnan and Hana Shalabi, both of whom protested against the combination of administrative detention and abusive arrest and interrogation procedures. It should be understood that administrative detention depends on accusations contained in secret evidence not disclosed to the detainee or defense lawyers and allows Israel to imprison Palestinians for six months at a time without bringing any criminal charges, with terms renewable as they expire. Both Mr. Adnan and Ms. Shalabi were released through last-minute deals negotiated at a time when their physical survival seemed in doubt, making death seem imminent. Israel apparently did not then want to risk agitating Palestinians by such martyrdom.

A fierce struggle of wills between the strikers and the prison authorities is underway between those with the advantages of hard-power domination and those relying on the soft-power resources of moral and spiritual courage, and societal solidarity. As the strikers repeatedly affirm, their acts are not meant for their own release alone, but on behalf of all prisoners, and beyond even this, in support of the wider Palestinian struggle for dignity, self-determination, and freedom from oppression.

The torment of these striking prisoners is not only a consequence of their refusal to accept food until certain conditions are met. Israeli prison guards and authorities are doing their best to intensify the torments of hunger. There are numerous reports that the strikers are being subjected to belittling harassment and a variety of punishments, including constant taunting, solitary confinement, confiscating personal belongings, denying family visits, disallowing examination by humanitarian NGOs, and hardhearted refusals to transfer medically threatened strikers to civilian hospitals, where they could receive the kinds of medical treatment their critical conditions urgently require.

There are also broader issues at stake. When in the past Palestinians resorted to violent forms of resistance they were branded by the West as terrorists and their deeds widely covered by dwelling upon their sensationalist aspects, but when Palestinians resort to nonviolent forms of resistance, whether hunger strikes, BDS, or an intifada, their actions fall mainly on deaf ears and wooden eyes, or worse, there is a concerted propaganda spin to depict a particular tactic of nonviolent resistance as somehow illegitimate, either as a cheap trick to gain sympathy or as a dirty trick to subvert the state of Israel by drawing its legitimacy into question. All the while, Israel's annexation plans move ahead, with settlements expanding. More than 100 settler outposts, formerly illegal even under Israeli law, are now in the process of being retroactively legalized. Such moves signal once and for all that the Netanyahu leadership exhibits not an iota of good faith when it continues to claim that it seeks to negotiate a conflict ending peace treaty with the Palestinians. It is a pity that the Palestinian Authority has not yet had the diplomatic composure to call it quits when it comes to heeding the hollow calls of the Quartet to resume direct talks with Israel. It is long past time to crumble this long bridge to nowhere.

That rock star of liberal pontificators, Thomas Friedman, has for years been preaching nonviolence to the Palestinians, implying that Israel, as a democratic country with a strong moral sensitivity, would surely yield in the face of such a principled challenge. Yet when something as remarkable as this massive expression of Palestinian commitment to nonviolent resistance takes place, Friedman and his liberal brothers and sisters are silent as stones. The *New York Times* was unable to find even an inch of space to report on these dramatic protests against Israel's use of administrative detention and abusive treatment until weeks after Khader Adnan and Hana Shalabi had ended their hunger strikes. Not until the sixty-fifth day of the continuing strikes of Bilal Diab and Thaer Halahleh, along with the 1,500 or so Palestinian prisoners who commenced refusing food on April 17 or later, did the *Times* report on the strikes.

Robert Malley, another influential liberal voice who was a Middle East advisor to Bill Clinton when he was president, suggests that any sustained display of Palestinian nonviolence, if met with Israeli violence, would be an embarrassment for Washington. Malley insists that if the Palestinians were to take to the streets in the spirit of Tahrir Square and Israelis responded violently, as the Netanyahu government could be expected to do, it "would put the United States in an . . . acute dilemma about how to react to Israel's reaction."[20] Only a confirmed liberal would call this a genuine dilemma, as any informed and objective observer would know that the U.S. government

---

20. Helene Cooper, "The Quiet Corner of the Mideast (Surprise)," *New York Times*, June 11, 2011, http://www.nytimes.com/2011/06/12/weekinreview/12palestinians.html?pagewanted=all&_r=0.

would readily accept, as it has repeatedly done in the past, an Israeli claim that force was needed to maintain public order, especially during a heated presidential campaign. In this manner Palestinian nonviolence would be once more disregarded and the super-alliance of these two partners in crime once more reaffirmed.

Let there be no mistake about the moral and spiritual background of the challenge being mounted by these Palestinians. Undertaking an open-ended hunger strike is an inherently brave act that is fraught with risks and uncertainties and is only undertaken in situations of extreme frustration or severe abuse. It is never undertaken lightly or as a stunt. For anyone who has attempted to express protest in this manner—and I have, for short periods during my decade of opposition to the Vietnam War—it is both scary and physically taxing even for a day or so. To maintain the discipline and strength of will to carry on such a strike for weeks at a time requires a rare combination of courage and resolve. Very few individuals have the psychological makeup needed to adopt such an extreme tactic of self-sacrifice and witness. For a hunger strike to be done collectively on this scale underscores the horrible ordeal of the Palestinians, which has been all but erased from the political consciousness of the West in the hot aftermath of the Arab Spring. It also suggests that a new Palestinian uprising may be in the offing, which would present Washington with the dilemma Malley worries about.

The world has long refused to take notice of one-sided Palestinian efforts over the years to reach a peaceful outcome. It is helpful to keep reminding ourselves that in 1988 the PLO officially accepted Israel within its 1967 borders, a huge territorial concession, leaving the Palestinians with only 22 percent of historic Palestine on which to establish an independent and sovereign state. In recent years, the main tactics of Palestinian opposition to the occupation, including on the part of Hamas, have largely turned away from violence, adhering to a diplomacy and practice that look toward long-term peaceful coexistence between two peoples. Israel has refused to take note of either development and has instead continuously thrown sand in Palestinians' eyes. The official Israeli response to Palestinian moves toward political restraint and away from violence has been to embark upon a program of feverish settlement expansion, extensive targeted killing, and excessive retaliatory violence, as well as intensifying the various forms of oppression that gave rise to these hunger strikes. One expression of this oppression is the 50 percent increase in the number of Palestinians held under administrative detention during the last year, along with an officially mandated worsening of conditions throughout its prison system.

Palestinian Hunger Strikes: Fighting Ingrained Duplicity

May 12, 2012
by Richard Falk and Noura Erakat[21]

On the seventy-third day of his hunger strike, Thaer Halahleh is vomiting blood and bleeding from his lips and gums, while his body weighs in at 121 pounds—a fraction of its pre-hunger strike size. The thirty-three-year-old Palestinian follows the still-palpable footsteps of Adnan Khader and Hana Shalabi, whose hunger strikes resulted in release. He also stands alongside Bilal Diab, who is entering his seventy-third day of visceral protest. Together, they inspired nearly 2,500 Palestinian political prisoners to go on hunger strike in protest of Israel's policy of indefinite detention without charge or trial.

Ayed Dudeen is one of the longest-serving administrative detainees in Israeli captivity. First arrested in October 2007, Israeli officials renewed his detention thirty times without charge or trial. After languishing in a prison cell for nearly four years without due process, prison authorities released him in August 2011, only to re-arrest him two weeks later. His wife Amal no longer tells their six children that their father is coming home, because, in her words, "I do not want to give them false hope anymore; I just hope that this nightmare will go away."[22]

Twenty percent of the Palestinian population of the occupied Palestinian territories has at one point been held under administrative detention by Israeli forces. Israel argues these policies are necessary to ensure the security of its Jewish citizens, including those unlawfully resident in settlements surrounding Jerusalem, Area C, and the Jordan Valley—in flagrant contravention of the Fourth Geneva Convention's Article 49(6), which explicitly prohibits the transfer of one's civilian population to the territory it occupies.

The mass hunger strike threatens to demolish the formidable narratives of national security long propagated by Israeli authorities. In its most recent session, the United Nations Committee on the Elimination of Racial Discrimination concluded that Israel's policy of administrative detention is not justifiable as a security imperative, but instead represents the existence of two laws for two peoples in a single land. The committee went on to state that such policies amount to arbitrary detention and

---

21. A version of this post was originally published in *Jadaliyya* on May 11, 2012, http://bit.ly/1lX7f7i.

22. Addameer, "Ayed Mohammed Salem Dudeen," undated, http://bit.ly/1qrNfL2.

contravene Article 3 of the International Convention on the Elimination of All Forms of Racial Discrimination, which prohibits "racial segregation and apartheid."[23] Nevertheless, this apartheid policy has so far escaped the global condemnation it deserves.

Although there has not been a principled or total abandonment of armed struggle by Palestinians living under occupation, there has been a notable and dramatic shift in emphasis to the tactics of nonviolence. For years, liberals in the West have been urging the Palestinians to make such a shift, partly for pragmatic reasons. Even President Obama echoed this suggestion in his 2009 Cairo address when he said, "Palestinians must abandon violence. . . . For centuries black people in America suffered the lash of the whip as slaves and the humiliation of segregation. But it was not violence that won full and equal rights. It was a peaceful and determined insistence upon the ideals at the center of America's founding."[24]

But when Palestinians act in this recommended manner, the West averts its gaze and Israel responds with cynical disregard. Today, Palestinians have epitomized the best of American values that reflect the global history of nonviolent resistance, as they wage a mass hunger strike, engage in a global BDS movement against Israeli apartheid, and risk their bodies on a weekly basis in peaceful protests against the annexation wall. The latter continues to expand its devastating encroachment upon and around Palestinian lands in defiance of a near-unanimous advisory opinion by the International Court of Justice as well as countless Security Council resolutions.

Yet the United States chooses to label the hunger strikers' prison guards, the architects of racist laws and policies, and the engineers of the apartheid wall the sole and exemplary democracy in the Middle East. Rather than condemn Israel's colonial practices, which constitute the core of Arab grievances and explain the widespread resentment of the United States' role in the Middle East, a House of Representatives panel has just now approved nearly one billion dollars in additional military assistance to augment Israel's anti-missile defense program. If passed, Israel will receive a record amount of four billion dollars in military aid next year—more than any country in the world.

---

23. UN Committee on the Elimination of Racial Discrimination, *Report of the Committee on the Elimination of Racial Discrimination*, 80th session (February 13–March 9, 2012), March 9, 2012, A/67/18, p. 21, http://www.refworld.org/docid/50a0edab2.html.

24. Barack Obama, "Remarks by the President on a New Beginning," speech delivered in Cairo, Egypt, June 4, 2009, http://www.whitehouse.gov/the_press_office/Remarks-by-the-President-at-Cairo-University-6-04-09.

What is more, such hunger strikes are part of a broader Palestinian reliance on a powerful symbolic appeal to the conscience of humanity in their quest for long-denied rights under international law. Said deprivations include a disavowal of a peace process that has gone nowhere for decades, while a pattern of settlement expansion has made any realization of the widely endorsed "two-state solution" increasingly implausible. The prolonged nature of the occupation also steadily transforms what was supposed to be a temporary occupation into a permanent arrangement best understood as a mixture of annexation and apartheid.

In the face of this opportunity to place pressure upon Israel to comply with international law and human rights norms, the international community of governments and intergovernmental institutions has been grotesquely silent as Palestinians place their very lives at sacrificial risk. For its part, the United Nations' most senior officials said nothing until a group of forty young protestors blocked the entrance of UN offices in Ramallah on May 8, demanding the issuance of a statement on behalf of the hunger striking prisoners. Together with the help of a global social media campaign to trend #UNclosed, UN Secretary-General Ban Ki-moon and the director of the UN Relief and Works Agency (UNRWA), Filippo Grandi, have finally issued statements expressing deep concern. Grandi has gone the farthest, urging that Israel either provide trials for the detainees or release them, though his statement has been conspicuously removed from UNRWA's website.

It is hard to deny the irony of tacit approval, at worst, or timid condemnation, at best, in the United Nations, the United States, and elsewhere. In its 2008 *Boumedienne v. Bush* decision, the U.S. Supreme Court declared that (arguably) the world's most villainous and immoral persons are entitled to habeas corpus review in U.S. courts in order to avoid the cruelty of indefinite detention. Yet, Israel's policy of detaining indigenous Palestinians who inhabit the lands the state has sought to confiscate and settle for more than four decades has denied those Palestinians exactly such legal protection. What are Palestinians to do in the face of such frustrating circumstances? What message does the lack of international support for their strong displays of nonviolence, self-sacrifice, and personal bravery send to them and to their Arab and Muslim counterparts, who are once more exposed to blatant U.S. hypocrisy in the region?

Palestinian civil society is now mainly opting for explicit acts of collective nonviolent resistance to register their dissatisfactions with the failures of the United Nations—or intergovernmental diplomacy in general—to produce a sustainable peace that reflects Palestinian rights under international law. The main expression of this embrace of nonviolence is the adoption of tactics used so successfully by the anti-apartheid campaign to change the political climate in racist South Africa, yielding a nonviolent path to multiracial constitutional democracy. At the present time the growing BDS movement is working to achieve similar results.

Let us recall that successful global nonviolent movements are not restricted to fasts and marches, but include the boycott, noncooperation, and civil disobedience tactics Palestinians are deploying today. Though President Obama, encumbered as he may be by a domestic election cycle, may feel compelled to ignore Palestinian responses to his call, the rest of the world should not. Certainly, U.S.-based and global citizens should demand that the Western media begin to act responsibly when dealing with injustices inflicted on the Palestinian people, and not sheepishly report human rights abuses only when committed by the adversaries of their state. The media itself is a tactical target and a residual problem. In solidarity with the hunger strikers, civic allies should address the institutional edifice upholding administrative detention. It extends from a discriminatory core, and therefore its requisite treatment includes ensuring the enjoyment of internationally guaranteed rights—rights enshrined by the BDS call to action and reified by the movement's steady and deliberate progression.

Reflecting on the Great Palestinian Hunger Strikes of 2012
May 15, 2012[25]

Ché Guevara was once asked what was at the root of his revolutionary commitment. His response, upon which we should all take some moments to reflect: "It is about love." Reading the words of Khader Adnan ("Open Letter to the People of the World") and Thaer Halahleh ("Letter to my Daughter"), or the comments of Hana Shalabi's mother and sister and Bilal Diab's father, led me to recall Guevara's illuminating comment. Only those with closed minds can read such words of devotion without feeling that the animating hunger of these Palestinians is for peace and justice, for love and dignity, and that their heroic strikes would have been impossible without cherishing life and future freedom for the people of Palestine.

The nature of extreme self-sacrifice, provided it is autonomous and nonviolent, is an inherently *spiritual* undertaking, even when its external appearance is *political*. For Christians and others moved to tears by the life

---

25. Originally published as "Reflections on the Great Palestinian Hunger Strikes of 2012," http://bit.ly/1vf27N6.

of Jesus, the crucifixion exemplifies this encounter between the political and the spiritual.

We can only marvel at the duplicitous double standards of the media. Without the Internet and Al Jazeera, the West, especially the United States, would have rendered invisible these challenges to Israeli abuses of human rights and international humanitarian law. Only the settlement of the strike and, to some extent, fear of Palestinian unrest should one of these hunger strikers die while in detention were deemed somewhat newsworthy by the Western press.

As many have observed, the media treatment of the Chinese dissident Chen Guangcheng or the global attention given to Gilad Shalit, the Israeli soldier held captive in Gaza, underscores the media's victimization of the Palestinian struggle and exposes the illegitimacy of an information regime that rests upon such a flagrant disregard for objectivity, taking refuge in ill-disguised double standards: magnifying Israeli grievances, disappearing Palestinian wrongs.

The Israeli media did have a cynical preoccupation with the hunger strikes, wavering between worries of seeming to give in to fears of a third intifada and the characteristic concern of an oppressor: that accommodating grievances would be treated as a show of weakness and encourage further Palestinian resistance activity. For this reason, right-wing Israeli politicians have sharply criticized the agreement reached to end the main strike.

Israel is not alone in addressing prison hunger strikes in a detached manner that refuses to acknowledge the moral motivation, physical courage and discipline, and righteousness of the demands for reforms. A 2011 protest hunger strike in California's notorious Pelican Bay State Prison and other prisons around the state led to this monumentally icy reaction from Nancy Kincaid, director of communications for the California Correctional Health Services: "They have the right to choose to die of starvation if they wish."[26] And as the late Kurt Vonnegut so memorably reflected on the terror bombing of Dresden during World War II: "And so it goes."

The ending of the hunger strikes on the eve of the sixty-fourth observance of *Nakba* Day is above all a protest against the *particular* reality of these protests against administrative detention, arrest procedures, and unacceptable prison regulations. It also needs to be understood as part of the *general* Palestinian struggle for protection and rights, above all the

---

26. Justin Berton, "Calif. Sees Gang Ties in Prisoners' Hunger Strike," *San Francisco Chronicle*, July 13, 2011, http://www.sfchronicle.com/news/article/Calif-sees-gang-ties-in-prisoners-hunger-strike-2354572.php.

inalienable right of self-determination, which is accorded to every people by virtue of Article 1 of both Human Rights Covenants.

Throughout this period of hunger strikes, I and others have taken notice of the IRA strike in the Maze Prison in Northern Ireland in which ten Irish prisoners fasted unto death, including the martyred Irish hero, Bobby Sands. What I have learned of while following the developments in the Palestinian strikes was the earlier, celebrated hunger strike of Terence MacSwiney, the elected lord mayor of County Cork who was arrested, charged, and convicted of his activism in the Irish struggle against British colonial rule.

MacSwiney, upon conviction, told a stunned court, "I shall be free, alive, or dead, within a month." He died on October 25, 1920, in the Brixton Prison after an extraordinary seventy-four-day hunger strike and has been part of the proud tradition of Irish revolutionary iconography ever since. Unlike the blanket of denial and silence that has accompanied the Palestinian acts of protest, the MacSwiney story "became a worldwide sensation, causing workers to lay down tools on the New York waterfront, sparking riots in Barcelona and mass demonstrations from Buenos Aires to Boston. The international press covered his decline on a daily basis, raising the profile of the cause of Irish Independence to previously unheard-of heights." [27]

Aside from the contrast in media coverage, there is the notable fact that MacSwiney faced charges in an open court and was allowed to speak in his own defense. Governments that claim to be democracies and respectful of human rights and the rule of law should waste no time in abolishing administrative detention provisions. And if that is not done, at least the pretension of constitutional democracy should be abandoned. Is it not time we demanded that power speak truth to the people?

---

27. For a detailed account, see Dave Hannigan's *Terence MacSwiney: The Hunger Strike that Rocked an Empire* (Dublin: O'Brien Press, 2010).

Beyond the Politics of Invisibility: Remembering Not to Forget Palestinian Hunger Strikers

May 28, 2012[28]

With a certain amount of fanfare in Israel and Palestine, although still severely underreported by the world media and relatively ignored by the leading watchdog human rights NGOs, the Palestinian hunger strikes were brought to an end by agreement between the strikers and Israel. At least, that is what most of us believed who were following this narrative from outside the region— but like so much else in the region, our understanding was a half-truth, if that. Whether Israel abides by its assurances remains to be seen, and although these strikes were courageous acts of nonviolent resistance it is not clear at this point whether they will have any longer term effects on the Israel's occupation, arrest, and prison policy or on the wider Palestinian struggle.

Two things are certain, however. First, the strikes raised a much wider awareness that Israel's reliance on administrative detention, its abusive arrest procedures, and its prison system deserve wider scrutiny than in the past, and that this dimension of the prolonged occupation of Palestine has inflicted great suffering on many Palestinians and their families ever since 1967. Whether such a structure of imprisonment of an occupied people should be viewed as a hitherto-neglected dimension of state terrorism is an open question that should be further investigated. Second, the hunger strike as a mode of resistance is now part of the Palestinian culture of resistance, and an option that engages Palestinian political consciousness in a manner that did not exist prior to Khader Adnan's hunger strike.

Supposedly Israeli prison authorities agreed under the pressure of these latter strikes to reduce reliance on solitary confinement in its prisons and to allow more family visits, especially from Gaza. What was this pressure? It was not moral suasion. It seemed to be a calculated decision by Israeli prison authorities that it would be better to make small concessions than risk angry reactions to the death of any hunger strikers. Israel only *seemed* to give in. It needs to be understood that Israel retains all the prerogatives to rely on administrative detention in the future and continues to have unmonitored, exclusive control over prison life.

These uncertainties about the results of these past strikes should certainly be kept in mind. What is presently of more urgent concern is the failure even to realize that long-term hunger strikes were never ended by at

---

28. Originally published at http://bit.ly/1iDeAKu.

least two prisoners, Mahmoud Sarsak, without food for seventy days, and Akram al-Rakhawi on strike for forty days. Both are currently in danger of dying, yet hardly anybody seems to know. Sarsak, who is twenty-five and a resident of the Rafah refugee camp in Gaza, is hardly a nobody: when arrested in July 2009 he was a member of the Palestine National Football Team on his way to a match in the West Bank. He was arrested under the Incarceration of Unlawful Combatants Law, which offers a detained person even less protection than is provided by "administrative detention." It is aimed at Palestinians living in Gaza, a part of Palestine that Israel (but not the international community) has treated as no longer occupied since implementing Sharon's "disengagement plan" in 2005. Imad Sarsak has bemoaned his brother's fate: "My family never would have imagined that Mahmoud would have been imprisoned by Israel. Why, really why?"[29]

There is reason to believe that rather than some conjured up security concern, Sarsak was arrested as part of a broader effort to demoralize the Palestinians, especially those long entrapped in Gaza. During the savage attacks on Gaza at the end of 2008, the national stadium used for football and the offices of the Palestine Football Association were targeted and destroyed, and three members of the Palestine team killed. All along the team has been handicapped by curfews, checkpoints, and harassments, as well as the blockade of Gaza, which has forced the team to forfeit many games. The goalkeeper, Omar Abu Rwayyes, has said, "If you degrade the national team you degrade the idea that there could ever be a nation."[30] Football (what we Americans call soccer) plays a vital symbolic role in the self-esteem and national consciousness of peoples throughout the Arab world and elsewhere in the South, to a degree unimaginable even for a sports-crazy country like the United States.

The football world has taken some slight notice of the plight of the Palestinian team. A few years ago Michel Platini, president of the Union of European Football Associations (UEFA), warned Israel that it was risking its own membership in UEFA if it continued to interfere with Palestinian efforts to field the best possible team for international competition. But as with many international gestures of protest against Israel, there was no follow-through. In fact, a disturbing reversal of approach took place. Not long afterward, Platini actually presided over a process that awarded Israel the honor of hosting the 2013 Under-21 European Championships. A British NGO, Soccer without Borders, was not so easily seduced: it urged

---

29. Dave Zirin, "What If Kobe Bryant Were an Imprisoned Palestinian Soccer Player?" *Nation*, May 10, 2012, http://www.thenation.com/blog/167827/what-if-kobe-bryant-were-imprisoned-palestinian-soccer-player.

30. Ibid.

a boycott of the event, declaring that its organization "stands in solidarity with Mahmoud Sarsak and all Palestinian political prisoners."[31]

As is usually the case, the Israeli response was self-justifying and cynical. A Shin Bet official insisted that Israel "can't play by the rules of bridge where everyone else is playing rugby."[32] This kind of assertion papers over the degree to which Israeli society in recent years has enjoyed peace, prosperity, and security while Palestinians have been enduring the rigors of a cruel occupation and the severe vulnerabilities of a rights-less existence. Palestinians have also been experiencing the split reality of observing one set of protective laws applied to Israeli settlers (all of whom are part of an unlawful enterprise) while an unregulated military structure is applied arbitrarily to the indigenous residents of the West Bank, East Jerusalem, and Gaza.

With national athletes being such objects of interest, this "politics of invisibility" is effective in keeping the world from knowing the harm being done to the Palestinian people and how they are resisting, often at great risk and self-sacrifice, as epitomized by these long hunger strikes. One can be certain that if such repressive measures were taken by China or Myanmar there would be a mighty cascade of interest, coupled with high-minded denunciations from the global bully pulpits of political leaders and an array of moral authority figures. But when the Palestinians experience abuse or resist by reliance on brave forms of nonviolence, there is a posture of almost total disregard; if a few voices are raised, such as that of Archbishop Desmond Tutu, they are either ignored as "partisan" or discredited by allegations of "anti-Semitism," a denunciation whose meaning has been conflated so as to apply to any critic of Israel. Even such a globally respected figure as Jimmy Carter could not escape the wrath of Israeli loyalists, merely because he used the word "apartheid" in the title of a book urging a just peace between the two peoples.

The politics of invisibility is cruel and harmful. It is cruel because it does not acknowledge a pattern of injustice, because the victims have been effectively stigmatized. It is harmful because it sends a strong signal that victimization will only be given some sort of visibility if it shocks the conscience with its violence against those who seem innocent. Such visibility has a largely negative and stereotyping impact, allowing the oppressor to escalate state violence without risking any kind of backlash or even notice and validating perceptions of the victim population as undeserving or even

---

31. Ibid.

32. Irris Makler, "Khader Adnan—A Palestinian Hungering for Justice," *Deutsche Welle*, May 28, 2012, http://www.dw.de/ khader-adnan-a-palestinian-hungering-for-justice/a-15981455.

as evil endorsers of an ethos of terrorism. Israeli *hasbara* has worked hard over many years to stereotype the Palestinians as "terrorists" and, by doing so, to withdraw any sympathy from their victimization, which is portrayed as being somehow deserved. These hunger strikers, despite all indications to the contrary, are so described, their supposed association with Islamic Jihad attributed to an embrace of terrorism. A more objective look at the evidence suggests that Islamic Jihad has itself for several years abandoned tactics of violence against civilian targets and is part of a broader shift in Palestinian tactics of resistance in the direction of nonviolence. Such shifts are totally ignored by the politics of invisibility so as to keep the negative stereotype before the public.

It is one more challenge to global civil society to do what international law is currently incapable of doing: treating equals equally. If the world media renders visible the plight of Chinese human rights activists who are abused by the state, might not human rights NGOs at least note the emergency plight of Palestinian hunger strikers on the edge of death? And if these NGOs are afraid to do so, should not those with eyes able to see such torment start screaming at the top of our lungs?

U.S. Military Suicides and Palestinian Hunger Strikers
June 12, 2012[33]

There is some awareness in the United States that suicides among U.S. military personnel are at their highest level since the Vietnam War. It is no wonder. The sense of guilt and alienation associated with taking part in the Afghanistan war, especially multiple postings to a menacing war zone for a combat mission that is increasingly hard to justify and almost impossible to carry out successfully, seems sufficient to explain such a disturbing phenomenon. These tragic losses of life, now outnumbering battlefield deaths—about one per day since the start of 2012—are not hidden from the American public, but neither do they provoke an appropriate sense of concern, or better, outrage. This contrasts with the Vietnam years, especially toward the end of the war, when many families with children at risk in a war that had lost its way and was being lost took to the streets, pressured their congressional representatives, spoke at antiwar rallies,

---

33. Originally published at http://richardfalk.wordpress.com/
2012/06/12/u-s-military-suicides-and-palestinian-hunger-strikers.

and supported their sons' unwillingness to take part. Now there is a stony silence in American society, which seems to be a confirmation that we now are "citizens" of, or "patriots" in, an authoritarian democracy—or, more urbanely, "subjects" of a constitutional democracy. We are less cognizant than ever of the Jeffersonian imperative: the health of this democracy depends on the conscience and vigilance of its citizens.

Anthony Swofford, a former marine seeking to comprehend what *Newsweek* acknowledges to be "an epidemic" of suicides among combat veterans, takes note of the resistance to self-scrutiny on the part of the governmental branches most involved. In his words, "the Department of Veterans Affairs and the military shy away from placing blame directly on the psychological and social costs of killing during combat."[34] There is some attention given, apparently, to improving the screening process so that potential suicides are not inducted, but no sensitivity to the deeply alienating experience of being assigned to kill in an utterly unfamiliar human environment that is naturally hostile to occupation. If you have seen pictures of heavily armed American foot soldiers on patrol in an Afghan village, feelings of surreal misfit seem inescapable. Yet there is no national sense of responsibility associated with sending young Americans into situations where the harm done to themselves not only puts their lives and well-being in jeopardy as a result of being exposed to enemy weapons, but also subjects them to often-invisible traumatic wounds that rarely heal altogether, even many years after leaving the war zone.

These wounds are far more widespread than even the high incidence of suicide suggests, often expressed in less dramatic and terminal ways. It is a monumental expression of insensitivity to the well-being of our youth that we put them in harm's way to carry out a war effort that has long been drained of meaning and that our leaders are at a loss to explain. True patriotism in this century should produce an angry uproar and public debate before acquiescing to such cruel indifference to the fate of our young warriors, who are disproportionately poor and frequently members of marginalized minorities. This insensitivity is far less pervasive than when the victims are "others." This is illustrated by the national failure to raise questions about the state terror associated with drone attacks on village communities in foreign countries that undoubtedly spread acute fear and feelings of vulnerability to the entire population, not just to those who might imagine themselves to be selected by an American president as a kill target.

---

34. Anthony Swofford, "We Pretend the Vets Don't Exist," *Newsweek*, May 21, 2012, http://bit.ly/1m0E6E3.

The relationship of these suicides to the recent wave of Palestinian hunger strikers objecting to Israeli detention, arrest, and prison practices is worth commenting upon. The hunger strikers are arousing widespread sympathy and a growing commitment among Palestinians to protest their confinement and celebrate their courage, embracing their acts as essential expressions of Palestinian nonviolent resistance to occupation, annexation, and apartheid conditions. Unlike suicides among veterans, which are lonely acts of desperation because the conditions of living have become unendurable, the hunger strikers are willingly and knowingly engaging in a punishing, self-decreed refusal to accept food as the only means available to call attention to their severe grievances. Their acts express an intense desire for life, not death, but their statement to the world is that when conditions become so dreadful, it is preferable to die than to be further humiliated by intolerable mistreatment.

The first hunger striker, Khader Adnan, released in April, tells why he engaged in such extreme violence against his body despite a deep attachment to his family and village life:

> The reasons behind my hunger strike were the frequent arrests and treatment received when arrested and the third was the barbaric methods of interrogation in prison—they humiliated me. They put dust of their shoes on my moustache, they picked hairs out of my beard, they tied my hand behind my back and to the chair which was tied to the floor. They put my picture on the floor and stepped on it. They cursed my wife, and my daughter who was less than a year and four months old with the most offensive words they could use.[35]

The hunger strikes have finally brought to light such patterns of humiliation, long imposed on imprisoned Palestinians. What Adnan did inspired many others among Palestinian prisoners, and at present there remain at least three Palestinians risking death to abide by their plea for life and dignity. These include a prominent member of the Palestinian national football team who has been held as an "unlawful combatant" since July 2009, Mahmoud Sarsak, now ninety days without food; the two others are Akram al-Rakhawi, seventy days, and Sunar al-Berq.

These dual sad sets of circumstances both involve fundamental wrongs associated with the violence of states. The American suicides are essentially sacrifices of lives at the altar of the Martian god of war, while the

---

35. Khader Adnan, "Khader Adnan Speaks," transcript of speech given via Skype to Palestine Place, London, June 3, 2012, http://palestineplace.wordpress.com/2012/06/08/khader-adnan-speaks-video-link-up-transcript-part-1-3-2.

Palestinian hunger strikes are struggles to survive in the face of state terror, imposed in darkness on those who show any signs of resistance to an occupation that has gone on for forty-five years and has become more and more oppressive with the passage of time. As Adnan said of his experience of arrest in the middle of the night and release: "They are trying to hurt our dignity . . . and released me in the dark, late at night . . . they only work in the darkness."[36]

Despite this darkness, we should be able to see what is happening and respond with whatever means are at our disposal. In the United States, we are mostly kept in the dark with respect to Palestinian suffering; as for our American victims of war, we are informed but not enlightened and thus are caught in the headlights, supposing that these military suicides are an unfathomable mystery rather than inevitable byproducts of wars fought in strange foreign lands for no credible defensive purpose.

---

36. Ibid.

4

Global Solidarity: Initiatives and Obstacles

Suddenly, the relevance of global solidarity to the Palestinian national struggle has come to be seen as crucial to the success of this increasingly robust movement. Ali Abunimah ends the preface of his recently published *The Battle for Justice in Palestine* with these words: "The victory against Israeli apartheid, colonialism, and racism that I am convinced the Palestinians and their allies have it within their power to make will not be theirs alone. It will belong to everyone who believes in, and fights for, equality and justice."[1] These are stirring words with two messages: that a potential Palestinian victory will come primarily *from below*, from the people—Palestinians and non-Palestinians—not through maneuverings *from above* by governments and special interests, and that the Palestinian struggle is linked to the wider quest for justice and equality throughout the world—and a victory in Palestine will strengthen prospects elsewhere.

The dramatic growth of the global Palestinian solidarity movement in recent years has been due to Israel's blatant defiance of international law and the shift in Palestinian resistance strategy strongly in the direction of waging a legitimacy struggle. This shift is related both to the failures of the early efforts in the period from 1948 to 1973 to achieve a Palestinian victory based on liberation *from without*, by warfare conducted by Arab neighbors of Israel in support of Palestinian claims to the land, exhibiting a refusal by the Arab world to accept the outcome of the 1948 War from which the sovereign state of Israel emerged. Israel's defeat of these Arab efforts led to a shift in Palestinian strategy, emphasizing armed resistance by the Palestinians themselves, which continued until the expulsion of the PLO

---

1. Ali Abunimah, *The Battle for Justice in Palestine* (Chicago: Haymarket Books, 2014), xiv.

from Lebanon in 1982. Then came the First Intifada in 1987, which was the beginning of nonviolent resistance *from below* as expressive of the essence of the Palestinian struggle. The subsequent 2005 call by a large coalition of Palestinian NGOs for a worldwide BDS movement did not have political traction at the outset, but in the last several years the BDS campaign has been gaining momentum on many fronts and may be reaching a tipping point. The comparison with the global, UN-endorsed campaign against apartheid in South Africa is natural to make, although there are many fundamental differences in circumstances, including the makeup and goals of the contesting parties.

At the same time, non-Palestinian supporters of a just and sustainable peace must remember to leave the center stage to the Palestinians. Underneath all the commentary on the conflict, we all need to appreciate that this struggle is, at its core, of, by, and for a people seeking to realize their long-denied inalienable right of self-determination, a struggle blocked by cruel and prolonged occupation and dispossession, unlawful military actions, and geopolitical interferences. The Palestinian people have been hurt over the decades by decisions made by others to shape the political future of Palestine, starting with the Balfour Declaration in 1917, a commitment by a British official to the Zionist movement to encourage the establishment of a Jewish homeland in historic Palestine. The UN partition plan, essentially a revision of the colonialist vision of the British Peel Commission, went along the same lines, devising a solution for conflict in Palestine without deferring to, or even taking into account, the wishes of the people resident in the territory.

What is called for at this time is solidarity with the Palestinian struggle, for the reasons Abunimah suggests, but humility about proposing what kind of political arrangement the Palestinians should agree to as the basis of a peace that promises to be sustainable and just—that is, more than a truce. Similarly, for Israelis, the future should be a matter shaped by their own processes, not a *diktat* from abroad. However unjust the Balfour Declaration was at the time, and however much suffering it has produced for the Palestinian people, the unfolding of history cannot be reversed. As Edward Said frequently observed, the Palestinian dispossession cannot be corrected by an Israeli dispossession. There must be a solution based on justice for both sides that is sensitive to competing rights under international law and in ways that are responsive to the imperatives of international morality.

The posts in this section depict and assess various dimensions of this new stage of conflict and explore the tactics of resistance and liberation being pursued beneath the banner of global solidarity with the Palestinian people and their struggle. Several selections discuss the relevance of Israel's persistent refusal to respect international law in different contexts and the degree to which the UN winks at such refusals by its failure to insist more credibly that Israel show respect for international law, especially in light of the vulnerability of so many Palestinians living under occupation and as refugees. It is also disillusioning that the UN has refused to exhibit even symbolic support for courageous civil society initiatives seeking to break the blockade of Gaza.

The two final selections consider the politics and tactics of legitimacy struggles. "The Pros and Cons of Solidarity with the Palestinian Struggle" does so in relation to the nature of global solidarity initiatives that reflect the efforts of non-Palestinians and that, without proper sensitivity, risk undermining Palestinians' control over their own national destiny, which is the essence of the right to self-determination. Second, "Divestment at the University of California, Santa Barbara" considers the especially sensitive mobilizing experience associated with the divestment campaigns being mounted in universities, churches, labor unions, and other venues around the world. The multiplication of such divestment efforts during the last two years, especially in the United States and Europe, has become a central battleground for advocates of the legitimacy approach to peace and justice. From another perspective, the purpose of divestment, indeed of BDS generally, is to create a political climate in which intergovernmental negotiations might produce more positive outcomes. In effect, the current imbalance in capabilities is so great as to undermine Israeli incentives to reach an agreement reflective of equality between the people of Israel and of Palestine.

Israel's Violence against Separation Wall Protests: Along the Path of State Terrorism
January 7, 2011[2]

One of the flashpoints in occupied Palestine in recent years has involved nonviolent weekly protests against continued Israeli construction of a separation wall extending throughout the whole of the West Bank. A particularly active site for these protests has been the village of Bil'in near the city of Ramallah, where the Israeli penchant for using deadly force to disrupt nonviolent demonstrations raises deep legal and moral concerns.

Way back in 2004, the International Court of Justice (the highest judicial body in the UN system), in a rare near-unanimous ruling, declared the

---

2. Originally published at http://bit.ly/1nWD5RW.

construction of the wall on occupied Palestinian territory to be unlawful and ordered Israel to dismantle it and compensate Palestinians for the harm done. Israel has defied this ruling and so the wall remains, and work continues on segments yet to be completed.

Against this background, the world should take note of the shocking death of Jawaher Abu Rahmah on the first day of 2011 as a result of suffocation resulting from tear-gas inhalation; she was not even taking part in the Bil'in demonstration. Witnesses confirm that she was standing above the actual demonstration as an interested spectator. It was a large year-end demonstration that included 350 Israeli and international activists. There was no excuse for using such a harsh method to disrupt a protest against a feature of the occupation pronounced unlawful by an authoritative international body. As it happens, Ms. Rahmah's brother had been killed a few months earlier by a tear-gas canister fired at high velocity from a close range. There are many other reports of casualties caused by Israel's extreme methods of crowd control. International activists have also been injured and harshly detained, including the Irish Nobel Peace laureate Mairead Maguire. Together these deaths exhibit a general and unacceptable Israeli disposition to use excessive force against Palestinians living under occupation. Just a day after Ms. Rahmah's death, an unarmed young Palestinian, Ahmed Maslamany, was shot to death at a West Bank checkpoint while peacefully commuting to work because he failed to follow an instruction given in Hebrew, a language he did not understand.

When this lethal violence is directed against unarmed civilians seeking to uphold fundamental rights to land, routine mobility, and self-determination, it dramatizes just how lawless a state Israel has become and how justifiable and necessary is the growing world campaign of delegitimation centered upon BDS. Each instance of excessive and criminal Israeli violence inflicts suffering on innocent Palestinian civilians, but is a form of martyrdom in the nonviolent legitimacy struggle that the Palestinians have been waging within Palestine and on the symbolic global battlefields of world public opinion, with growing success.

Israel knows very well how to control unruly crowds with a minimum of violence. It has demonstrated this frequently by the way it deals gently, if at all, with a variety of settler demonstrations that pose far greater threats to social peace than do these anti-wall demonstrations. It is impossible to separate this excessive use of force on the ground against Palestinians from the indiscriminate use of force against civilians in Israel's larger occupation policy, as illustrated by the cruel, punitive blockade it has imposed on the people of Gaza since 2007 and by the criminal manner in which it carried out attacks for three weeks on the defenseless population of Gaza beginning in late 2008. Is it not time for the international community to step in and offer this long-vulnerable Palestinian population protection against Israeli violence?

Underneath Israel's reliance on excessive force as a matter of strategic doctrine are thinly disguised racist ideas: that Israeli lives are worth many times the value of Palestinian lives; that Palestinians, like all Arabs, only understand the language of force. This last is an essentially genocidal idea launched influentially years ago in a notorious book, *The Arab Mind* by Raphael Patai, published in 1973. It is also part of a punitive approach to the occupation, especially in Gaza, where WikiLeaks cables confirm what was long suspected: "As part of their overall embargo plan against Gaza, Israeli officials have confirmed to [U.S. embassy economic officers] on multiple occasions that they intend to keep the Gaza economy on the brink of collapse without quite pushing it over the edge."[3] Prime Minister Ehud Olmert, in a January 2008 speech, said of the blockade: "We will not harm the supply of food for children, medicine for those who need it and fuel for institutions that save lives. But there is no justification for demanding we allow residents of Gaza to live normal lives while shells and rockets are fired from their streets and courtyards [at southern Israel]."[4]

This is a clear confession of collective punishment of a civilian population by Israel's political leader at the time, violating the unconditional prohibition of Article 33 of the Fourth Geneva Convention. Such gross criminality should subject Israeli political leaders to international mechanisms designed to impose accountability on individuals responsible for the commission of crimes against humanity. It also makes it evident that the blockade is punitive, not a response to cross-border violence—which, incidentally, was at all times far more destructive of Palestinian lives and property than Israeli. Beyond this, the Hamas leadership in Gaza had, since its election, repeatedly attempted to establish a ceasefire along its border, which with the help of Egypt reduced casualties on both sides to almost zero after being established in mid-2008. Israel provocatively disrupted this ceasefire on November 5, 2008, to set the stage for launching massive attacks on Gaza, on December 27, 2008.

In that war, if such a one-sided conflict can be so described, the criminality of the IDF's tactics has been abundantly documented by the Goldstone Report, by a comprehensive fact-finding mission headed by John Dugard under the auspices of the Arab League, and by detailed reports issued by

3. The cable, published by the Norwegian daily newspaper *Aftenposten* on January 5, 2011, can be read in full at http://bit.ly/1pJveqw.

4. Jeffrey Heller, "Israel Said Would Keep Gaza near Collapse: WikiLeaks," Reuters, January 5, 2011, http://reut.rs/1oaUJBk.

Amnesty International and Human Rights Watch. There is no reasonable basis for any longer doubting the substance of the allegations of criminality associated with those three weeks of all-out attacks on the people and civilian infrastructure of Gaza, including UN schools and buildings.

The Goldstone Report correctly noted that the overall impression left by the attacks was an extension of the "Dahiya doctrine," attributed to an Israeli general during the 2006 Lebanon War, in which Israel destroyed a district in South Beirut from the air, a deliberately excessive response at the expense of civilian society, because it was an alleged Hezbollah stronghold and in response to a border incident with Hezbollah in which ten Israeli soldiers lost their lives. The 2009 Goldstone Report quoted IDF Northern Command chief Gadi Eisenkot, who said:

> What happened in the Dahiya quarter of Beirut in 2006 will happen in every village from which Israel is fired on. We will apply disproportionate force on it and cause great damage and destruction there. From our standpoint, these are not civilian villages, they are military bases. . . . This is not a recommendation. This is a plan. And it has been approved.[5]

In effect, the civilian infrastructure of adversaries such as Hamas or Hezbollah are treated as permissible military targets, which is not only an overt violation of the most elementary norms of the law of war and of universal morality, but an avowal of a doctrine of violence that needs to be called by its proper name: state terrorism.

We have reached a stage where the oppressiveness of the Israeli occupation of the West Bank, East Jerusalem, and the Gaza Strip, extending now for more than forty-three years and maintained by multiple daily violations of international humanitarian law should be understood and condemned as being, in its essence and by design, *state terrorism*, as exhibited both in structure and practice.

---

5. UN Fact-Finding Mission on the Gaza Conflict, "Human Rights in Palestine and Other Occupied Territories" [Goldstone Report] (New York: United Nations, September 25, 2009), 254, http://www2.ohchr.org/english/bodies/hrcouncil/docs/12session/A-HRC-12-48.pdf.

The Legal Flaws of the Palmer Commission Flotilla Report

September 13, 2011

by Richard Falk and Phyllis Bennis[6]

When the UN Secretary-General announced on August 2, 2010, that a panel of inquiry had been established to investigate Israel's May 31 attacks on the *Mavi Marmara* and five other ships carrying humanitarian aid to the beleaguered people of Gaza, there was widespread hope that international law would be vindicated and the Israelis would finally be held accountable. With the release of the Palmer Commission Report, these hopes have been largely dashed; the report failed to address the central international law issues in a credible and satisfactory manner. Turkey, not surprisingly, responded strongly that it was not prepared to live with the central finding of the 105-page report, which reached the astonishing conclusion that the Israeli blockade of the Gaza Strip was lawful and could be enforced by Israel against a humanitarian mission even in international waters.

Perhaps this outcome should not be so surprising after all. The panel, as appointed, was woefully ill-equipped to render an authoritative result. Geoffrey Palmer, its chair, although a respected public figure as the former prime minister of New Zealand and an environmental law professor, was not particularly knowledgeable about either the international law of the sea or the law of war. Incredibly, the only other independent member of the panel was Álvaro Uribe, the former president of Colombia, who holds no professional credentials relevant to the issues under consideration and is notorious both for his horrible human rights record in office and for forging intimate ties with Israel by way of arms purchases and diplomatic cooperation. The latter was acknowledged by the American Jewish Committee with its Light Unto the Nations Award, which should have been sufficient by itself to cast doubt on Uribe's suitability for this appointment. His presence on the panel compromised the integrity of the process and makes one wonder how such an appointment could even be explained, let alone justified. Turkey's agreement to participate in such a panel was in itself, it now becomes clear, a serious diplomatic failure. It should have insisted on a panel with more qualified and less aligned members.

The other two members of the panel were designated by the governments of Israel and Turkey, and predictably appended partisan dissents

---

6. Originally published at http://richardfalk.wordpress.com/2011/09/13/
   the-legal-flaws-of-the-palmer-commission-flotilla-report.

to those portions of the report that criticized the positions taken by their respective governments. Another unacceptable limitation of the report was that the panel was constrained by its terms of reference, which prohibited its members from relying on any materials other than what was presented in the two national reports submitted by the contending governments. With these considerations in mind, we can only wonder why the Secretary-General would have established a formal process so ill-equipped to reach findings that would put the legal controversy to rest and resolve diplomatic tensions, both of which it has certainly failed to do. Such deficient foresight is one of the notable outcomes of this unfortunate UN effort to achieve the peaceful resolution of an international dispute.

Even such an ill-conceived panel did not altogether endorse Israel's behavior on May 31. The panel found that Israel used excessive force and was legally and morally responsible for the deaths of nine passengers on the *Mavi Marmara*, and instructed Israel to pay compensation and issue a statement of regret.[7] In other words, the Palmer Report seems to fault the manner by which Israel enforced the blockade seriously, but nevertheless upheld the underlying legality of both the blockade and the right of enforcement—and that is the rub. Such a conclusion contradicted the earlier finding of a more expert panel established by the Human Rights Council, as well as rejecting the overwhelming consensus expressed by qualified international law specialists on these core issues. Another gross inadequacy of the report was that it separated its assessment of the blockade, as if exclusively concerned with Israeli security, and ignored the blockade's essential role in imposing an intolerable regime of collective punishment on the population of Gaza.

While the panel delayed the report several times to give diplomacy a chance to resolve the contested issues, Israel and Turkey could never quite reach closure. There were intriguing reports along the way that unpublicized discussions between representatives of the two governments had led to a compromise arrangement, with Israel ready to offer Turkey a formal apology and to compensate the families of those killed and wounded during the attack, but when the time came for announcing such a resolution, Israel refused to go along. In particular, the Israeli prime minister, Benjamin Netanyahu, seemed unwilling to take the last step, claiming that it would demoralize the citizenry of Israel and signal weakness to Israel's enemies in the region. More cynical observers believed this was a reflection of domestic politics, especially Netanyahu's rivalry with an even more extremist political figure, Foreign Minister Avigdor Lieberman, who was forever accusing Netanyahu of being a wimpy leader and made no

---

7. A tenth passenger died of his injuries in May 2014.

secret of his own ambition to be the next Israeli head of state. Whatever the true mix of reasons, the diplomatic track failed, despite cheerleading from Washington that openly declared resolving this conflict to be a high priority for U.S. foreign policy. And so the Palmer Report assumed a greater role than might have been anticipated for what was supposed to be no more than a technical inquiry about issues of law and fact. After the feverish diplomatic efforts failed, the Palmer panel seemed to offer a last chance for the parties to reach a mutually satisfactory resolution based on the application of international law and resulting recommendations that would delimit what must be done to overcome any violations during the attack on the flotilla.

But to be satisfactory, the report had to interpret the legal issues in a reasonable and responsible manner. This would mean, above all else, finding that the underlying blockade imposed more than four years ago on the 1.6 million Palestinians living in Gaza was unlawful, and should be immediately lifted. On this basis, enforcing the blockade by way of the May 31 attacks was unlawful, an offense aggravated by the gross interference with freedom of navigation on the high seas, by producing nine deaths among the humanitarian workers and peace activists on the *Mavi Marmara*, and by Israeli soldiers' harassing and abusive behavior toward the rest of the passengers. The panel should have reached such conclusions without difficulty; these determinations were so obvious from the perspective of international law as to leave little room for reasonable doubt. But this was not to be, and the report as written is a step backward from the fundamental effort of international law to limit permissible uses of international force to situations of established *defensive necessity*, and even then to ensure that the scale of force employed is *proportional*, respectful of civilian innocence, and weighs security claims against harmful humanitarian effects. It is a further step back to the extent that it purports to allow a state to enforce, on the high seas, a blockade condemned around the world for its cruelty and its damaging impact on civilian mental and physical health, a blockade that has deliberately deprived the people of Gaza of the necessities of life as well as locking them into a crowded and impoverished space and mercilessly attacking them with modern weaponry from time to time.

Given these stark realities, it is little wonder that the Turkish government reacted with anger and disclosed its resolve to proceed in a manner that would not only express its sense of law and justice, but also reflect Turkish efforts in recent years to base regional relations on principles of fairness and mutual respect. The Turkish foreign minister, Ahmet Davutoğlu, realizing that the panel's results were unacceptable, formulated his own Plan B. This consisted of responding not only to the report, but to Israel's failure to act responsibly and constructively on its own by offering a formal apology and setting up adequate compensation arrangements. Israel had more than a year to meet these minimal Turkish demands and showed its unwillingness to do so. As Mr. Davutoğlu made clear, this Turkish response was not intended to produce an encounter with Israel, but to put the relations between the countries back on the "right track." I believe that this is the correct approach under the circumstances, as it takes international law seriously and rests policy on issues of principle and prudence rather than opting for geopolitical opportunism. As Davutoğlu said plainly, "The time has come for Israel to pay a price for its illegal action. The price, first of all, is being deprived of Turkey's friendship."[8]

This withdrawal of friendship is not just symbolic. Turkey has downgraded diplomatic representation, expelling the Israeli ambassador from Ankara and maintaining intergovernmental relations at the measly level of second secretary. Beyond this, all forms of military cooperation are suspended, and Turkey indicated that it intends to strengthen its naval presence in the eastern Mediterranean. As well, Turkey has indicated that it will initiate action within the General Assembly to seek an advisory opinion from the International Court of Justice as to the legality of the blockade. What is sadly evident is that Israeli internal politics have become so belligerent and militarist that the political leaders in the country are hamstrung, unable to take a foreign policy initiative that is manifestly in their national interest. For Israel to lose Turkey's friendship is second only to losing U.S. support; coupled with the more democratically driven policies of the Arab Spring, alienating Ankara is a major setback for Israel's future in the region, as has been underscored during the last several days by the angry anti-Israeli protests in Cairo.[9]

What is more, Turkey's refusal to swallow the findings of the Palmer Report indicates a political posture that is bound to have a popular resonance throughout the Middle East and beyond. At a time when some of Turkey's earlier diplomatic initiatives have run into difficulties, most evidently in Syria, this stand on behalf of the victimized population of Gaza represents a rare display of a government placing values above interests. The people of Gaza are weak, abused, and vulnerable. In contrast, Israel is a military powerhouse, economically prosperous, a valuable trading partner for Turkey, and has in the background an ace in the hole—the

---

8. Mohammed Ayoob, "Turkey's Hardline Stance on Israel Just Tip of the Iceberg," *Mail & Guardian*, September 19, 2011, http://mg.co.za/article/2011-09-19-turkeys-hardline-stance-on-israel-just-tip-of-the-iceberg.

9. These protests occurred in the heady days following the overthrow of President Husni Mubarak in early 2011 and have become a distant memory by 2014, especially after the military coup of July 3, 2013.

United States, ever ready to pay a pretty penny to induce a rapprochement, thereby avoiding the awkwardness of dealing with this breakdown between its two most significant strategic partners in the Middle East. We should also keep in mind that the passengers on these flotilla ships were mainly idealists, seeking nonviolently to overcome a humanitarian ordeal that the UN and the interplay of national governments have been unable and unwilling to address for several years. This initiative by civil society activists deserved the support and solidarity of the world, not discouragement from the UN and a slap on the wrist, being chastened by the Palmer Report's view that their actions were irresponsible and provocative rather than empathetic and courageous.

Israel has managed up to now to avoid paying the price for defying international law. For decades it has been building unlawful settlements in the occupied West Bank and East Jerusalem. It has used excessive violence and relied on state terror on numerous occasions in dealing with Palestinian resistance and has subjected the people of Gaza to sustained and extreme forms of collective punishment. It attacked villages and neighborhoods in Beirut mercilessly in 2006, launched its massive campaign from land, sea, and air for three weeks (December 27, 2009-January 18, 2009) against a defenseless Gaza, and then shocked world opinion with its violent nighttime attack against the *Mavi Marmara* in 2010. It should have been made to pay the price long ago for this pattern of defying international law, above all by the United Nations. If Turkey sustains its position, it will finally send a message to Tel Aviv that Israel's future well-being and security will depend on a change of course in its relations to the Palestinians, its regional neighbors, and the international community. The days of flaunting international law and fundamental human rights are no longer policy options with no downside for Israel. Turkey is dramatically demonstrating that there can be a decided downside to flagrant Israeli lawlessness.

A Shameless Secretary-General versus Freedom Flotilla 2

June 2, 2011[10]

It is expected that at the end of June, Freedom Flotilla 2 will set sail for Gaza carrying various forms of humanitarian aid, including medical, educational, and construction materials. This second flotilla will consist of fifteen ships, including the *Mavi Marmara* sailing from Istanbul but also vessels departing from several European countries and carrying as many as 1,500 humanitarian activists as passengers. If these plans are carried out, as seems likely, it means that the second flotilla will be about double the size of the first, which was so violently and unlawfully intercepted by Israeli commandos in international waters on May 31, 2010, resulting in nine deaths on the Turkish lead ship.

Since that shocking incident a year ago, the Arab Spring has been transforming the regional atmosphere, but it has not ended the blockade of Gaza or the suffering inflicted on the Gazan population over the four-year period of coerced confinement. Such imprisonment of an occupied people has been punctuated by periodic violence, including Israel's sustained all-out attack for three weeks at the end of 2008, during which even women, children, and the disabled were not allowed to leave the deadly killing fields of Gaza. It is an extraordinary narrative of Israeli cruelty and deafening international silence, a silence broken only by the brave civil society initiatives in recent years that have brought both invaluable symbolic relief in the form of empathy and human solidarity, as well as token amounts of substantive assistance in the form of much-needed food and medicine. It is true that the new Egypt opened the Rafah crossing a few days ago (but not fully or unconditionally), allowing several hundred Gazans to leave or return to Gaza on a daily basis. At best, this opening, even if sustained, provides only partial relief. Rafah is not currently equipped to handle goods and is available only to people, so the blockade of imports and exports continues in force and may even be intensified as Israel vents its anger over the Fatah–Hamas unity agreement.

The Greek coordinator of Freedom Flotilla 2, Vangelis Pisias, has expressed the motivation of this new effort to break the blockade: "We will not allow Israel to set up open prisons and concentration camps." Connecting this Gazan ordeal to the wider regional struggles, Pisias added, "Palestine is in our heart and could be the symbol of a new era in the

---

10. Originally published at http://richardfalk.wordpress.com/2011/06/02/
a-shameless-secretary-general-versus-freedom-flotilla-2.

region."[11] Such sentiments reinforce the renewal of Palestinian militancy, as exhibited in the recent *Nakba* and *Naksa* Day[12] demonstrations.

A highly credible assessment of the 2010 Israeli attack on the first Freedom Flotilla, conducted by a fact-finding mission appointed by the UN Human Rights Council, concluded that the Israelis had violated international law in several respects: by using excessive force, by wrongfully attacking humanitarian vessels in international waters, and by unacceptably claiming to be enforcing a blockade that was itself unlawful. Such views have been widely endorsed by a variety of respected sources throughout the international community, although the panel appointed by the UN Secretary-General to evaluate the same incident has not yet made its report public, and apparently its conclusions will be unacceptably muted by the need to accommodate its Israeli member.

In light of these circumstances, including Israel's failure to live up to its promise, announced after the attack in 2010, to lift the blockade, it shocks our moral and legal sensibilities that the Secretary-General should be using the authority of his office to urge member governments to prevent ships from joining Freedom Flotilla 2. Ban Ki-moon, shamelessly, does not even balance such a call, purportedly to avoid the recurrence of violence, by at least sending an equivalent message to Israel insisting that the blockade end and demanding that Israel use no force in response to such humanitarian initiatives. Instead of protecting those who would act on behalf of unlawfully victimized Palestinians, the Secretary-General disgraces the office by taking a one-sided stand in support of one of the most flagrant and longest-lasting instances of injustice allowed to persist in the world. True, his spokesperson tries to soften the impact of such a message by vacuously stating that "the situation in the Gaza Strip must be changed, and Israel must conduct real measures to end the siege."[13] We must ask: why were these thoughts not expressed by the Secretary-General himself directly to Israel? Public relations is part of his job, but it is not a cover for crassly taking the wrong side in the controversy over whether or not

---

11. Erisa Dautaj Şenerdem, "Second Gaza Flotilla to Sail from Turkey by the End of June," *Hürriyet Daily News*, May 30, 2011, http://bit.ly/T1cNm9.

12. The *Nakba*, Arabic for "disaster" or, more commonly, "catastrophe," refers to the 1948 War and the accompanying massive dispossession of Palestinians; *Naksa*, or "setback," is used to reference Israel's victory in the 1967 Six-Day War. In my view, *Nakba* should also be understood as a *process* continuing into the present, not merely a historical *event*.

13. Saed Bannoura, "Ban Ki-moon Calls For Obstructing Freedom Flotilla Heading To Gaza," International Middle East Media Center, May 28, 2011, http://www.imemc.org/article/61331.

Freedom Flotilla 2 is a legitimate humanitarian initiative, courageously undertaken by civil society without the slightest credible threat to Israeli security and in the face of Israel's warnings of dire consequences.

Appropriately, and not unexpectedly, the Turkish government refuses to bow to such abusive pressures even when backed by the UN at its highest level. Ahmet Davutoğlu, the widely respected Turkish foreign minister, has said repeatedly in recent weeks, when asked about Freedom Flotilla 2, that no democratic government should ever claim the authority to exercise control over the peaceful initiatives of civil society as represented by NGOs. Davutoğlu has been quoted as saying "Nobody should expect from Turkey . . . to forget that nine civilians were killed last year. Therefore, we are sending a clear message to all those concerned. The same tragedy should not be repeated again." Underscoring the unresolved essential issue, he asked rhetorically, "Do we think that one member state is beyond international law?" Noting that Israel has still not offered an apology to Turkey or compensation to the families of those killed, Davutoğlu makes clear that until such reasonable preconditions for diplomatic normalization are met, Israel should not be accepted as "a partner in the region."[14]

In the background of this sordid effort to interfere with Freedom Flotilla 2 is the geopolitical muscle of the United States, which blindly (and dumbly) backs Israel no matter how outrageous or criminal its behavior. Undoubtedly this geopolitical pressure helps explain the UN's attempted interference with a brave and needed humanitarian initiative that deserves its strong support rather than its condemnation. Despite the near-universal verbal objections of world leaders, including even Ban Ki-moon, to the Israeli blockade, no meaningful action has yet been taken by either governments or the UN. Israel's undisguised defiance in Gaza of the requirements of belligerent occupation, as set forth in the Fourth Geneva Convention of 1949 and the First Additional Protocol appended thereto in 1977, is an unacknowledged scandal of gigantic proportions.

Liberating Palestine from oppressive occupation and refugee regimes should become a unifying priority for peoples and leaders during this second stage of the Arab Spring. Nothing could do more to manifest the external as well as the internal turn to democracy, constitutional governance, and human rights than displays of solidarity by new and newly reformist governments in Arab countries with this unendurably long Palestinian struggle for justice and sustainable peace. It would also offer the world a contrast with the subservience to Israel recently on display in

---

14. Tulay Karadeniz and Simon Cameron-Moore, "Turkey Saves Ire for Israel, Concern for Syria," Reuters, May 30, 2011, http://mobile.reuters.com/article/worldNews/idUSTRE74T3ZP20110530.

Washington, highlighted by Benjamin Netanyahu's invitation to address an adoring U.S. Congress, a rarity in the country's treatment of foreign leaders. Its impact was heightened by President Barack Obama's pandering speech to AIPAC, the notorious Israeli lobbying organization, at about the same time. It is unprecedented in the history of diplomacy that a leading sovereign state would so jeopardize its own global reputation and sacrifice its values to avoid offending a small allied partner. It is in the American interest, as well as in the interest of the peoples of the Arab world, particularly the Palestinians, to end the conflict.

The U.S. government has long discredited itself as an intermediary in the conflict. Its partisanship, driven mainly by domestic politics, represents a costly sacrifice of its own interests but is also objectionable as lending support to intolerable Israeli policies of apartheid, occupation, and colonialist expansionism. It is time to shift the locus of diplomatic responsibility for resolving the conflict from Washington to the far more geopolitically trustworthy auspices of Brazil, Turkey, the Nordic countries, and even possibly Russia or China and to encourage a more active regional role. If the encouraging recent Fatah–Hamas unity arrangements hold up and move forward, Palestinian representation will be regarded as increasingly credible, and will, it can be hoped, actively incorporate elements of the refugee communities in the bordering countries into their diplomacy. It is time for the world to realize, and the Palestinians to highlight, that the conflict is not just about territory ("land for peace") or even to ensure an adequate Palestinian presence in Jerusalem: it is most fundamentally about people. Insisting on respect for the moral, legal, and political rights of Palestinian refugees is the litmus test of a people-centered approach to the conflict and should not be allowed to drift off into peripheral space, as has happened in the past.

The Pros and Cons of Solidarity with the Palestinian Struggle
July 11, 2012[15]

The posture of solidarity with the struggle of "the other" is more complex than it might appear at first glance. It seems a simple act to join with others in opposing severe injustice and cruelty, especially when experiencing and witnessing its reality firsthand, as I have for several decades in relation to the

---

15. Originally published at http://richardfalk.wordpress.com/2012/07/11/
    pros-and-cons-of-solidarity-with-the-palestinian-struggle/.

Palestinian struggle. I was initially led to understand the Palestinian (counter-) narrative by friends while still a law student in the late 1950s. But my engagement was more in the spirit of resisting what Noam Chomsky would later teach us to call "indoctrination in a liberal society," a matter of understanding how the supposedly objective media messes with our minds in key areas of policy sensitivity. None in the West, especially in North America, has turned out to be more menacingly stage-managed than the presentation of Palestinians and their struggle, which merge with sinister forms of racial and religious profiling under the labels of "the Arab mind" and "Muslim extremism." The intended contrast to be embedded in Western political consciousness is between the bloodthirsty Arab–Palestinian–Muslim and the Western custodian of morality and human rights.

For very personal reasons, I had since childhood taken the side of the less privileged in whatever domain the issue presented itself: in sports or family life, in relation to race and sexual identity, and, professionally, in foreign policy. Despite being white and sexually attracted only to women, I found myself deeply moved by the ordeals faced in democratic America by African Americans, gays, and later, members of indigenous communities. I have sustained these affinities despite a long career that involved swimming upstream in the enclaves of the privileged as a longtime member of the Princeton University faculty.

In recent years, partly by chance, most of these energies of solidarity have been associated with the Palestinian struggle, which in my case has mainly involved bearing witness to the abuses endured by the Palestinian people living under occupation or in varying forms of exile, especially in my role as UN Special Rapporteur. This is an unpaid position, which affords me a much higher degree of independence than is enjoyed by normal UN career civil servants or diplomats serving a particular government. Many of these individuals work with great dedication and take on dangerous assignments, but they are expected to conform to institutional discipline that is exercised in a deadly, hierarchical manner that often links the UN to the grand strategy and geopolitical priorities of a West-centric world order. This structure itself seems more and more out of step with the rise of the non-West in the last several decades. Just days ago, India's representative at the UN called for restructuring the Security Council to get rid of its anachronistic characteristics that overvalue the West and undervalue the rest.[16]

---

16. UN General Assembly, "Calling for Security Council Reform, General Assembly President Proposes Advisory Group to Move Process Forward," 68th Plenary (46th & 47th Meetings), Nov. 7, 2013, http://www.un.org/News/Press/docs/2013/ga11450.doc.htm.

Bearing witness involves being as truthful and factually accurate as possible, regardless of what sort of consensus is operating in the corridors of power. In a biased media and a political climate that is orchestrated from above, the objectivity of bearing witness will itself be challenged as "biased" or "one-sided" whenever it ventures onto prohibited terrain. In actuality the purpose of bearing witness is to challenge bias, not to perpetuate it, but in our Orwellian media world, it is bias that is too often presented as balanced and truth witnessing that is either ignored or derided.

The witness of unwelcome truths should always exhibit a posture of humility, not making judgments about the tactics of struggle employed by those fighting against oppression, not supplying the solutions for those whose destinies are directly and daily affected by a deep political struggle. To do otherwise is to pretend to purvey greater wisdom and morality than those enduring victimization. In the Palestine–Israel conflict it is up to the parties—the peoples themselves and their authentic representatives—to find the path to a sustainable and just peace, although it seems permissible for outsiders to delineate the distribution of rights that follow from an application of international law and to question whether the respective peoples are being legitimately represented.

These comments reflect my reading of a passionate and provocative essay by Linah Alsaafin entitled "How Obsession with 'Non-Violence' Harms the Palestinian Cause."[17] The burden of her excellent article is the insistence that it is for the Palestinians, and only the Palestinians, to decide on the forms and nature of their resistance. She writes with high credibility as a recent graduate of Birzeit University who was born in Cardiff, Wales, and has lived in England and the United States as well as Palestine. She persuasively insists that for sympathetic observers and allies to worship at the altar of Palestinian nonviolence means to cede to the West the authority to determine what forms of Palestinian struggle are acceptable and unacceptable. This is grotesquely hypocritical considering the degree to which Western militarism is violently unleashed around the planet so as to maintain structures of oppression and exploitation, more benignly described as "national interests." In effect, the culturally sanctioned political morality of the West indicates an opportunistically split personality: nonviolence for your struggle, violence for ours. Well-meaning liberals broadcasting such an insidious message are not to be welcomed as true allies.

In this connection, I acknowledge my own carelessness in taking positive note of this shift in Palestinian tactics in the direction of nonviolent

---

17. Linah Alsaafin, "How Obsession with 'Non-Violence' Harms the Palestinian Cause," *Electronic Intifada*, July 10, 2012, http://electronicintifada.net/content/how-obsession-nonviolence-harms-palestinian-cause/11482.

forms of resistance; I was being unwittingly paternalistic, if not complicit with an unhealthy "tyranny of the stranger." It is certainly not the case that Alsaafin is necessarily advocating Palestinian violence, but rather she is contending that the Palestinians realize that they must mobilize their own masses to shape their own destiny. This leads her to lament, because it is not yet happening, that nothing will change and the occupiers and oppressors will continue to dominate the Palestinian scene. In effect, Alsaafin is telling us that deferring to Western canons of struggle is currently dooming Palestinians to apathy and despair.

I find most of what Alsaafin has to say to be persuasive, illuminating, and instructive, although I feel she neglects to take note of the courage and mobilizing impact of the prison hunger strikes that have ignited the imaginations of many Palestinians in recent months. Also, to some extent, my highlighting nonviolence was never intended as input into the Palestinian discourse or favorable commentary, but to challenge and expose the untrustworthiness of Western liberals who have for years been lecturing the Palestinians to abandon violence for the sake of effectiveness, arguing that a supposedly democratic and morally sensitive society (such as they allege exists in Israel) would be responsive to a nonviolent challenge by the Palestinians, and this would in turn lead the Israelis to a more reasonable and fair negotiating approach out of which a just peace could emerge. As should have been understood by the harsh Israeli responses to both intifadas, Israel turns a blind eye to Palestinian nonviolence and even does its best to provoke Palestinian violence so as to have some justification for its own. And the usually noisy liberal pontificators such as Tom Friedman and Nicholas Kristof go into hiding whenever Palestinian creativity in resistance does have recourse to nonviolent tactics. These crown princes of liberal internationalism were both silent throughout the unfolding and dramatic stories of the long hunger strikes (see chapter 3). These were remarkable examples of nonviolent dedication that bear comparison with the challenges Gandhi hurled at the British Empire or the IRA's later efforts to awaken London to the horrors of prison conditions in Northern Ireland; they certainly were newsworthy.

At the same time, there are some universal values at stake that Alsaafin does not pause to acknowledge. Two of these truths are intertwined in bewildering complexity: no outsider has the moral authority or political legitimacy to tell those enduring severe oppression how to behave, and no act of violence, whatever the motivation, that is directed against an innocent child or civilian bystander is morally acceptable or legally permissible, even if it seems politically useful. Terrorism is terrorism, whether the acts are performed by the oppressor or the oppressed, and for humanity to move toward any kind of collective emancipation, such universal principles must be affirmed as valid and respected by militants.

Also absent from the article is any effort to situate the Palestinian struggle in its historical and geographic context. There are tactical realities in some situations of conflict that may make those who act in solidarity a vital part of the struggle, participating on the basis of their own political calculus. The Vietnamese recognized the importance of an autonomous Western peace movement in weakening the will of the American political establishment to continue with the Vietnam War. The global anti-apartheid campaign turned the tide in South Africa and allowed the internal forces led by the African National Congress to prevail in their long struggle against settler-colonial rule and racism. We all need to remember that each struggle has its own originality that is historically, politically, and culturally conditioned. The Palestinian struggle is no exception.

As Alsaafin powerfully reminds those of us who attempt to act in solidarity, even while she is addressing a related message to the Palestinians, it is for the Palestinians to exert leadership and find inspiration and for the rest of us to step to one side. We must be humble for our sake as well as theirs, they must be assertive, and then our solidarity might make a welcome contribution rather than unintentionally administering a mild depressant.

Divestment at the University of California, Santa Barbara
April 16, 2013[18]

A few days ago I spoke to a student audience in support of a divestment resolution that was to be submitted for adoption at the University of California at Santa Barbara (UCSB). This petition was narrowly defeated in the UCSB Student Senate, but this series of efforts to urge several campuses of the University of California to divest from corporations doing a profitable business selling military equipment to Israel represents an encouraging awakening on the part of American youth to the severe victimization of the Palestinian people by way of occupation, discrimination, refugee misery, and exile, a worsening set of circumstances that has lasted in its various forms for several decades and shows no signs of ending anytime soon.

---

18. Originally published at http://richardfalk.wordpress.com/2013/04/16/
divestment-at-ucsb.

Ever since the *Nakba* of 1948, neither traditional diplomacy nor the United Nations nor armed struggle have been able to secure Palestinian rights. As time has passed, Palestinian prospects are being steadily diminished by deliberate Israeli policies: establishing and expanding unlawful settlements, "ethnic cleansing" of East Jerusalem, constructing a separation wall (which the World Court found in 2004 was being unlawfully built on Palestinian territory), building a network of Israeli-only roads, maintaining a dualistic system of laws that have an apartheid character, widespread abuse of Palestinian prisoners, and systematic discrimination against the Palestinian minority living within Israel's pre-1967 borders.

Israel has been consistently defiant in relation to international law and the UN and has refused to uphold Palestinian rights under international law. Given this set of circumstances, which combine the failures of diplomacy to achieve a fair peaceful resolution of the conflict and the unwillingness of Israel to fulfill its obligations under international law, the only viable option consistent with the imperatives of global justice is a blend of continuing Palestinian resistance and a militant global solidarity campaign that is nonviolent, yet coercive.

The Palestinian struggle for self-determination has become the great international moral issue of our time, a successor to the struggle in South Africa a generation ago against its form of institutionalized racism, the original basis of the international crime of apartheid. It is notable that the Rome Statute of the International Criminal Court designates apartheid as one type of crime against humanity and associates it with any structure of discrimination that is based on ethnicity or religion—not necessarily a structure exhibiting the same characteristics as were present in South Africa. Increasingly, independent inquiry has concluded that Israel's occupation of Palestine is accurately considered to be a version of apartheid and hence an ongoing crime against humanity.

It is against this background that divestment initiatives and the wider BDS campaign take on such importance at this time, especially here in the United States where the governing authorities turn a blind eye to Israel's wrongdoing and yet continue to insist on their capacity to provide a trustworthy intermediary perspective they allege to be the only path to peace. This claim goes back to the aftermath of the 1967 War and is more definitively linked to the famous brokered handshake on the White House lawn affirming the 1993 Oslo Accords as the authoritative foundation for the resolution of the conflict. Oslo has turned out to be a horrible failure from the perspective of achieving Palestinian rights, yet a huge success from the standpoint of the Israeli expansionist blueprint, which includes annexing the most fertile and desirable land in the West Bank and consolidating unified control over the sacred city of Jerusalem.

Against this background, there is only a single way forward: transnational civil society must mobilize to join the struggle mounted by the Palestinians for an end to occupation in a manner that produces a just solution, including respect for the rights of Palestinian refugees. If this solidarity surge happens on a sufficient scale, it will weaken Israel internally and internationally and perhaps even lead to an altered political climate in Israel and the United States that would at long last be receptive to an outcome consistent with international law and morality. Such a posture would contrast with what these two governments have for so long insisted upon: a "solution" that translated Israel's hard-power dominance, including the "facts on the ground" it has steadily created, into arrangements falsely called "peace."

After I presented this argument supporting the divestment resolution, members of a generally appreciative student audience asked several important questions.

Q: *Some people object to this divestment effort as unfairly singling out Israel, when there are so many other situations in the world where unlawful behavior and oppressive policies have resulted in more extreme forms of victimization than that experienced by the Palestinians. Why single out the Israelis for this kind of hostile maneuver?*

There are several ways to respond. U.S. support of Israel is itself reason enough to justify the current level of attention. Despite Israel's relative affluence, American taxpayers foot the bill for more than three billion dollars per year, more than is given to the whole of Africa and Latin America. This amounts to $8.7 million per day. In addition to the financial contribution is the extraordinary level of diplomatic support that privileges Israel above any other allied country and extends to pushing policies that reflect Israeli priorities even when they are adverse to U.S. national interests. This is the case with respect to Iran's nuclear program. The most stabilizing move would be to propose a nuclear-free zone for the entire Middle East, but the United States will not even mention such an option for fear of occasioning some kind of backlash orchestrated by an irate leadership in Tel Aviv.[19]

The world community as a whole, particularly the UN, undertook a major responsibility for the future of Palestine when it adopted General Assembly Resolution 181 proposing the partition of historic Palestine, giving 55 percent for a Jewish homeland and 45 percent to the Palestinians;

---

19. Although not acknowledged officially, it seems clear that the reluctance of the U.S. government to move in this otherwise sensible direction is due to Israel's refusal to consider any conflict-resolving pattern that requires it to acknowledge formally and then eliminate its arsenal of nuclear weapons.

ever since the Balfour Declaration in 1917, the wishes of the indigenous population of Palestine have been disregarded in favor of colonialist ambitions. Palestine remains the last and most unfortunate instance of an ongoing example of settler colonialism, exemplified by the dispossession and subjugation of the indigenous population as a result of violent suppression. The "settlers," in this usage, are all those who displace the indigenous population, depriving such people of their right of self-determination, and should not be confused with "settlers" from Israel who establish enclaves of domination within occupied Palestine.

Q: Some people have said that we should not push for divestment because it makes Jewish students on campus uncomfortable. Is there some basis for taking such sensitivities into account?

It is important not to allow Zionist propaganda to make us believe that being critical of Israel is tantamount to anti-Semitism and hostility to Jews as a religious and ethnic minority in this country and elsewhere. Because anti-Semitism did produce such horrible historical abuses of Jews, it is a cruel and opportunistic tactic to mislead public opinion in this manner. Not only Jews but all of us must learn that we are *human* before we are Jews or any other ethnicity. I am Jewish, but it is more important to privilege human interests and to avoid the narrow partisanship of tribal loyalties. If we are to survive on this crowded planet we must learn, in the words of W. H. Auden (in "September 1, 1939"), to "love one another or die." It would be odd if, as citizens of the United States, we were to refrain from criticizing the government in Washington because we didn't want to make Americans feel uncomfortable. At this stage, we have an obligation to make those who shield Israel from criticism feel uncomfortable—not because they are Jewish, but because they are complicit in the commission of crimes against a vulnerable people who have long endured unimaginable levels of abuse.

Q: Is there any reason to believe that the Israeli government will change its policies as a result of the pressures mounted by divestment measures of this kind even if implemented, which seems highly unlikely?

The importance of this divestment campaign is partly symbolic and partly substantive. Such initiatives are only undertaken after a prolonged failure of traditional means of overcoming international situations of extreme injustice. As such, it sends a message of distress as well as seeking to discourage corporations from making profits from transactions relating to unlawful activities in Israel, especially relating to uses of force against the Palestinian civilian population. Beyond this, we never know whether a combination of factors produces such pressure that those responsible for policy recalculate their interests and make a drastic change that could not have been anticipated. This happened to the white leadership in South Africa, leading to the release of Nelson Mandela from prison after twenty-seven years and a reconciliation process that allowed the oppressed black majority to assume leadership of the country on the basis of a constitutionally mandated, inclusive democracy. No one now expects an analogous transformation in Israel, but it will surely not come about without making the status quo increasingly unsustainable for the oppressor, as it has long been for the oppressed.

5

The United States,
the United Nations,
and International Law

There is a complicated relationship between international law and the Palestinian struggle. From a superficial perspective, the Palestinians' major claims in relation to borders, settlements, refugees, Jerusalem, and water are supported by the norms and principles embodied in international law, which are generally endorsed by the UN and by most independent experts. This support also extends to the main Palestinian grievances associated with the Israeli occupation since 1967. Yet, on closer examination, it seems that after forty-seven years of occupation and Israel's continuing violation of these norms and principles, it would be easy to conclude that international law is at best irrelevant to the realities of the Palestinian situation. More realistically, it would appear that Israel has been able to transform its unlawful appropriations of Palestinian rights (e.g., relating to occupied territory, the nature of Jerusalem, and the probable location of permanent borders) into altered expectations about the future that favor its claims.

In the circumstances of a legitimacy struggle, the significance of international law is far more complicated. It is true that international law cannot be implemented if opposed by strong geopolitical actors. There is a circumstance of defiance and impunity that has spared Israel direct adverse consequences from even flagrant violations of international law. At the same time, in the framework of a legitimacy struggle, international law is of great importance, as is the UN's political disposition toward an unresolved political conflict. The intensifying victimization of the Palestinian people can be expressed through inquiry into the acute and specific denial of Palestinian rights; such perceptions have given the Palestinians most of the moral high ground in the conflict, displacing the early perception of

Israel as a necessary post-Holocaust haven for victimized Jews, which gave rise to sympathy with the Zionist project of establishing a state to secure its homeland in historic Palestine.

Israel's use of excessive force in the Lebanon War of 2006, the tactics it employed in the massive military operation against Gaza in 2008 and 2009, its attack on the *Mavi Marmara* in international waters in 2010, and its refusal to accept the international law finding of a near-unanimous International Court of Justice advisory opinion[1] in 2004 have contributed to an image of Israel as a rogue state in the Middle East and helped mobilize global civil society in support of BDS and other initiatives associated with militant nonviolence.

The posts in this section seek to acknowledge the limits of international law with respect to the Palestinian national struggle while recognizing its importance in identifying the contours of a just and sustainable peace and its usefulness in influencing the climate of global public opinion relevant to diplomacy and perceptions of the relative justice of the two sides' positions. Israel's furious response to the Goldstone Report and its acknowledgement of the threats posed by what its think tanks call "the delegitimation project" is an indirect confirmation of the relevance of international law. At the same time, it needs to be understood that the Palestinian legitimacy struggle is not an assault upon the legitimacy of Israel itself, but rather on its unlawful practices and policies, including an unlawful occupation that has long exceeded all rules of reason, inflicting a cruel and rights-less regime upon those Palestinians residing in the West Bank, Gaza, and East Jerusalem.

Interwoven with these world-order concerns and their relationship to Palestinian legitimacy claims is the ceaseless effort of the U.S. government to reaffirm its unconditional support for Israel and its diplomatic claim to provide neutral auspices for a neutral "peace process." U.S. leaders' bobbing and weaving was recently exhibited in the tension between Obama's efforts to strike a balanced approach, as between Israelis and Palestinians, and his conflicting need to convince Israeli leaders, but also the Israeli lobby, that he is a pro-Israel partisan. Given the power disparity between Israel and Palestine, it has been clear that Obama has been more committed to demonstrating that alliance relations with Israel are as strong as ever than to showing the Palestinians and the world that he is prepared to uphold the U.S. claim to be "an honest broker." Such a posture of leaning to one side is evident in several of the posts that follow: opposing the

---

1. United Nations, "International Court of Justice Finds Israeli Barrier in Palestinian Territory is Illegal," UN News Centre, http://www.un.org/apps/news/ storyasp?NewsID=11292&#.U6WqTajt47A.

Goldstone Report, punishing UNESCO for allowing Palestine to become a member, speaking at AIPAC meetings in an appeasing manner, and talking to young Israelis in Jerusalem almost as though he is one of them. It may be that as legitimacy pressures mount, the United States will step slowly to one side, allowing others to play the intermediary role. Israel will oppose such a fundamental shift in the diplomatic framing of negotiations, but will it have a choice?

Discrimination in Occupied Palestine: Validating the Obvious Is Necessary
December 21, 2010[2]

In 2010 only the most diehard Zionist would deny the presence of multiple forms of Israeli discrimination being daily inflicted upon the Palestinians in the course of an occupation that has gone on for more than forty-three years. It is hardly a secret that Israel lavishes every kind of benefit on the settler population of the West Bank, while subjecting Palestinians to severe torments that bring cruel suffering and produce an atmosphere of unalleviated anxiety, which inevitably accompanies a situation in which the oppressor can do anything it wants whenever it pleases with impunity, up to and including dispossession and murder, while the oppressed is left utterly vulnerable, without the protection of law, and placed in a no-law vacuum of utter subjugation—or declared subject to Israeli military law, which is roughly the equivalent. (When victimized, no law; when accused, one-sided oppressive law.)

The release a few days ago of an exhaustive Human Rights Watch report, *Separate and Unequal: Israel's Discriminatory Treatment of Palestinians in the Occupied Palestinian Territories*,[3] is a major event. It exhaustively documents the forms of discrimination against Palestinians in the West Bank and enjoys the credibility of an NGO that has an impeccable global reputation for getting the facts and applicable law right and for exercising restraint with respect to political implications. When Human Rights Watch speaks, the media listens (although media bias is such that it keeps

---

2. Originally published at http://richardfalk.wordpress.com/2010/12/21/ discrimination-in-occupied-palestine-validating-the-obvious-is-necessary.

3. Human Rights Watch, *Separate and Unequal: Israel's Discriminatory Treatment of Palestinians in the Occupied Palestinian Territories* (New York: Human Rights Watch, 2010), http://www.hrw.org/sites/default/files/reports/iopt1210webwcover_0.pdf.

its mouth mostly shut if the target is Israel). The public has every reason to believe that whatever allegations Human Rights Watch makes are fully supported by reliable evidence. For all these reasons, and in the setting of the global Palestinian solidarity movement and specifically the BDS campaign, those who support the Palestinian struggle should welcome this publication and do their best to make it as widely known as possible. This is so even though, in important respects, *Separate and Unequal* (an ironic play on the Jim Crow doctrine supported for years by the U.S. Supreme Court under the rubric "separate but equal") doesn't tell us anything we didn't know before, or at least should have known. If you are "shocked" after reading this report, it means that for more than four decades your ears have been filled with wax and your eyes blindfolded.

But the report is more than a conclusive demonstration that acute and pervasive discrimination against Palestinians is a salient feature of the Israeli occupation. It also brings abstractions and statistics to life by relating stories of specific individuals and particular communities that have endured the occupation or enjoyed the privileges of being a settler living in a settlement. It is an aspect of the ugly atmosphere that still prevails in the United States that whenever it issues a report critical of Israel, Human Rights Watch is described as "courageous." In a democratic society that supposedly values the rule of law, it should not require courage to depict patterns of practice that so flagrantly and systemically violate international humanitarian law norms as embodied in the Fourth Geneva Convention. But it is courageous. A human rights organization dependent on private funding and media access takes its life in its hands wherever it challenges Israeli policies toward the Palestinians.

In this respect, it is appropriate to acknowledge the principled leadership of Human Rights Watch that undertook to produce this report, knowing with the certainty of the cycles of the moon that a vicious counterattack designed to discredit it would undoubtedly greet the study at the moment of its publication—and, what is more, that the attack would be short on substance but adept at the politics of deflection. It would cleverly seek to redirect the reader's eye from the message to the supposedly perfidious messenger. A spokesperson from the office of Benjamin Netanyahu launched such an attack only a day after the report was released: "Unfortunately, over the last few years there has been a series of documented cases in which Human Rights Watch has allowed a blatant anti-Israeli agenda to pollute its reporting."[4] In fact, Human Rights Watch is scrupulously careful whenever it ventures on this treacherous ground

---

4. Tobias Buck, "Report Accuses Israel of Discrimination," *Financial Times*, December 19, 2010, http://on.ft.com/1jteaBg.

and leans over backward, as did the defamed Goldstone Report, in giving every possible benefit of the doubt to Israel's claims.

The group NGO Monitor characteristically shoots from the hip, trying its best to discredit NGOs and individuals who dare to be truthful about the situation of Palestinians living under occupation, even if their approach is methodical and mild. CNN gave TV exposure to Gerald Steinberg, the notorious founder and principal toxic voice of NGO Monitor, in an interview which he absurdly claimed that the Human Rights Watch report consists of "manufactured allegations" that ignore the supposedly intense ongoing conflict between Israel and the Palestinians and that Human Rights Watch is thus insensitive to the "legitimate security" of Israel. From this perspective, it is but a short leap to contend that "the report exploits human rights" and is part of the larger plan to turn Israel into a "pariah state." In essence, he criticizes the Human Rights Watch for relying on information gathered by such highly respected human rights NGOs as Al-Haq, BADIL, B'Tselem, and Yesh Din as well as the UN's Office for the Coordination of Human Affairs. Human Rights Watch is also accused of promoting the BDS agenda by recommending that outside sources of settlement funding be respectful of international law and withhold financial support. NGO Monitor also explicitly argues that outsiders should refrain from ever holding Israel accountable because it is an open society that engages in self-criticism and needs no external assessment as to law or morality. Without much effort at disguise, what irks these defenders of Israel is the claim that the international community holds Israel to higher standards than other countries in the region and is supposedly obsessed with Israel while turning a blind eye to the violations of others. There is a bit of truth to this claim, although it overlooks the degree to which it was a colonialist mentality (first Britain, then the United Nations) that inflicted a tragic destiny on the Palestinian people from a time long predating the independence of Israel as a sovereign state. What is also not considered is the degree to which the United States in particular, through an unprecedented network of public and private sector initiatives, has been regularly financing the settlement dynamic and Israeli militarism.

What is strange, although understandable given the oppressive structure of Israeli discrimination, is the lack of attention critics of the Human Rights Watch report have given to its most central contention: that the Israeli settlers unlawfully present and their settlements unlawfully established are given the fullest protection of the law and the maximum security possible, while Palestinians living under this occupation, who are, according to international humanitarian law, "protected persons," are abused constantly and compelled to live decade after decade without rights or the barest minimum of security, their land and prospects for a decent future constantly diminished by the expansion of the settlements.

Several shortcomings of its conclusions and recommendations show the moderation, and from my perspective, incompleteness of the Human Rights Watch report:

Time: Although the report is explicit about the length of the occupation aggravating patterns of discrimination, it accords no attention to the intrinsic unlawfulness of such a prolonged occupation.

International humanitarian law was designed for temporary occupations of short duration, not a quasi-permanent set of circumstances that includes ill-disguised tactics of land seizure and the incremental dispossession of long-term Palestinian residents. Any "right" of occupation should long since have lapsed. It is a serious flaw of international humanitarian law that it makes no provision in the event of this failure to bring a belligerent occupation to a timely and agreed end (here anticipated in accordance with Security Council Resolution 242, agreed upon in 1967, which points to an Israeli withdrawal).

Criminality: The report addresses violations of international and human rights law, but it holds back from describing these violations in terms of their criminal character. Surely, the structures of discrimination (roads, security, legal regime, access to water, mobility) establish the *prima facie* basis for allegations of apartheid arising from the dual structure of privilege (for Israeli settlers) and vulnerability and deprivation (for Palestinians). The Rome Statute, which established the International Criminal Court, treats apartheid (forms of systematic discrimination based on race) as one type of crime against humanity. This international crime of apartheid is deliberately conceived of as a distinct crime of generic character, not to be equated with the specific patterns of racist discrimination that existed in South Africa under the apartheid regime that operated there. The crime of apartheid is also embedded in customary international law, which makes it a crime even without any formal undertaking by the International Criminal Court. Additionally, these patterns of discrimination are rendering life unbearable for Palestinian residents in most of the West Bank. As many as 31 percent of those interviewed in the Human Rights Watch report said they were seeking to escape somehow from life under occupation. Such an outcome appears to qualify this occupation as a form of "ethnic cleansing," even if evidence of a blueprint or specific intent is lacking. An inference of ethnic cleansing follows from the deliberateness of the dual structures of law and administration producing direct and indirect forms of displacement of the indigenous population.

Language: The report speaks in terms of violations—not crimes, not the overall illegitimacy of persisting occupation that encroaches on the fundamental rights of the occupied—and leaves those living under occupation without a clear path to achieving their most fundamental of rights, the right of self-determination. I believe it is necessary to use harsher language than is usual in mainstream circles in describing the situation. It is "annexation," not "occupation"; it is "ethnic cleansing," not "house demolitions"; not just "land seizures" but "settler-only roads"; not constraints on "mobility," but "settler colonialism." In keeping with the BDS campaign, it is time for the peoples of the world to perceive the ongoing Palestinian *Nakba* clearly, without evasive or legalistic terminology that obscures and normalizes rather than illuminating the abnormality of the situation and giving rise to a mobilizing sense of outrage.

The U.S. Stands Alone with Israel at the UN Security Council: How (Dis)Honest Is the "Honest Broker"?
February 19, 2011[5]

The United States reluctantly stood its ground on behalf of Israel and, on February 18, 2011, vetoed a resolution to censure Israel for illegally continuing to build settlements in the West Bank and East Jerusalem. All fourteen of the other members of the UN Security Council supported the resolution in what appears to be as close to a consensus as the world community can ever hope to achieve. The resolution was also sponsored by 130 UN member countries before being presented to the Council. In the face of such near-unanimity, the United States might have been expected to show some respect for the views of every leading government in the world, including all of its closest European allies, or to have had the good grace to at least abstain from the vote. Indeed, such an obstructive use of the veto builds a case for its elimination, or at least for restricting its use. Why should an overwhelming majority of member countries be held hostage to the geopolitical whims of Washington, or some other outlier member trying to shield itself or its ally from a Security Council decision enjoying overwhelming support? This U.S. veto is not some idiosyncratic whim but an expression of the sorry pro-Israeli realities of domestic politics, suggesting that Israel is the real holder of the veto in this situation; the U.S. Congress and the Israel lobby are merely enforcers.

---

5. Originally published at http://bit.ly/TkJbAt.

Susan Rice, the chief U.S. representative in the Security Council, appeared to admit as much when she lamely explained that casting the veto on this text "should not be misunderstood to mean support for settlement construction," adding that, on the contrary, the United States "rejects in the strongest terms the legitimacy of continued Israeli settlement activity."[6] Why then? The formal answer is that the United States, agreeing with Israel, believes that only in the context of direct negotiations can the issue of settlements be addressed alongside other unresolved matters such as refugees, borders, and the status of Jerusalem. This seems absurdly arrogant—and geopolitically humiliating. If the fourteen other members of the Security Council believe that Israel should be censured for continuing to build unlawful settlements and that no negotiations can proceed until it ceases, then a united front would seem to be the most effective posture to resume negotiations. This is especially so here; it is a no-brainer to realize that every additional settlement unit authorized and constructed makes it less likely that a truly independent and viable Palestinian state can ever be brought into being, and that there exists the slightest intention on the Israeli side to do so.

In view of this feverish Israeli effort to create still more facts on the ground, for the Israelis to contend that negotiations should resume without preconditions is for them to hope that the Palestinian Authority will play the fool forever. After all, for more than forty-three years, they have been whittling away at the substance of the two-state consensus embodied in the unanimous Security Council Resolution 242 (1967), contending at every phase of the faux peace process that an agreement must incorporate "subsequent developments": that is, unlawful settlements and ethnic cleansing. In the end, the Israelis may turn out to have been cleverer by half, creating an irresistible momentum toward the establishment of a single secular, democratic state of Palestine that upholds human rights for both peoples and brings to an end the Zionist project of an exclusive "Jewish state." With great historic irony, such an outcome would seem to complete the circle of fire ignited by Lord Balfour's secret 1917 promise to the Zionist movement of "a Jewish homeland" in historic Palestine, a process that caused a Palestinian catastrophe along the way and brought war and bloodshed to the region.

The disingenuousness of the Israeli position was confirmed by the recent publication of the Palestine Papers, which showed beyond a shadow of a doubt that even when the Palestinian Authorities caved in on such

---

6. Richard Roth, "U.S. Vetoes U.N. Resolution Declaring Israeli Settlements Illegal," CNN.com, February 18, 2011, http://www.cnn.com/2011/WORLD/meast/02/18/un.israel.settlements.

crucial issues as Jerusalem, settlements, and refugees, their Israeli counterparts—including the Netanyahu administration's supposedly more
moderate predecessors—displayed no interest in reaching even an agreement so heavily weighted in Tel Aviv's favor.[7] What seems inescapable,
from any careful reading of these negotiating positions behind closed
doors during the prior decade, is that the public negotiations are a sham
designed to buy time for Israel to complete its illegal dirty work of de facto
annexation in the West Bank. This is a position it has long adopted in the
form of *de jure* annexation of the entire expanded city of Jerusalem, in
defiance of the will of the international community and the understanding
of international law, objectively considered. To contend that stopping the
unlawful encroachments of continuing settlement activity on occupied
Palestinian territory, an assessment that even the United States does not
question substantively, is an inappropriate Palestinian demand seems so
excessive as to humiliate any Palestinian representatives who would stoop
so low as to accept it. Equally so is the Israeli claim that this demand has
not been made in the past, which, to the extent that it is accurate, is not
an argument against freezing further settlement activity but a disturbing
comment on the Palestinian failure to insist upon respect for their rights
under international law.

In the context of this latest incident in the Security Council, the
Palestinian Authority deserves praise for holding firm and not folding
under strong U.S. pressure, which reportedly included President Obama
warning President Mahmoud Abbas by phone of adverse "repercussions"
if the text calling for an end to illegal settlement-building was brought
before the Security Council for a vote. Obviously, the U.S. government
realized its predicament. It did not want to be isolated and embarrassed
in this way, caught between its international exposure, as willing to support even Israel's most unreasonable defiance of the UN, and its domestic
vulnerability to a pro-Israeli backlash should it fail to do Israel's bidding in
this matter of largely symbolic importance.

We should not forget that, had the Security Council resolution been
adopted, there is not the slightest prospect that Israel would have curtailed,
let alone frozen, its settlement plans. Israel has defied a near-unanimous
World Court vote (with the U.S. judge casting the lone negative vote
among the fifteen judges, hardly a surprise) in 2004 on the unlawfulness
of the separation wall. Here, an American dissent could not bring Israel
in from the cold for its refusal to abide by this ruling; thankfully, there is
no veto power in judicial settings. Israel wasted no time denouncing the
advisory opinion of the highest UN judicial body, declaring its refusal to

---

7. Available at http://www.aljazeera.com/palestinepapers.

obey this clear finding that the wall built on occupied Palestinian territory should be dismantled forthwith and Palestinians compensated for any harm done. Instead, despite brave nonviolent Palestinian resistance, work on finishing the wall continues to this day.

With respect to the settlements, it is no wonder that American diplomats wanted to avoid blocking an assertion of unlawfulness to which it was on record as agreeing, a fact Ambassador Rice awkwardly acknowledged in the debate, knowing that the resolution would not have the slightest *behavioral* impact on Israel in any event. As much as Israel defies the UN and international law, it still cashes in its most expensive diplomatic chips to avoid censure whenever possible. I believe that this is an important, although unacknowledged, Israeli recognition of the legitimizing role of international law and the UN. It is also connected with an increasing Palestinian reliance on soft power, especially the BDS campaign. This partial shift in Palestinian tactics worries Israel. In the last several months, Israeli think tanks close to the government have been referring to BDS as "the delegitimation project" with growing anxiety. The Palestinian global solidarity movement's approach is what I have been calling a legitimacy war. For the last several years it has been waged and won by the Palestinians, joining the struggles of those living under occupation and in exile.

The Palestinian Authority side was reported to be anxious that withdrawing the resolution in this atmosphere would amount to what was derisively referred to as a possible "Goldstone 2," a reference to the Palestinian Authority's inexcusable effort back in October 2009 to have the Human Rights Council defer consideration of the Goldstone Report for several months as a prelude to its institutional burial, which has now more or less taken place thanks to American pressures behind the scene. It has even been suggested that, had the Palestinian Authority withdrawn the resolution, Abbas would have been driven from power by an angry popular backlash among the Palestinian populace. In this sense the Palestinian Authority was, like the United States, squeezed from both sides: by the Americans and by its own people.

In the background of this incident at the UN are the tumultuous developments taking place throughout the region, which are all adverse to Israel and promising in relation to the Palestinian struggle, even though many uncertainties exist. It is not only the anti-autocrat upheavals in Tunisia and Egypt, the outcomes of which are still not clear from the perspective of genuine regime change (as distinct from recasting the role of dictator), but also wider regional developments. These include the political rise of Hezbollah in Lebanon, Turkish diplomacy that refuses to toe the Washington line, the failure of U.S. interventional diplomacy in Iraq, and the beleaguered authoritarian governments in the region, some of whom are likely to give more active support on behalf of Palestinian goals to shore up their own faltering domestic legitimacy in relation to their own people.

In many ways, the failed Security Council resolution condemning Israeli settlement activity is a rather trivial event in the broader setting of the underlying conflict. At the same time, though, it is a significant show of forces operative in Washington and Ramallah; above all, it is an unseemly display of the influence Israel wields with respect to the Obama administration. Is it not time that the United States either revisits its Declaration of Independence or begins to treat the Fourth of July as a day of mourning?

Obama's AIPAC Speech:
A Further Betrayal of the Palestinian People
May 24, 2011[8]

On Sunday, May 22, 2011, three days after giving a decidedly pro-Israel speech on his broader Middle East foreign policy at the State Department. U.S. president Barack Obama spoke at a conference held by the American Israel Public Affairs Committee, more commonly known as AIPAC. It was a shockingly partisan speech to an extremist lobbying group that has the entire U.S. Congress in an unprecedented headlock that has become the envy of even the National Rifle Association. I assume that Obama's handlers regarded a speech to AIPAC as obligatory, given the upcoming 2012 presidential election. The dependence of political candidates for almost any significant elected office in the United States on Jewish electoral and funding support has become an article of secular political faith, particularly for a national office like the presidency. Nevertheless, Obama's enactment of this political ritual seemed so excessive, even taking full account of the role of the Israel lobby, as to be worth noting and decrying.

What is worse, the mainstream media typically misconstrued the AIPAC event in a manner that compounded the outrage of the speech itself. For instance, the *New York Times* headline says it all: "Obama Challenges Israel to Make Hard Choices for Peace." As Obama pointed out himself in his remarks, "There was nothing particularly original in my proposal; this basic framework for negotiations has long been the basis for

---

8. Originally published at http://richardfalk.wordpress.com/2011/05/24/
   obama's-aipac-speech-a-further-betrayal-of-the-palestinian-people.

discussions among the parties, including previous U.S. administrations."[9] These "hard choices" involve Israeli withdrawal to the 1967 borders with agreed land swaps—a simple restatement of the generalized international consensus that U.S. leaders have often articulated in a variety of authoritative settings. This is hardly a hard choice, especially as interpreted by the White House's former special envoy, George Mitchell, as including Israel's perceived security requirements. That is, the land swaps now seem to embrace not only the unlawful settlement blocs that George W. Bush conceded, but also Netanyahu's over-the-top demands for strategic depth at the expense of Palestinian land, demanding the appropriation of portions of the Jordan Valley along with the deployment of Israeli troops within a hypothetical demilitarized Palestinian state.

What is more, these alleged hard choices are never set against the background of the aftermath of the 1948 War, which deprived Palestinians of about half of the territory they were given according to the UN partition plan embodied in General Assembly Resolution 181. As is widely known, the Palestinians rejected that partition plan as being grossly unfair, imposed from without, and awarding the Jewish minority population about 56 percent of historic Palestine. In effect, the Palestinians' willingness, first expressed by the 1988 session of the Palestinian National Council, to live within the 1967 borders meant agreeing to have their Palestinian state on 22 percent of the British mandate. This was indeed a hard choice! The land swaps involving settlement blocs, their bypass roads, and further security zones all encroach upon that 22 percent, and the fact that such further Palestinian concessions can be proposed indicates just how unfair the U.S.-led approach to resolving the underlying conflict has become. It is also notable that this fundamental territorial redefinition of the two-state consensus is never acknowledged or even mentioned. In effect, what was thought to be two states in 1947 was dramatically diminished by what became the contours of two states after the 1967 war and has been further diminished in dramatic form ever since by the settlement process and the various unilateral changes Israel has introduced in the course of administering Jerusalem.

Obama's speech to AIPAC is significant not for these nonexistent "hard choices," but for the scandalously obsequious, pleading tone adopted by a U.S. president who acknowledges with pride everything about the U.S. government's relationship to the conflict that should disqualify it from ever again having a shred of diplomatic credibility as a third-party intermediary. Obama started with a fawning "What a remarkable, remarkable

---

9. The text of Obama's speech was reprinted in the *National Journal*, May 22, 2011, http://www.nationaljournal.com/whitehouse/text-obama-s-aipac-speech-20110522.

crowd" and proceeded to heartfelt words of sympathy for Israeli victims of violence—without even a scintilla of empathy for the far, far greater suffering daily endured by the entire Palestinian people: dispossessed, living under occupation, blockade, in refugee camps and exile, or as persons displaced physically and psychologically.

The passage on military assistance to a prosperous Israel should have come as a shock to American taxpayers, but passed without notice by the Western media. I will quote it in full because it so shamelessly overlooks Israel's defiance of international law and its militarist outlook toward the future:

> I and my administration have made the security of Israel a priority. It's why we've increased cooperation between our militaries to unprecedented levels. It's why we're making our most advanced technologies available to our Israeli allies. It is why, despite tough fiscal times, we've increased foreign military financing to record levels. And that includes additional support—beyond regular military aid—for the Iron Dome anti-rocket system.[10]

It is not surprising that there was loud applause after each sentence in the paragraph just quoted, but it is surprising that a U.S. president would try to please even an AIPAC audience in this abject manner. After all, others are listening—or should be!

Obama similarly brushed aside any concern about the unlawfulness of the Israeli occupation or its uses of force against a defenseless population in Gaza. He also dismissed the Goldstone Report by name, suggesting that its assessment of Israel's wrongdoing somehow challenges Israel's right of self-defense when in actuality the Goldstone legal analysis does just the opposite (and far more ardently and unconditionally than appropriate, in my view). He said not a word about the flotilla incident a year ago or the recent excessive use of lethal force at the Israeli borders in response to the "right of return" demonstrations associated with the 2011 Palestinian remembrance of the *Nakba*.

Going beyond the negativity of his State Department comments, Obama mimicked Netanyahu in condemning the moves toward reconciliation and unity between Fatah and Hamas. He had the temerity to insist that "the recent agreement between Fatah and Hamas poses an enormous obstacle to peace."[11] Actually, reasonably considered, the agreement

---

10. Ibid.

11. "Palestinian Unity Arose from Ruins of Peace Talks," Ma'an News Agency, May 23, 2011, http://www.maannews.net/eng/ViewDetails.aspx?ID=390498.

should have been welcomed as an indispensable step toward creating the possibility of peace.

Obama uttered not a word of challenge in front of this AIPAC audience about settlements, Jerusalem, or refugees. Not a word about the Palestinian ordeal, or diminished horizons of possibility, and no White House plan announced to give a talk before a Palestinian audience. The Obama talk was so outrageously one-sided, so contrary to U.S. strategic interests, that it implicitly suggests that the Palestinians are so weak and passive as to let it slip by in silence. Only a justifiable outburst of Palestinian rage could begin to counter this impression of diplomatic surrender.

Palestinian prudence would go further than an angry reaction. After such a speech, the only responsible response by the Palestinian leadership is to conclude once and for all, however belatedly, that it is no longer possible to look to Washington for guidance in reaching a peaceful, just, and sustainable resolution of the conflict. Indeed, to allow such a framing of peace at this point, in light of Obama's and Netanyahu's posturing, would further disclose the incompetence and illegitimacy that have long handicapped the Palestinian struggle for self-determination based on a just and sustainable peace and founded on respect for Palestinian rights under international law.

Reflections on Mahmoud Abbas's Statehood Speech
September 29, 2011[12]

There is a natural disposition for supporters of the Palestinian struggle for self-determination to suppose that the Palestinian statehood bid must be a positive initiative because it has generated such a frantic Israeli effort to have it rejected. Despite the high costs to U.S. diplomacy in the Middle East at this time of regional tumult and uncertainty, the United States has committed itself to exercising its veto on Israel's behalf if that turns out to be necessary. To avoid the humiliation of disregarding the overwhelming majority opinion of most governments in the world, the United States has rallied the former European colonial powers to stand by its side while leaning on Bosnia and Colombia to abstain, thereby hoping to deny Palestine the nine votes it needs for a Security Council decision without technically casting a veto. On the side of Palestinian statehood one finds

---

12. Originally published as "Reflections on the Abbas Statehood/Membership Speech to the UN General Assembly" at http://bit.ly/1jHBeft.

China, Russia, India, South Africa, Brazil, Lebanon, Nigeria, and Gabon, the leading countries of the South, the main peoples previously victimized by colonial rule. Is not a comparison of these geopolitical alignments sufficient by itself to resolve the issue of taking sides on such a litmus test of political identity? The old West versus the new South!

Add to this the drama, eloquence, and forthrightness of Mahmoud Abbas's historic September 23 speech to the General Assembly, which received standing ovations from many of the assembled delegates.[13] Such a favorable reception was reinforced by its contrast with the ranting polemic delivered by the Israeli prime minister, Benjamin Netanyahu, who insulted the UN by calling it "the theater of the absurd" while offering nothing of substance that might make even mildly credible his strident rhetoric claim to support "peace," "direct negotiations," and "a Palestinian state."[14] Netanyahu's deviousness was made manifest when a few days later the Israeli government announced that it had approved 1,100 additional housing units in the major East Jerusalem settlement of Gilo. This was a bridge too far even for Hillary Clinton, who called the move "counterproductive." Europeans regarded it as deeply disappointing and confidence-destroying, so much so that Netanyahu was openly asked to reverse the decision. There are a variety of other indications that additional settlement expansion and ethnic cleansing initiatives will be forthcoming from Israel in the weeks ahead. Are not such expressions of Israeli defiance, which embarrass even its most ardent governmental supporter, enough to justify a Security Council recommendation of Palestine statehood? Would it not be worthwhile at this crucial moment to demonstrate the wide chasm separating increasing global support for the pursuit of justice on behalf of the Palestinian people from the United States's domestically driven reliance on its ultimate right of veto to block Palestinian aspirations? Would it not be well to remind Americans across the country, including even a captive Congress, that their own Declaration of Independence wisely counsels "a decent respect for the opinions of mankind"? If ever the use of the veto seems ill-advised and deeply illegitimate, it is in this instance—which the Obama administration seems to acknowledge, or otherwise why would it use its leverage to induce allies and dependent states to go along with its opposition to Palestinian membership in the UN?

Turning to the speech itself, the language of recognition may be more notable than the substance. Never before in an international forum has the

---

13. Mahmoud Abbas, speech to UN General Assembly, New York, NY, September 23, 2011, transcript reproduced in *Haaretz*, http://bit.ly/1ixszkN.

14. Benjamin Netanyahu, speech to UN General Assembly, New York, NY, September 24, 2011, transcript reproduced in *Haaretz*, http://bit.ly/T1nxRk.

voice of the Palestinian Authority spoken of Israel's occupation policies so unabashedly—as "colonial," as involving "ethnic cleansing," as imposing an unlawful "annexation wall," as creating a new form of "apartheid." With admirable directness, Abbas accused Israel of carrying out the occupation in a manner that violated fundamental rules of international humanitarian law and cumulatively amounts to committing crimes against humanity.

In the course of his speech, Abbas tried hard to reassure the Palestinian diaspora on two matters of deep concern: that the PLO will continue to represent the Palestinian people, and that the Palestinian people are the ultimate beneficiaries of the right of self-determination. The issue here is lost on almost all observers of the conflict: the Palestinian Authority, of which Abbas is president, is a subsidiary body that was created by the PLO with a temporary mandate to administer Palestinian territory under occupation. Thus it was important to allay suspicions that the PLO was an intended casualty of the statehood bid, so as to territorialize the conflict and give Abbas and the Palestinian Authority leadership complete representational control over the Palestinian role at the UN. The deep concern here relates to the adequacy of representation for Palestinians living in refugee camps in neighboring Arab countries and in exile around the world. In the Palestinian National Council, 483 of 669 members are drawn from Palestinians *not* living under occupation. President Abbas used the clearest possible language to reaffirm the PLO's position just prior to enumerating the five conditions guiding his leadership role, confirming that he spoke "on behalf of the PLO, the sole legitimate representative of the Palestinian people, which will remain so until the end of the conflict in all its aspects and until the resolution of the final status issues."[15]

In the background of this representation issue is an anxiety that Palestinian refugee rights will be forgotten or marginalized in the course of striking a deal built around a "land for peace" formula. Again Abbas inserted some reassuring language in his speech to the effect that peace will depend on "a just and agreed-upon solution to the Palestine refugee issue in accordance with resolution 194," which unconditionally affirms a Palestinian right of return. Relevantly, Netanyahu, in his speech, alluded to the "fantasy of flooding Israel with millions of Palestinians," which is his way of both dismissing the rights of Palestinian refugees, especially as derived from the massive dispossession of Palestinians in 1948, and insisting that Palestinians recognize Israel as a "Jewish state."

This insistence combines demographics with democracy, contending that ever since Lord Balfour's promise on behalf of the British government to a leader of the Zionist movement in 1917, there have been continual

---

15. Available at http://bit.ly/1ixszkN.

acknowledgements that Israel was a Jewish state. Netanyahu made short shrift of the claims to dignity and equality of the 1.5 million Palestinians existing under an array of discriminatory burdens by saying merely that Israel treats its minorities in a manner that respects their human rights. It should be recalled that the Balfour Declaration, with its notoriously colonial disposition, did not promise the Jewish people a state but rather "a national home," to be established in a manner that did not interfere with the "civil and religious rights of existing non-Jewish communities in Palestine."[16] Human rights and democracy have become significantly universalized during the last several decades. This development implies that the governing structures of society embodied in the state must renounce any claim of ethnic or religious particularity. Political legitimacy in the twenty-first century should not be accorded to any state that claims to be a Jewish state, an Islamic state, or a Christian state. Such statist neutrality should be set forth as an element of legitimate statehood by formal action at the United Nations. Such a declaration would impose a limit on the right of self-determination by denying to peoples the right to establish ethnic or religious states. In a globalizing world, ethnic and religious diversity are present in every major state and need to be respected by unfurling a banner of equality that grants religious freedom to all faiths and allows collective identities to be expressed without prejudice.

For some widely respected Palestinian activists and NGOs, these assurances were not enough. With the formidable intellectual support of Oxford professor Guy Goodwin-Gill, the very idea of Palestinian statehood compromises the representational rights of diaspora Palestinians within UN arenas of decision and potentially deforms future negotiations by according predominance to territorial priorities. Goodwin-Gill's analysis is built around the general view that a state could never adequately represent people outside its borders. Given existing realities, this would mean disenfranchising the Palestine refugee and exile population, which comprises a majority of "the Palestinian people," who are, as a collectivity, the holders of the overarching entitlement embodied in the right of self-determination. Such a view may be technically correct and operationally prudent, but it overstates the clarity of the legal implications of Palestinian statehood and UN membership while understating the degree to which what are being questioned are the psycho-political priorities of the current Palestinian Authority–PLO leadership. To further strengthen and promote the unity of the Palestinian global solidarity movement, it is crucial to continue to seek accommodation between territorial and nonterritorial

---

16. The full text of the Balfour Declaration can be found at http://news.bbc.co.uk/2/hi/
in_depth/middle_east/israel_and_the_palestinians/key_documents/1682961.stm.

dimensions of the Palestinian struggle, and thus to minimize intra-Palestinian divergences, including the ongoing rift with Hamas. Here again, Abbas had some reassuring words to say about the future implementation of the reconciliation agreement reached between the PLO and Hamas in June, but Hamas's failure to endorse the statehood–membership bid at this time raises doubts about whether cooperation between these two political tendencies of Palestinians living under occupation will be forthcoming in the future.

There are, against this background, some further grounds for concern that result from gaps or disappointing formulations in the Abbas speech. One glaring gap was the failure to address the accountability issues associated with the Goldstone Report's recommendations arising out of war-crimes allegations associated with Operation Cast Lead. In an important statement, the Palestinian Centre for Human Rights, jointly with several respected human rights NGOs, assigned the PLO responsibility for doing its best to see that these recommendations for referral to the International Criminal Court be carried out. In the words of the statement, "Should the PLO choose not to pursue the accountability process initiated by the Report of the UN Fact-Finding Mission—at the expense of the Statehood initiative—this will amount to the prioritisation of political processes over victims' fundamental rights; indicating acceptance of the pervasive impunity that characterises the situation in Israel and the occupied Palestinian territory."[17]

Although implicitly recognized in the Abbas speech, Israel's systematic refusal to comply with international law was not accorded the emphasis it deserves. Given this reality, it was comic irony for Netanyahu to invoke international law in relation to the captivity of a single Israeli soldier, Gilad Shalit; of course international law should be observed in relation to every person, but when Israel subjects the whole of Gaza to a punitive blockade for more than four years, imprisons thousands of Palestinians in conditions below international legal standards, and refuses to implement the World Court's near-unanimous advisory opinion on the unlawfulness of its annexation wall, it has lost all credibility to rely on international law on those few occasions when it works to Israel's advantage.

Even more disturbing, because so relevant to the present posture of the conflict, was the PLO's rather bland expression of willingness to resume direct negotiations provided that Israel imposes "a complete cessation

---

17. Palestinian Centre for Human Rights, International Federation for Human Rights, and Al-Haq, "Human Rights Organisations Demand PLO and International Community Uphold Victims' Rights," press release, September 29, 2011, http://bit.ly/1nSD29K.

of settlement activities." As there is no chance that this condition will be met, it may not be so important for Abbas to question the value of direct negotiations, given their repeated failure to move the parties any closer to peace during the past eighteen years. In fact, Israel has cloaked settlement expansion, ethnic cleansing, and a variety of encroachments on what might have at one time become a viable Palestinian state with the charade of periodic peace talks held under the non-neutral auspices of the United States. What Abbas could have done more effectively, given the unlikelihood of an affirmative Security Council recommendation on UN membership, is to couple the statehood–membership bid with a demand for a new framework for future negotiations that includes an Israeli commitment to abandoning settlement expansion in East Jerusalem as well as the West Bank and, more importantly, selects a state or regional organization to provide nonpartisan auspices for the talks. Such a demand would have made clear that the PLO and Palestinian Authority were no longer willing to play along with the Oslo game, which has more than doubled the settler population and allowed Israel to invest in an expensive settler-only infrastructure that is unlikely ever to be voluntarily dismantled. It is past time to declare the Oslo framework of direct negotiations terminally ill, futile, illegitimate, and incapable of drafting a roadmap that leads anywhere worth going! For the UN to be one of the four Quartet members, especially given U.S. hegemonic control over the diplomacy on the conflict, also warranted a harsh comment by Abbas.

What the future holds is more uncertain than ever. The mainstream media has tended to criticize both Israel and the Palestinian Authority–PLO as if their respective behavior was equivalent. For instance, it treats the Palestinian statehood–membership initiative as being equally provocative to Israel's announced intention to expand the unlawful Gilo settlement. Such an attitude does belong in the theater of the absurd, equating a completely legal, arguably overdue plea for upgraded status at the UN with a criminal encroachment on basic Palestinian rights associated with territory under occupation, as recognized by Article 49(6) of the Fourth Geneva Convention.

Whether Israel will follow through on its threats to "punish" the Palestinian Authority for undertaking this completely legal initiative remains to be seen. Already there is a troublesome indication of widespread settler violence in the West Bank that is either unopposed or backed by Israeli military and security units. As President Peres has observed, Israel will never have a more moderate partner for peace than the Ramallah leadership; if it undermines the viability of that leadership, Israel will be demonstrating once again that it has lost its capacity to promote its national interests. It has showed this aspect of decline most dramatically by picking a fight with a resurgent Turkey, then missing one opportunity after another to repair the damage, which is what Ankara had earlier hoped would happen. As regional developments move toward greater support for the Palestinian struggle, Israel is allowing what might have been a historic opportunity for a sustainable peace to slip away. An acute problem with extremism, whether of the Likud or Tea Party variety, is that it subordinates interests and rationality to the dictates of an obsessive and emotive vision that is incapable of calculating the balance of gains and losses in conflict situations. It is preoccupied with all-or-nothing outcomes, which are the antithesis of diplomacy. This is a path that inevitably produces acute human suffering and often leads to disaster. It is time for Israelis to abandon such a path, for their own sake and the sake of others.

An American Awakening?
October 5, 2011[18]

The exciting presence of protestors on Wall Street (and the spread of the #OccupyWallStreet protests across the country) is a welcome respite from years of passivity in the United States, not only in relation to the scandalous legal and illegal abuses of comprador capitalists but also to the prolongations of wars in Iraq and Afghanistan, a shocking disregard of the impinging challenges of climate change, a rising Islamophobic tide at home, and a presidency that seems less willing to confront hedge-fund managers than jobless masses. But will this encouraging presence be sustained in a manner that brings some hope of restored democracy and law-oriented leadership abroad?

There is little doubt that this move to the streets expresses a deep disillusionment with ordinary politics based on elections and governing institutions. Obama's electoral victory in 2008 was the last hope of the young in the United States, who poured unprecedented enthusiasm into his campaign that promised so much and delivered so little. Perhaps worse than Obama's failure to deliver was his refusal to fight, or even to bring into his entourage of advisors some voices of empathy and mildly progressive outlook. From his initial appointment of Rahm Emanuel onward, it was clear that the Obama presidency would be shaped by the old Washington games played by special interests and abetted by a Republican Party leaning ever

18. Originally published at http://richardfalk.wordpress.com/2011/10/05/
an-american-awakening-2.

further to the right, a surging Tea Party pushing the opposition to the outer extremes of irrational governance, and a Democratic Party trying to survive mainly by mimicking Republicans. It is a wonder that a more radical sense of the future of the United States took so long to materialize, or even to show these present signs of displeasure with what is and engagement with what might be.

For those of us with our eyes on the Middle East, two observations follow. Obama's falling back from his 2009 Cairo speech was extraordinary. The speech was, contrary to how it was spun by the pro-Israel media, a very cautious approach to the Israel–Palestine conflict, but at least forward looking in its realization that something more had to be done if negotiations were ever to be more than a charade. It contained lots of reassurances for Israel, treating the dispute as essentially territorial, and only seemed to project balance when it insisted on a suspension of settlement expansion as a confidence-building step toward a new cycle of negotiations. It really was a most modest request to insist that Israel temporarily stop expanding illegal settlements that pose a real threat to the viability of an independent Palestinian state. When Israeli leaders and their zealous American backers indicated "no go," the Obama administration backpedaled with accelerating speed, gradually isolating the United States on the global stage by its unconditional support for Israel. Besides this, a few months ago the leaked Palestine Papers underscored Israel's disinterest in a negotiated solution to the conflict even in the face of huge Palestinian Authority concessions behind closed doors. Obama should not take the whole blame, as Congress has outdone him when it comes to support for partisan positions that often seem to outdo the Knesset.

The latest phase in U.S. foreign policy in relation to the conflict is associated with its threat to veto Palestine's statehood bid in the UN Security Council, coupled with its arm-twisting efforts to induce others to vote with it or at least abstain, so that Palestine will not get the nine affirmative votes it needs and the U.S. will be spared the embarrassment and backlash of casting a veto. It should finally be understood: Time is not neutral. It helps Israel and hurts Palestine.

Disavowing American party and institutional politics and situating hope with the arousal of progressive forces in civil society is different from concluding that the Occupy Wall Street protests are more than a tantalizing flash in the pan at this stage. Even this cautionary commentary should make it obvious that the events owe their primary inspiration to Tahrir Square (with a surprising initial push from the Canadian anticonsumerist organization Adbusters, previously known for its irreverent and vaguely anarchistic magazine by the same name), especially the ethos of a nonviolent, leaderless, programless, spontaneous rising that learns day by day what it is about, who it is, and what is possible. The stakes for activists are much lower than in Egypt or elsewhere in the Middle East, as there is little risk of death at this point on American streets. At the same time, the monsters of Wall Street are not quite as potent a unifying target for a militant opposition as was the grim personage of Hosni Mubarak, cruel autocrat of more than three decades, and so it may be harder to transform the protests into a sustainable movement.

In the end, we must hope and engage. The beginnings of hope are rooted in the correctness of analysis, so we can be thankful that this initiative places its focus on financial and corporate structures and not on the state. Further along these lines, if the struggle gains momentum, it will be totally thanks to politics from below. The implicit, not-so-subtle point is that the center of power over the destinies of the American people has shifted its locus from Washington to New York, and from the penthouse to the basement.

Goldstone's Folly: Disappointing and Perverse
November 4, 2011[19]

Surely, the *New York Times* would not dare turn down a piece from the new Richard Goldstone, who has recast himself as the self-appointed guardian of Israel's world reputation even as he was earlier anointed as the distinguished jurist who admirably put aside his ethnic identity and personal affiliations to carry out his professional work as a specialist in international criminal law and conduct high-profile investigative and fact-finding missions. Goldstone even seemed willing to confront the Zionist furies of Israel when criticized for chairing the UN panel appointed to consider allegations of war crimes during Operation Cast Lead.

A few months ago Goldstone took the unseemly step of unilaterally retracting a central conclusion of the Goldstone Report. The former judge wrote, in the *Washington Post*, that the Goldstone Report would have been different if he had known then what he came to know now.[20] This was an arrogant assertion considering that he was but one of four panel members designated by the UN Human Rights Council; the other three

---

19. Originally published at http://richardfalk.wordpress.com/2011/11/04/ goldstones-folly-disappointing-and-perverse.

20. Richard Goldstone, "Reconsidering the Goldstone Report on Israel and War Crimes," *Washington Post*, April 1, 2011, http://wapo.st/TPnIAe.

publicly reaffirmed their confidence in the report's original conclusion. What should have discredited Goldstone's effort to restore his tarnished Zionist credentials was this failure to consult with other members of the team before rushing into print with his seemingly opportunistic change of heart. It is also of interest that he chooses to exhibit this new role on the pages of the newspapers of record in the United States, and reportedly escalated the tone and substance of his retraction after the *Times* rejected the original version as too bland. To get into print with this wobbly change of position, Goldstone went to these extraordinary lengths.

Now, on the eve of the third session of the Russell Tribunal on Palestine, scheduled to be held in Cape Town between November 5 and 7, Goldstone has again come to the defense of Israel in a highly partisan manner, with a *New York Times* op-ed piece that abandons any pretense of respect for either the legal duties of those with power or the legal rights of those in vulnerable circumstances.[21] Recourse to a quality tribunal of the people, in this instance constituted and participated in by those with the highest moral authority and specialized knowledge, is a constructive and serious response to the failure of governments and international institutions to declare and implement international criminal law over the course of many years. People of good will should welcome the Russell Tribunal's laudable efforts as overdue rather angrily dismissing them, as Goldstone does, because of their supposed interference with nonexistent and long-futile negotiations between the parties. Those who will sit as jurors to assess these charges of apartheid against Israel are world-class moral authority figures whose response to the apartheid charge will be assisted by the testimony of experts on the conflict and by jurists of global stature. It should embarrass Goldstone to write derisively of such iconic South African personalities as Archbishop Emeritus Desmond Tutu and Ronnie Kasrils or internationally renowned figures such as the morally driven novelist Alice Walker, Nobel Peace Prize winner Mairead Maguire, former member of the U.S. Congress Cynthia McKinney, and the ninety-three-year-old Holocaust survivor and French ambassador Stephane Hessel, as well as several other persons of high repute.

A further imprimatur of respectability is given to the Russell Tribunal by the participation of Goldstone's once-close colleague John Dugard, who is internationally regarded as South Africa's most trusted voice whenever legal comparisons are made between apartheid as practiced in South Africa and alleged in Palestine. Professor Dugard will play a leading

---

21. Richard Goldstone, "Israel and the Apartheid Slander," *New York Times*, October 31, 2011, http://www.nytimes.com/2011/11/01/opinion/ israel-and-the-apartheid-slander.html?_r=0.

role in the Russell proceedings by offering expert testimony in support of the legal argument for charging Israel with the crime of apartheid. A widely esteemed international lawyer and UN civil servant, Dugard acted for seven years as Special Rapporteur for the UN Human Rights Council and was scrupulous in his efforts to report truthfully on the situation of occupied Palestine. His experience in that role led him, despite his cautious legal temperament, to allege the apartheid character of the occupation in the formal reports he submitted to the United Nations.

Goldstone condemns the venture before it begins without acknowledging the participation of these distinguished participants, scorning this inquiry by contending that it is intended as an "assault" on Israel with the "aim to isolate, demonize and delegitimize" the country. In the most aggressive prosecutorial style, Goldstone demonizes these unnamed Russell jurors as biased individuals who hold "harsh views of Israel." The new Goldstone adopts the standard Israeli practice of denigrating the auspices and condemning any critical voices, however qualified and honest, without bothering to take a serious look at the plausibility of the apartheid allegations. The fact that those familiar with Israel's policies are sharp critics does not invalidate their observations but raises substantive challenges that can only be met by producing convincing countervailing evidence. Unbalanced realities can only be accurately portrayed by a one-sided assessment, if truthfulness is to be the guide to decide whether bias is present or not. If the message contains unpleasant news then it deserves respect precisely *because* it is delivered by a trustworthy messenger. It should be reflected upon with respect rather than summarily dismissed, because this particular messenger has the credibility associated with an impeccable professional reputation, strengthened in the context of the Russell Tribunal by a wealth of prior experience that predisposed and prepared her or him to compose a message with a particular slant.

Goldstone's central contention is that to charge Israel with the crime of apartheid is a form of "slander" that, in his words, is not only "false and malicious" but also "precludes, rather than promotes, peace and harmony." It is necessary to await the deliberations of the Russell Tribunal to determine whether allegations of apartheid are irresponsible accusations by hostile critics or are grounded, as I believe, in the reality of a systematic legal regime of discriminatory separation of privileged Israelis, especially several hundred thousand unlawful settlers, from rightless and often dispossessed Palestinians who are indigenous to the land so long occupied by Israel.

The Rome Statute of the International Criminal Court treats apartheid as one among several types of crime against humanity and associates its commission with systematic and severe discrimination. Although the crime derives its name from the South African experience that ended in 1994, it has now been generalized to refer to any condition that imposes an oppressive regime based on group identity and designed to benefit a dominating collectivity that coercively through its control of the legal system abuses a subjugated collectivity. It is true that "race" is the basis for drawing the dividing line between the two collectivities, but the legal definition of race has been expanded to make it clear beyond reasonable doubt that the practice of apartheid can be properly associated with any form of group antagonism that is translated into a legal regime incorporating inequality as its core feature. This includes regimes that base their human classifications of belonging to a group on reference to national and ethnic identity, as is the case with regard to Israelis and Palestinians. The government of Israel has itself drawn attention to this ethno-religious divide by demanding that its Palestinian minority and the Palestinian Authority formally accept its character as "a Jewish state."

The overwhelming evidence of systematic discrimination is impossible to overlook in any objective description of Israel's current occupation of the West Bank, and to a lesser degree, East Jerusalem.[22] The pattern of establishing settlements for Israelis throughout the West Bank not only violates the prohibition in international humanitarian law against transferring members of the occupying population to an occupied territory, it also creates an operational rationalization for Israel's establishment of a legal regime of separation and subjugation. From this settlement phenomenon follows an Israeli community protected by Israeli security forces, provided at great expense with a network of settler-only roads, enjoying Israeli constitutional protection, and given direct, unregulated access to Israel. What also follows is a Palestinian community subject to often-abusive military administration without the protection of effective rights, living with great daily difficulty due to many burdensome restrictions on mobility, and subject to an array of humiliating and dangerous conditions that include frequent use of arbitrary and excessive force, house demolitions, and nighttime arrests and detentions that subject Palestinians as a whole to a lifetime ordeal of acute human insecurity. The contrast of these two sets of conditions, translated into operative legal regimes, for two peoples living side by side makes the

---

22. The encroachment on Palestinian rights in Jerusalem is also flagrantly unlawful, involving settlements, cleansing edicts by way of undermining residency security of many Palestinian residents, and an array of other abuses by Israel as the occupying power. Indeed, Israel has unilaterally transformed by its domestic law the city of Jerusalem into an integral part of Israel, which completely negates the central rule of international law prohibiting the acquisition of territory by force.

allegations of apartheid seem persuasive. If a slander is present, then it can be attributed to those who, like Goldstone, seek to defame and discredit the Russell Tribunal's heroic attempt to challenge the scandal of silence that has allowed Israel to perpetrate injustice without accountability.

Goldstone's preemptive strike against the Russell Tribunal is hard to take seriously. It is formulated in such a way as to mislead and confuse a generally uninformed public. For instance, he devotes much space in the column to painting a generally rosy (and false) picture of recent conditions of life for by the Palestinian minority in Israel, without even taking note of their historic experience of expulsion, the *Nakba*. He dramatically understates the deplorable status of Palestinian Israelis, who live as a discriminated minority despite enjoying some of the prerogatives of Israeli citizenship. Goldstone's main diversionary contention is that apartheid cannot be credibly alleged in a constitutional setting where Palestinians are currently accorded citizenship rights; he never dares to raise the question of what it means to ask Palestinian Muslims and Christians to pledge allegiance to "a Jewish state," by its nature a fracturing of community through racially based inequality.[23] Few would argue that this pattern of unacceptable inequality adds up to an apartheid structure within Israel. However, the Russell Tribunal is likely to forgo making the apartheid charge associated with the events surrounding the founding of Israel in the late 1940s, because, from an international law perspective, they took place before apartheid was criminalized in the mid-1970s.

The Tribunal is focusing its attention on the situation existing in the West Bank, which has been occupied since 1967. John Dugard has issued a statement to the press to clear the air, indicating that his testimony will be devoted exclusively to the existence of conditions of apartheid obtaining in the occupied territories, which reflects his special competence.[24] That Dugard felt compelled to issue such a statement is a kind of backhanded tribute to the success of the Goldstone *hasbara* effort to divert and distort. For Goldstone to refute the apartheid contention by turning to the *present* situation within Israel itself, while at the same time virtually ignoring the allegation principally concerned with the occupation, is a stunning display of bad faith. He knows better. Goldstone avoids any reference to the mass expulsion of Palestinians from their land in 1948 and the subsequent destruction of hundreds of Palestinian villages when he attempts to refute

---

23. For a list of more than 50 Israeli laws that discriminate against non-Jewish citizens, see "Discriminatory Laws in Israel," Adalah, http://adalah.org/eng/ Israeli-Discriminatory-Law-Database.

24. See John Dugard, testimony to the Russell Tribunal on Apartheid in the Occupied Palestinian Territory, November 1, 2011, video available at http://bit.ly/V26mRz.

the apartheid allegation, though this would likely be viewed as legally dubious because of its retroactivity.

With shameless abandon, Goldstone relies on a debater's trick, insisting that apartheid is a narrowly circumscribed racial crime of the exact sort that existed in South Africa, which is certainly disingenuous. He takes scant account of the explicit legal intent, as embodied in the authoritative Rome Statute and in the International Convention on the Crime of Apartheid, to understand race in a much broader sense that applies to the Israeli–Palestine interaction if its systematic and legally encoded discriminatory character can be convincingly established, as I believe is the case.

The sad saga of Richard Goldstone's descent from the pinnacle of respect and trust to this shabby role as legal gladiator recklessly jousting on behalf of Israel is as unbecoming as it is unpersuasive. It is undoubtedly a process more personal and complex than caving in to Zionist pressures, which were even nastier and more overt than usual as well as clearly defamatory, but what exactly has led to his radical shift in position remains a mystery. As yet there is neither an autobiographical account nor a convincing third-party interpretation. Goldstone himself has been silent on this score, seeming to want us to believe that he is now as much a man of the law as ever but only persisting in his impartial and lifelong attempt to allow the chips to fall where they may. His polemical manipulation of the facts and arguments makes me doubt any such self-serving explanation. It is my judgment that enough is now known to acknowledge Goldstone's justifiable fall from grace, and for his own sake it is unfortunate that Goldstone did not choose a silent retreat from the fray rather than reinventing himself as a prominent Israeli apologist.

Palestinian suffering and denial of legal rights is sufficiently grounded in reality that the defection of such an influential witness amounts to a further assault not only on Palestinian well-being but also on the wider struggle to achieve justice, peace, and security for both peoples. Contrary to Goldstone's protestations about the Russell Tribunal striking a blow against hopes for resolving the conflict, it is the Goldstones of this world who are producing the smokescreens behind which the very possibility of a two-state solution has been deliberately destroyed by Israel's tactics of delay while it is accelerating its policies of expansion and encroachment.

In the end, if there is ever to emerge a just and sustainable peace, it will be thanks to many forms of Palestinian resistance and a related campaign of global solidarity, to which the Russell Tribunal promises to make a notable contribution. We should all remember that it is hard to render the truth until we render the truth, however ugly it may turn out to be.

On (Im)Balance and Credibility in America: Israel–Palestine

November 18, 2011[25]

I could not begin to count the number of times friends, and adversaries, have given me the following general line of advice: Your views on Israel–Palestine would gain a much wider hearing if they showed more sympathy for Israel's position and concerns, that is, if they were more "balanced." Especially on this set of issues, I have always found such advice wildly off the mark for two main reasons.

First, if the concern is balance, we should not begin with me but with the absurd pro-Israel balance that pervades the response to the conflict in Washington, in the Congress, at the White House and State Department, and among Beltway think tanks, as well as in the mainstream media. There is a serious problem of balance, or I would say distortion, that undermines diplomatic credibility. Such a toxic imbalance here in the United States makes the U.S. claim to mediate the conflict and provide neutral auspices futile, if not ridiculous, or at best a reliance on geopolitical "justice" in place of legal justice (based on rights). When the Goldstone Report is rejected before it has been read and the World Court's near-unanimous advisory opinion condemning the separation wall is repudiated without a serious critical argument, it is clear that bias controls reason.

But what of the *imbalance* that is consistent with the evidence, with the law, with the "facts on the ground" as observers arrive at their findings and conclusions? What of the continuous expansion of settlements in the West Bank and East Jerusalem, the denial of Palestinian refugees' right of return, the apartheid legal structure of occupation, discrimination against the Palestinian minority living as Israeli citizens, the appropriation of scarce Palestinian water reserves, the abuse of prisoners and children, the long siege imposed on the people of Gaza as a sustained collective punishment? What of the continuous defiance of international law by Israeli reliance on excessive and disproportionate uses of force in the name of security? In light of this record, is not such imbalance, particularly in the inflamed American atmosphere, the only possible way for truth to speak to power? Stated more strongly, is not a circumstance of imbalance written into the fabric of the conflict and exhibited in the daily suffering and thrall of the Palestinian people, whether living under occupation or in refugee camps in neighboring countries, in exile as a subjugated minority?

---

25. Originally published at http://richardfalk.wordpress.com/2011/11/18/ on-imbalance-and-credibility-in-america-israelpalestine.

Finally, the idea of balance and symmetry should also "see" the structures of life that describe the contrasting conditions of the two peoples: Israelis living in conditions of near-normalcy, Palestinians enduring, for an incredible six-decade period, a variety of daily hardships and abuses that is cumulatively experienced as *acute human insecurity*. To be structurally blindfolded and blind is to adopt a common yet deforming appearance of balance that perpetuates an unjust imbalance between oppressor and oppressed.

In relation to self-determination for Palestinians and Israelis, I favor a stance of "constructive imbalance," which I believe is the only truthful manner of depicting *this* reality. Truth and accuracy are my litmus tests of objectivity, and as such, they knowingly defy that sinister god who encourages the substitution of balance for truth.

What Was Wrong with Obama's Jerusalem Speech
March 24, 2013[26]

It was masterfully crafted as an ingratiating speech by the world's most important leader and the government that has most consistently championed Israel's cause over the decades. Enthusiastically received in Israel and by Jews around the world, President Obama's words in Jerusalem will clear the air somewhat in Washington. Obama may now have a slightly better chance to succeed in his second, legacy-building presidential term, despite a deeply polarized U.S. Congress and a struggling U.S. economy (if assessed from the perspective of workers' distress rather than on the basis of robust corporate profits).

As for the speech itself, it was not without several redeeming features. It did acknowledge that alongside Israeli security concerns the "Palestinian people's right of self-determination, their right to justice must also be recognized."[27] This affirmation was followed by the strongest assertion of all: "Put yourself in their shoes. Look at the world through their eyes." To consider the realities of the conflict through Palestinian eyes

26. Originally published as "What Was Wrong with Obama's Speech in Jerusalem" at http://richardfalk.wordpress.com/2013/03/24/ what-was-wrong-with-obamas-speech-in-jerusalem.

27. Barack Obama, "Remarks of President Barack Obama to the People of Israel," March 21, 2013, http://www.whitehouse.gov/the-press-office/2013/03/21/ remarks-president-barack-obama-people-israel.

is to confront the ugly realities of prolonged occupation, annexationist settlement projects, an unlawful separation wall, generations confined to the misery of refugee camps and exile, second-class citizenship in Israel, ethnic cleansing in Jerusalem, and a myriad of regulations that make the daily life of Palestinians a narrative of humiliation and frustration. Obama did not dare to do this. He specified none of these realities, leaving them to the imagination of his audience of Israeli youth, but at least his general injunction to see the conflict through the eyes of the other pointed the way toward empathy and reconciliation.

Obama also encouraged, in a helpful way, Israeli citizen activism on behalf of a just peace based on two states for two peoples. A bit strangely, he urged that they should "for the moment, put aside the plans and process" by which this goal might be achieved, and "instead . . . build trust between people." Is this not an odd bit of advice? It seems a stretch to stress trust when the structures and practice of occupation are, for the Palestinians, unremittingly cruel and exploitative, and whittle away day after day at the attainability of a viable Palestinian state. But this far-fetched entreaty was coupled with a more plausible plea: "I can promise you this: Political leaders will never take risks if the people do not push them to take some risks. You must create the change that you want to see. Ordinary people can accomplish extraordinary things." There is some genuine hope to be found in these inspirational words, but to what end, given the present situation?

In my opinion the speech was deeply flawed in three fundamental respects.

First, by speaking only to Israeli youth and not arranging a parallel talk in Ramallah to Palestinian youth, the role of the United States as "dishonest broker" was brazenly confirmed; it also signaled that the White House was more interested in appealing to the folks in Washington than to those Palestinians trapped in the West Bank and Gaza. This interpretation was reinforced by Obama laying a wreath at the grave of Theodor Herzl but refusing to do so at the tomb of Yasser Arafat. This disparity of concern was further exhibited when Obama spoke of the children of Sderot in southern Israel, "the same age as my own daughters, who went to bed at night fearful that a rocket would land in their bedroom simply because of who they are and where they live." To make such an observation without even mentioning the trauma-laden lives of children on the other side of the border in Gaza, who have been living for years under conditions of blockade, violent incursions, and total vulnerability year after year, is to subscribe fully to the one-sided Israeli narrative of the insecurity being experienced by the two peoples.

Second, by speaking about the possibility of peace based on the two-state consensus, the old ideas, without mentioning developments that have made more and more people skeptical about Israeli intentions is to lend credence to what seems more and more to be a delusionary approach to resolving the conflict. Coupling this with Obama's perverse injunction to the leaders of the Middle East that seems willfully oblivious to the present set of circumstances makes the whole appeal seem out of touch: "Now's the time for the Arab world to take steps towards normalizing relations with Israel." How can now be the time, when just days earlier Benjamin Netanyahu announced the formation of the most right-wing, pro-settler government in the history of Israel, selecting a cabinet that is deeply dedicated to settlement expansion and resistant to the very idea of a genuine Palestinian state? It should never be forgotten that the Palestinian Liberation Organization announced back in 1988 that it was prepared to make a sustained peace with Israel on the basis of the 1967 borders. By doing this, the Palestinians were making an extraordinary territorial concession that has never been reciprocated. The move meant accepting a state limited to 22 percent of historic Palestine, or less than half of what the UN had proposed in its 1947 partition plan contained in General Assembly Resolution 181. To expect the Palestinians to be willing now to accept less than these 1967 borders to reach a resolution of the conflict seems unreasonable and probably unsustainable.

Third, by endorsing the formula "two states for two peoples," Obama was consigning the Palestinian minority in Israel to permanent second-class citizenship without even being worthy of mention as a human rights challenge facing the "democratic Israel" Obama was celebrating. As David Bromwich has pointed out, Obama was also endorsing a tribalist view of statehood that seem inconsistent with a globalizing world and with secularist assumptions that the state should not be exclusivist in either religious or ethnic character.[28] His words repeated the core Zionist idea of a statist homeland where all Jews can most fully embrace their Jewishness: "Israel is rooted not just in history and tradition, but also in a simple and profound idea: the idea that people deserve to be free in a land of their own."

Such a regressive approach to identity and statehood was also by implication attributed to the Palestinians, also affirmed as entitled. But this is highly misleading, a false symmetry. The Palestinians have no guiding ideology that is comparable to Zionism. Their quest has been to recover rights under international law in the lands of their habitual residence, the exercise of the right of self-determination in such a manner as to roll back the wider claims of settler colonialism so grandiosely part of the vision and practice of the Netanyahu government. Indeed, Obama's speech was also

---

28. David Bromwich, "Tribalism in the Jerusalem Speech," *Mondoweiss*, March 23, 2013, http://mondoweiss.net/2013/03/tribalism-jerusalem-speech.html.

an affront to many Israeli post-Zionists and secularists who do not affirm the idea of living in a hypernationalist state with pretensions of religious endowments.

In my view, there are two conclusions to be drawn. First, until the rhetoric of seeing the realities of the situation through Palestinian eyes is matched by a consideration of the specifics, there is a misleading impression created that both sides hold equally the keys to peace, and both are equally at fault for being unwilling to use them. Second, it is a cruel distraction to urge a resumption of negotiations when Israel clearly lacks the political will to establish a Palestinian state within the 1967 borders, and in circumstances in which the West Bank has been altered by continuous settlement expansion, settler-only roads, and the separation wall, and all signs suggest more of the same to come. Making matters even worse, Israel is taking many steps to ensure that Jerusalem never becomes the capital of whatever Palestinian entity eventually emerges.

In retrospect, worse than the speech was the visit itself. Obama should never have undertaken such a visit without an accompanying willingness to treat the Palestinian reality with at least equal dignity and without some indication of how to imagine a just peace based on two states for two peoples, given the severe, continuing Israeli encroachments on occupied Palestinian territory that give every indication of permanence. Obama made no mention of the wave of recent Palestinian hunger strikes or the degree to which Palestinians have shifted their tactics of resistance away from a reliance on violence. It is perverse to heap praise on the oppressive occupier and then call on both peoples to move forward toward peace by building relations of trust with one another. On what planet has Mr. Obama been living?

Northern Ireland and the
Israel–Palestine "Peace Process"

December 22, 2013[29]

Having visited Belfast over the last few days during some negotiations about unresolved problems between unionist and republican (or nationalist) political parties, I was struck by the process's absolute dependence for any kind of credibility upon the unblemished perceived neutrality of

---

29. Originally published at http://richardfalk.wordpress.com/2013/12/22/
   northern-ireland-and-the-israelpalestine-peace-process.

the mediating third party. It would have been so totally unacceptable to rely on Ireland or Britain to play such a role; the mere suggestion of such a partisan intermediary would have occasioned ridicule by the opposing party and confirmed suspicions that its intention must have been to scuttle the proposed negotiations. In the background of such a reflection is the constructive role played by the United States more than a decade ago when it actively encouraged a process of reconciliation through the antagonists' historic abandonment of violence. That peace process was based on the justly celebrated Good Friday Agreement, which brought the people of Northern Ireland a welcome measure of relief from the so-called "Time of Troubles" even if the underlying antagonisms remain poignantly alive in the everyday realities of Belfast and some inclination toward violence lingers among those extremist remnants of the struggle on both sides who reject all moves toward accommodation. The underlying tensions persist: the republicans still long for a united Ireland and the unionists feel more British than ever and threatened by any intimation that Northern Ireland might be absorbed by the Republic of Ireland at some point.

The current round of negotiations going on in Belfast involve seemingly trivial issues: whether the flag of the United Kingdom will be flown from the Parliament and other government buildings on eighteen official holidays or every day; whether the Irish tricolor will be flown when leaders from the Republic of Ireland are visiting Belfast; the degree to which annual unionist parades passing through republican neighborhoods of the city will be regulated to avoid provocations; and how the past might be addressed so as to bring belated solace to those who have grievances, especially associated with deaths of family members that were never properly addressed by those in authority at the time. Apparently, in recollection of the achievements attributed to George Mitchell, the distinguished American political figure principally associated with developing the proposals that produced the Good Friday Agreement, the present phase of an evolving accommodation process is being presided over by another notable American, Richard Haass. Haass is a former State Department official and currently serves as president of the Council on Foreign Relations, the influential establishment NGO in the foreign policy domain. In this setting the U.S. government is seen as an honest broker (as are its leading citizens), and although the government is not now directly involved, an individual closely associated with the established order has been chosen and seems acceptable to the five Northern Ireland political parties participating in the negotiations. This effort to ensure the continuation of stability in Northern Ireland seems responsive to the natural order: that negotiation in circumstances of deep conflict do benefit from third-party mediation, provided it is perceived to be nonpartisan, neutral, and competent and acts credibly and diligently as a check on the gridlock of partisanship.

The contrast of this experience in Northern Ireland with what has emerged during the past twenty years in the effort to resolve the Israel–Palestine conflict could not be more striking. The negotiating process between Israel and Palestine is generated by an avowedly partisan third party, the United States, which makes no effort to hide its commitment to safeguarding Israeli state interests even at the expense of Palestinian concerns. This critical assessment has been carefully documented in Rashid Khalidi's authoritative *Brokers of Deceit* (2013). Beyond this taint, the White House repeatedly throws sand in Palestinian eyes with its gall in designating AIPAC-related special envoys to oversee the negotiations, as if it is primarily Israel that needs reassurances that its national interests will be protected in the process while Palestinians' greater concerns do not require any such indication of protective sensitivity.

How can we explain these contrasting American approaches in these two major conflict-resolving undertakings? The first line of explanation would be domestic politics in the United States. Although Irish Americans by and large have republican sympathies, Washington's multiple bonds with the United Kingdom ensure it will strike a posture of impartiality from the perspective of national interests. The United States had most to gain in Ireland by being seen to help the parties move from a violent encounter to a political process in pursuing their rival goals. Such would also seem to be the case in Israel–Palestine but for the intrusion of domestic politics, especially in the form of the AIPAC's lobbying leverage. Can anyone doubt that if the Palestinians had countervailing lobbying capabilities, either the United States would be excluded as the diplomatic arbiter or it would do its best to appear impartial?

There are other secondary explanatory factors. Especially since the 1967 War, it has been a matter of agreement within U.S. policymaking circles that Israel is a reliable strategic ally in the Middle East. Interests may diverge from time to time, as seems recently to be the case in relation to Iran's nuclear-weapons program, but overall the alliance patterns in the region put the United States and Israel on the same side: counterterrorist operations and tactics, counterproliferation, containing Iran's influence, opposing the spread of political Islam, supporting Saudi Arabia and conservative governments in the Gulf. Since 9/11, in particular, Israel has been a counterterrorist mentor to the United States and others in the world, offering expert training and what it calls "combat-tested weaponry," which means tactics and weapons it has used over many years in controlling the hostile Palestinian population, especially in Gaza.

A third, weaker explanation is purported ideological affinity. Israel promotes itself, and this is endorsed by the United States, as the "sole democracy" or "only genuine democracy" in the Middle East. There is much hypocrisy and deception embedded in such an assertion that implies a U.S. bias toward democracy. It is hardly consistent with the close positive relations that the United States sustains with the reactionary and autocratic monarchy that rules in Saudi Arabia or the overt silence and covert approval given by the Obama presidency to the Egyptian coup and its bloody aftermath. And the affirmation of Israel is hardly consistent with the wide-eyed refusal of Washington to take note of Israeli's legalized pattern of discrimination against the 20 percent Palestinian minority living within Israel. It has been persuasively suggested that part of the reason that Arab governments are reluctant to support the Palestinian struggle is the fear that its success would destabilize authoritarian regimes in the region. In this regard, it was the First Intifada, back in 1987, that seems in retrospect to have been the most important antecedent cause of the 2011 Arab Spring. It is also notable that despite its profession of democratic values in the Middle East, Israel showed no regrets when the elected government in Egypt was overthrown by a military coup whose leadership then proceeded to criminalize those chosen only a year earlier by the national electorate to run the country.

These weighty reasons, when considered together, help us understand why the Oslo framework, its Roadmap sequel, and the various negotiating sessions have not produced an outcome that remotely resembles what might be fairly described as "a just and sustainable peace" from a Palestinian perspective. Israel has evidently not perceived such a conflict-resolving outcome as being in its national interest and has not been given any sufficient incentive by the United States or the UN to scale back its ambitions, which include continuous settlement expansion; control over the whole of Jerusalem; denying Palestinian rights of return; appropriating water and land resources; intrusive, one-sided, and excessive security demands; and an associated posture that opposes a viable Palestinian state ever coming into existence and is even more opposed to giving any credence to proposals for a single, secular, binational state. What is more, despite this unreasonable diplomatic posture, which attains plausibility only because of Israel's disproportionate influence on the intermediary mechanisms and its own media savvy in projecting its priorities, Palestine and its leadership are mainly blamed for the failures of the "peace process" to end the conflict by a mutually agreed-upon solution. This is a particularly perverse perception given Israel's extreme unreasonableness in relation to resolving the conflict, U.S. partisanship, and Palestine's passivity in asserting its claims, grievances, and interests.

Finally, we must ask why Palestinian leaders have been willing to give credibility for so long to a diplomatic process that seems to offer their national movement so little. The most direct answer is the lack of the power to say no. This can be further elaborated by pointing to the lack of a preferable alternative. A further indication of Palestinian diplomatic dependence is the degree to which the United States exerts pressure on Ramallah because it finds the management of this peace-process bridge to nowhere useful, despite its many frustrations and failures, in that it allows Washington to exhibit a commitment to both peace and Israel. U.S. secretary of state John Kerry has in recent months pressured the parties to resume peace talks, talking often of "painful concessions" that both sides would have to make if the negotiations are to succeed. This misleading appeal to symmetry overlooks the gross disparity in position and capabilities of the two sides. Whether such a disparity is so great as to make it dubious to use the language of conflict is itself an open question. Would it not be more forthright and revealing to ask, due to the degree of inequality, whether Palestine has any capability to say anything about the terms of a resolution other than "yes" or "no" to what Israel is prepared at any time to offer? In this sense it more closely resembles the end of a war in which there is a winner and loser, except that here the loser at least retains the sovereign right to say no. This perception is also deeply misleading because it overlooks the legitimacy struggle, which the Palestinians are winning and which, given the history of decolonization, seems to have a good chance of controlling the political outcome of the struggle.

Returning to the intergovernmental approach, it should also be noticed that the diplomacy does not take account of the historical background. Did not Palestine concede more than enough before the negotiations even began? We should also take account of the relevance of the supposed basic UN policy against the acquisition of territory by the use of force. The implication of Kerry's painful concession rhetoric is that Israel would only be expected to remove some isolated settlements and outposts in the West Bank and could retain the valuable land it has appropriated for the settlement blocs established since 1967, despite both being unlawful. In other words, Palestine is expected to give up fundamental *rights* while Israel is supposed to abandon some relatively minor unlawful aspects of its prolonged occupation of the West Bank and retain most of its ill-gotten gains.

What do we learn from such an analysis?

Third-party intermediation only works if it is perceived to be nonpartisan by both sides.

1. Partisan intermediation can only succeed if the stronger side is able to impose its vision of the future on the weaker side.

2. Analyzing the Palestine–Israel diplomacy underscores the relevance of the second explanation and should not be confused with its claimed character as an instance of the first.
3. Perhaps in the aftermath of a Palestinian victory in the legitimacy struggle, a framework for constructive diplomacy similar to that achieved in Northern Ireland could be devised, but its credibility would depend on nonpartisan intermediation.

6

The Larger Picture

The concerns of this volume focus on the Palestinian struggle, the forms it has taken, and the obstacles it has faced. I have also offered criticisms of Israel's policies and practices from the perspective of international law, international morality, and political prudence. This section seeks to generalize about these interactions. It depicts in several posts the new direction the Palestine national movement is adopting. It also discusses the basic Israeli tactic of deflection and fragmentation to frustrate Palestinians by diverting attention from the substantive merits of their struggle and to weaken their movement by fragmenting it in multiple ways. It is vital to understand the interplay between the Palestinian strategic embrace of legitimacy struggle and the Israel strategic reliance on tactics that weaken the Palestinian will and present images to the world of a Palestinian inability to function as a coherent whole.

This larger picture seeks to portray the overall character of the interaction between Palestine and Israel as of June 2014. The uncertainties arising from the regional turbulence in the Middle East are likely to bring changes in the approaches of both sides of this continuing struggle. At present, Israel is seeking to consolidate its gains via expanding its settlements in the West Bank, completing the separation wall as an encroaching potential border, and shifting the ethnic composition of East Jerusalem. On the Palestinian side, the governmental actors appear to be treading water, hoping for the best, while the Palestinian justice movement shifts its center of gravity to hopes for populist resistance and global solidarity, a sign of confidence in the eventual triumph of its soft-power capabilities and legitimacy-war strategies.

If the Palestinian approach succeeds in altering the political climate, especially in Israel and the United States, intergovernmental diplomacy may finally be able to play a constructive role in resolving the conflict. Pressure on Israel would likely create a greater incentive for accommodation and increase the likelihood that the U.S. government would view the conflict in a genuinely balanced manner. Such a prospect may be fanciful if Israel succeeds in further implementing its expansionist vision, making any political reversal impossible and suggesting that the only way forward would be a secular unified state that encompasses the entirety of historic Palestine as administered between the two world wars.

International Day of Solidarity with the Palestinian People at the Arab League Headquarters in Cairo
November 29, 2012[1]

I delivered these remarks in Cairo in 2012 at the joint UN–Arab League ceremony observing the International Day of Solidarity with the Palestinian People, some ten hours before the historic vote on Palestinian statehood at the United Nations General Assembly.

It is an exceptional honor and challenge to speak on such an occasion. We meet at a tense historical moment with heavy potential consequences for the Palestinian people and for the peoples and governments of the region. I, along with many others throughout the world, share Nelson Mandela's view that the denial of Palestinian rights remains the "the greatest moral issue of our time." This 2012 International Day of Solidarity with the People of Palestine possesses a special significance. A ceasefire ending the latest orgy of violence afflicting the two societies, but especially affecting the people of Gaza, has been agreed upon just over a week ago and appears to be holding. And, in a few hours, the chairman of the Palestinian Liberation Organization and president of the Palestinian Authority, Mahmoud Abbas, is scheduled to ask the UN General Assembly to recognize Palestine as a nonmember observer state within the UN, a status similar to that of the Vatican. When this initiative is approved later today, it means an upgraded status for Palestine within the UN system, including probable access to other organs of the UN.

Meeting here in Cairo on this occasion has an added resonance. It was the Egyptian government that played such an instrumental role in producing the ceasefire in Gaza, and it is the democratization of Egypt that has done more to improve Palestinian prospects than any other recent regional or international development. It also raises expectations that Egypt will,

---

1. Originally published as "Observing the International Day of Solidarity with the Palestinian People in Cairo" at http://bit.ly/1wiAGVe.

in the future, exert its influence to bring this conflict that has lingered far too long to a just end by working toward a peaceful solution based on the recognition of Palestinian rights under international law. Nothing would better convey to the world that the Arab Spring represents a regional declaration of independence from the dominion of external influence. In doing so it would enlarge upon the earlier historic achievement of unexpectedly bringing about the downfall of a series of dictatorial regimes reigning throughout the Middle East.

Those innocent Palestinians who lost their lives and were injured during the latest Israeli military attack upon Gaza should be remembered and mourned on this day as martyred victims of Israel's latest onslaught. This attack was carried out with ferocity, using the most modern weaponry against an essentially entrapped and acutely vulnerable people. We should be thankful that this latest violent interlude has come to an end, and all of us should resolve to work toward the good-faith implementation of the ceasefire agreement, not only with respect to the violence but in its entirety. Such an implementation would uphold what was achieved through the energetic and flexible diplomacy of Egypt and other regional forces.

There are already disquieting signs that Israel is downplaying the conditions set forth in the ceasefire text, especially those pertaining to a prohibition on future targeted assassinations and on establishing the mechanisms mandating the opening of the Gaza crossings. The blockade of Gaza imposed by Israel in mid-2007 is nothing other than the collective punishment of the entire Gazan population, and hence a flagrant violation of Article 33 of the Fourth Geneva Convention. If the ceasefire agreement is faithfully carried out, the blockade will finally be brought to an end after more than five years of punitive closure. Goods and persons will be able to flow in both directions across the borders between Israel and Gaza. This is unlikely to happen without concerted pressure from Israel's neighbors. Israeli officials are whispering behind the scenes that nothing more was agreed upon, despite the clear language of the brief ceasefire text, beyond the cessation of the violence. The Israeli claim is that everything else was a mere pledge to discuss, without any obligation to act. Such a disappointing of Palestinian expectations must not be allowed to happen. Without implementation of the full agreement, this ceasefire will evaporate in a cloud of smoke, the rockets soon will again fall on Israel, and Gaza will again become a killing field while the world once more looks on helplessly at this awful spectacle of an ultramodern war machine killing and maiming at will, and once more terrifying with unforgiveable impunity the entire civilian population of Gaza.

Such a situation presents the regional and world communities with both a responsibility and an opportunity. As I have suggested, without pressure brought to bear, Israel is unlikely to implement the ceasefire. There are levers of influence that can be pulled and, if they are, it will convey a new seriousness on the part of Arab governments to take concrete measures to enforce the international legal rights of the Palestinian people. States such as Egypt and Jordan have peace treaties with Israel that can be suspended due to fundamentally changed circumstances or diplomatic relations downgraded or even drawn into question. The more affluent Arab governments could commit to supplying UN agencies with funds to offset any refusals to pay the normal assessed financial contributions of Israel and its friends. There are many concrete steps that can be taken if the political will to do so is present.

Shockingly, Michael Oren, Israel's ambassador at the United States, declared a few days ago that in this recent attack, "Israel was not confronting Gaza, but Iran." He added that the attack on Gaza should be understood as a "rehearsal" for militarily engaging Tehran. Such an acknowledgement is tantamount to a public confession by a high Israeli official to commit crimes against humanity, spilling Palestine blood so as to play what amounts to a war game to test how effective the Iron Dome would likely be in dealing with Iranian rockets expected to be released in the aftermath of an Israeli attack, if in fact Israel actually goes ahead with such a military venture at odds with the UN Charter.

This assertion by someone of Ambassador Oren's stature reinforces the call to the UN Human Rights Council to form a high-level fact-finding mission to Gaza that evaluates allegations of war crimes on all sides of the struggle, as was done with mixed results after the Gaza War of 2008 and 2009. Such a step has been proposed in a letter of November 22, 2012, to Navi Pillay, the High Commissioner for Human Rights, from the highly respected director of the Palestine Centre for Human Rights, Raji Sourani. I believe firmly that it is our responsibility as citizens of the world, especially those of us associated with the UN, to do whatever is necessary to avoid flagrant violations of international humanitarian law being swept under the diplomatic rug. Further, it is my hope that this time, unlike the unfortunate experience with the Goldstone Report four years ago, whatever recommendations are made to the UN do not get buried beneath the weight of geopolitical influence but are carried out in a timely and diligent manner. The UN, to be credible and relevant to the aspirations of the Palestinian people, must at this time move beyond its authoritative and oft-repeated affirmation of inalienable Palestinian rights under international law to undertaking concrete steps designed to implement those rights.

Ambassador Oren's comments are revealing in another way. They are an extreme example of Israel's frequent reliance on a "politics of deflection" to divert attention from its highest-priority concerns. Such deflection takes various forms. On a simple level it means attacking the messenger to avoid the message, or claiming that the UN is biased so as to avoid discussing the abuses alleged. Such a pattern was epitomized by the recent unlawful and criminal attack on journalists in Gaza, in effect eliminating the messenger to prevent delivery of the message. On a more complex level it means shifting attention away from the real drama of the occupation. Periodic attacks on Gaza totally redirect the attention of the world away from Israel's expansionist projects. It should be clear to all by now that Israel's highest priorities in occupied Palestine are associated with their controversial and unlawful settlement activity in the West Bank and East Jerusalem. Israel builds an unlawful security wall on occupied Palestinian territory, in the course of which it seizes additional Palestinian land, and when the World Court declares this unlawful wall should be torn down and Palestinians compensated for the harm done, Israel callously attacks the highest judicial body of the UN and carries on with its construction efforts without suffering any adverse effects.

Similarly, Israel continuously expands its settlements and has made a recent major move to legalize its approximately one hundred "outposts," smaller settlements that had previously been illegal even under Israeli law. The attention of the world is guided toward Gaza while settlement-building gets a free pass. The passage of time is not neutral. For Israel it allows expansionist policies to move forward uninterrupted; for the Palestinians it diminishes ever further their prospects for realizing their primary goal of sovereign territorial statehood. It is part of the Palestinian tragedy that the international community and the media are so easily manipulated. Responsible action requires vigilance, and it is a positive step in this regard that the HRC authorized a fact-finding mission to assess the settlement phenomenon from the perspective of international law and human rights standards. This is a concrete step that represents an effort to refocus world attention where it belongs. Make no mistake. Every additional settler, every new settlement outpost, is one more nail in the coffin of the two-state consensus.

In considering the Palestinian situation, it is misleading to become preoccupied, as is the case with the Western media, with pinning the blame on one side or the other for a particular breakdown of the precarious armed truce. More relevant is an appreciation of the broader context. As Sara Roy, a Harvard specialist on Gaza, reminds us, "The current crisis is framed in terms devoid of any real context. The issue goes far beyond which side precipitated the terrible violence that has killed innocents on both sides. The issue—largely forgotten—is one of continued occupation and blockade, a grossly asymmetrical conflict that has deliberately disabled Gaza's economy and people."[2] This defining reality of the occupation applies to all of occupied Palestine, but the asymmetry of human loss is particularly evident in relation to Gaza and is partly conveyed by a comparison of the grisly statistics of death: more than 160 Palestinians—and five Israelis. According to figures compiled by the Israeli human rights NGO B'Tselem, between the ceasefire established in January 2009 and the outbreak of this recent cycle of violence, not a single Israeli was killed, while Israeli violence was responsible for 271 Gazan deaths.

Looking at the overall casualty ratios, the Israeli journalist Gideon Levy observes: "Sometimes numbers do reflect reality, and this reality can no longer be ignored. Since the first Qassam rocket fell on Israel in April 2001, 59 Israelis have been killed—and 4,717 Palestinians. The numbers don't lie, as they say in less lethal fields, and this proportion is horrifying."[3] It should help us realize that Israel had an alternative to this turn once more toward mass mechanized violence directed against an occupied people enduring a siege that is crippling their society materially and bringing their mental and physical health to a point of near collapse.

In my role as UN Special Rapporteur on the situation of human rights in the occupied Palestinian territories, I have tried to move in this proposed direction—that is, from rhetoric to action—in my most recent report to the General Assembly. I have recommended a boycott of those corporations that do business with unlawful Israeli settlements, naming several of the prominent corporations making profits in this unacceptable manner. We also voiced support for the ongoing international civil society campaigns of boycott originated by a coalition of Palestinian NGOs in a call that dates back to 2004. These are practical steps taken only after efforts by way of confidential communications with these corporations had failed to persuade them to live up to their legal and moral responsibilities to respect human rights. This encouragement of civil society also recognizes that other political actors have failed to live up to their responsibility as members of the organized international community. When Israel, a member state of the UN, fails to cooperate and is guilty of persistent, gross violations of international law, then something should be done in reaction. It is notable—and regrettable—that the most direct challenges to the unlawful blockade of Gaza have come not

2. Sara Roy, "Where's Our Humanity for Gaza?" *Boston Globe*, November 23, 2012, http://www.bostonglobe.com/opinion/2012/11/23/roy/sctFniw6Wn2n9nTdxZ91RJ/story.html.

3. Gideon Levy, "An Accounting," *Haaretz*, November 25, 2012, http://www.haaretz.com/opinion/an-accounting.premium-1.480275.

from the UN or from member states in the region and beyond, but from civil society in the form of the Free Gaza Movement and the Freedom Flotilla. It is equally notable that the most serious challenges to Israel's archipelago of expanding settlements have been mounted by the BDS campaign of solidarity with the Palestinian people and not by states or international institutions.

We should also remember Rachel Corrie in this connection, an American peace activist who was brazenly killed by an Israeli bulldozer almost ten years ago while trying to stop the demolition of a Palestinian home in Rafah. Rachel was an idealistic young woman who pierced the dehumanizing myths surrounding the plight of the Palestinian people. In a letter to her mother back in Olympia, Washington, just days before her death, Rachel wrote, "I have bad nightmares about tanks and bulldozers outside our house and you and me inside." It is such brave persons who bear witness to the daily ordeal being experienced by Palestinians, not just for days or months or even years, but for decades and generations. It should not have been necessary for Rachel Corrie to sacrifice her life in this manner if the world system had done its job of enforcing the rights of the long-oppressed Palestinian people. We who have witnessed and documented these realities of oppression must do our best to honor Rachel Corrie's legacy.

The time has come for practical measures that back up UN assessments of Israeli unlawfulness. This unlawfulness is sustaining a cruel and prolonged occupation of Palestine that has over time assumed the character of territorial expansionism coupled with an apartheid structure of control. As many as 600,000 Israeli settlers are fully protected by the Israeli rule of law, while Palestinian residents of the West Bank and East Jerusalem are held captive decade after decade without rights and without the protection of law. Such conditions are often worsened by prison detentions and lifelong confinement in refugee camps, either within Palestine or in neighboring countries. It is an intolerable status quo, and has been for a period spanning several generations of Palestinians. The international community recently, with much fanfare, avowed the "responsibility to protect" as a new international norm intended to guide the UN in responding to situations of humanitarian catastrophe. Only the maliciousness of geopolitics can explain why the people of Palestine, and especially the residents of Gaza, have not been given the protection that they so desperately need and deserve. It seems time to challenge this maliciousness in the name of peace and justice and the dignity of a people whose inalienable right of self-determination has been too long denied. A starting point might be the deployment of UN peacekeepers to monitor adherence to the ceasefire. The Palestinians are the most glaring example in this postcolonial era of a people who have not managed to gain their independence and national sovereignty despite almost sixty-five years of struggle, strife, and humiliation.

Prolonged occupation is a special condition that deserves a special recognition it has not yet received. The occupation of the West Bank, East Jerusalem, and Gaza since 1967 exacts a terrible cost from the captive population. The framework provided by international humanitarian law, while helpful in situations of short-term occupation, falls far short of its claims to offer the protection needed when an occupation extends beyond ten years. One aspect of occupation is to silence those who represent the people of such a society. The UN General Assembly is being given an opportunity to take belated account of this situation on this very day by recognizing and acknowledging Palestinian statehood, something 132 governments have already done by establishing diplomatic relations with Palestine. The very least that a people living for more than forty-five years under occupation deserve is this right of access to the institutions of the world to present their grievances on a global stage, to have a voice and, if not a full-fledged seat at the tables of decision, at least a stool. Let us hope that the UN General Assembly will give us all something positive to celebrate on this International Day of Solidarity.

I think the most important lesson that can be learned by all sides is that political violence is not the answer. It brings neither security nor liberation. Such learning is particularly important for the militarily superior side that often wrongly associates its future security with a willingness to make use of its military dominance. What recent history has shown, and not only in relation to Israel–Palestine, is that political outcomes are at sharp odds with military outcomes. The United States essentially won every battle in Vietnam, yet lost the war. An Afghan saying makes the same point: "You have the watches, we have the time."

What follows from this is obvious: If political violence begets more political violence, then it is time for the stronger side to turn to diplomacy, compromise, respect for law and rights. Until Israel appreciates that its security can only be achieved by turning to peaceful means, there will be insecurity for both Israelis and Palestinians. The dance of death will go on. It was only when the British made this switch that the conflict in Northern Ireland changed from being "irreconcilable" to becoming "negotiable," and a substantial peace followed.

This is a time when the test of solidarity with the struggle of the Palestinian people needs to be expressed by deeds, by walking the walk, no longer being content with talking the talk. It is time for civil society actors throughout the world to lend robust support to the BDS campaign.

It is time for governments to consider the sort of economic sanctions so effectively imposed on the South African apartheid regime. It is time for the UN to accord recognition of statehood to any people that has been occupied for more than ten years, starting with the people of Palestine. It is time for the members of the Quartet, which includes the UN, the EU, Russia, and the United States, to explain to the world how it imagines a Palestinian state to be possible in light of Israel's continued settlement expansion and the related determined attempt to give East Jerusalem a distinctly Jewish character. Without such an explanation it is bad faith, and a trap for the Palestinians, to urge a return to another diversionary round of negotiations, a roadmap to nowhere.

In other words, it is time for us finally, wherever and whoever we are, to act responsibly toward the Palestinian people. The great Jewish religious teacher Abraham Heschel expressed this sentiment with memorable words: "Few are guilty, all are responsible."

I want to give the last words to the extraordinary Palestinian poet Mahmoud Darwish, some lines from his long prophetic poem "Silence for Gaza," written in 2007 but more relevant today than when written. These lines refer to the plight of Gaza, but they apply as well to all Palestinians, whether living under the yoke of occupation, in refugee camps, or consigned to an involuntary diaspora throughout the world:

> Enemies might triumph over Gaza (the storming sea might triumph
> Over an island . . . they might chop down all its trees)
> They might break its bones.
> They might implant tanks on the insides of its children and women.
> They might throw it into the sea, sand, or blood
> But it will not repeat the lies and say "Yes" to invaders.
> It will continue to explode
> It is neither death, nor suicide.
> It is Gaza's way of declaring that it deserves to live.
> It will continue to explode.
> It is neither death, nor suicide.
> It is Gaza's way of declaring that it deserves to live.[4]

4. Mahmoud Darwish, *Hayrat al-'A'id [The Returnee's Perplexity]*, trans. Sinan Antoon (Beirut: Riyad al-Rayyis, 2007), quoted in Henry Norr, "Mahmoud Darwish: 'Silence for Gaza,'" *Mondoweiss*, November 24, 2012, http://mondoweiss.net/2012/11/mahmoud-darwish-silence-for-gaza.html.

Israel's Politics of Deflection
September 30, 2013[5]

During my period as the UN Special Rapporteur for Human Rights in Palestine on behalf of the Human Rights Council, I have been struck by the persistent efforts of Israel and its strong civil society adjuncts to divert attention from the substance of Palestinian grievances and the consideration of the respective rights of Israel and Palestine under international law. I have also observed that many, but by no means all, of those who represent the Palestinians seem strangely reluctant to focus on substance or to take full advantage of opportunities to use UN mechanisms to challenge Israel on the terrain of international law and morality.

This Palestinian reluctance is more baffling than are the Israeli diversionary tactics. It seems clear that international law supports Palestinian claims on the major issues in contention: borders, refugees, Jerusalem, settlements, resources (water, land), statehood, and human rights. Then why not insist on resolving the conflict by reference to international law with such modifications as seem mutually beneficial? Those representing the Palestinians in international venues are aware of these opportunities and are acting on the basis of considerations that in their view deserve priority. It is disturbing that this passivity on the Palestinian side persists year after year, decade after decade. There are partial exceptions: support for recourse to the International Court of Justice to contest the construction of the separation wall, encouragement of the establishment of the Goldstone fact-finding inquiry, and complaints about settlement expansion in the West Bank and Jerusalem. But even here, Palestinian officialdom will not push hard to have these symbolic victories implemented in ways that alter the behavioral realities on the ground—and maybe, even if they did do their best, nothing would change.

On the Israeli side, diversion and the muting of legal and legitimacy claims are fully understandable as a way to blunt challenges from adversary sources: seeking to have the normative weakness of the Israeli side offset by an insistence that if there is to be a solution, it must be based on the facts on the ground, whether these are lawful or not, and upon comparative diplomatic leverage and negotiating skill in a framework that is structurally biased in favor of Israel. The recently exhumed direct negotiations between the Palestinian Authority and the government of Israel exemplify this approach: proceeding despite the absence of preconditions

---

5. Originally published at http://richardfalk.wordpress.com/2013/09/30/israels-politics-of-deflection.

as to compliance with international law even during the negotiations, reliance on the United States as the convening intermediary, and President Obama's appointment of an AIPAC-anointed special envoy, Martin Indyk, the latter underscoring the absurd one-sidedness of the diplomatic framework. It would seem that the Palestinians are too weak and infirm to cry foul but merely play along, as if good-natured, obedient, and frightened schoolchildren, while the bullies rule the schoolyard.

Such a pattern is discouraging for many reasons: It weights the diplomatic process hopelessly in favor of the materially stronger side that has taken full advantage of the failure to resolve the conflict by grabbing more and more land and resources; it makes it virtually impossible to imagine a just and sustainable peace emerging out of such a process at this stage; it plays a cruel game in which the weaker side is almost certain to be made to seem unreasonable because it will not accept what the stronger side is prepared to offer, which is insultingly little; and it allows the stronger side to use the process and time interval of the negotiations as an opportunity to consolidate its unlawful claims, benefiting from the diversion of attention.

There are two interwoven concerns present: the pernicious impacts of the politics of deflection as an aspect of conflictual behavior in many settings, especially where there are gross disparities in hard power and material position; the specific politics of deflection as a set of strategies devised and deployed with great effectiveness by Israel in its effort to attain goals with respect to historic Palestine that far exceed what the UN and the international community had conferred. The section that follows deals with the politics of deflection in the Israel–Palestine context.

The Specific Dynamics of the Politics of Deflection

Anti-Semitism: Undoubtedly the most disturbing behavior by Israel and its supporters is to deflect attention from the substance of the conflict and the abuses of the occupation by dismissing criticism of Israel as anti-Semitism or defaming the critic as an anti-Semite. This is pernicious for two reasons: first, it exerts a huge influence because anti-Semitism has been so totally discredited, even criminalized, in the aftermath of World War II, which featured the exposure and repudiation of the Holocaust; second, because by extending the reach of anti-Semitism to address hostile commentary on Israel, Israel shifts attention away from the core evil of ethnic and racial hatred to encompass the quite reasonable, highly critical appraisal of Israeli behavior toward the Palestinian people by reference to overarching norms of law and morality.

Israel also misuses language to attack Jewish critics of Israel by irresponsibly characterizing them as "self-hating Jews." Such people might exist, but to infer their existence because of their criticisms of Israel or opposition to the Zionist project functions as a means to inhibit open discussion and debate and avoid substantive issues. It tends to be effective as a tactic because few people are prepared to take the time and trouble to investigate the fairness and accuracy of such allegations, so once the shadow is cast, many stay clear of the conflict or come to believe that criticism of Israel is of less interest than the pros and cons of the personal accusations. Strong Zionist credentials will not insulate a Jew from such allegations, as Richard Goldstone discovered when he was vilified by the top tier of Israeli leadership after chairing a fact-finding inquiry that confirmed allegations of Israeli war crimes in the course of Operation Cast Lead. Even his much-publicized subsequent "retraction" did little to rehabilitate the man's reputation in Israeli eyes, although his change of heart as to the main allegation of his own report (a change rejected by the other three members of the inquiry group) was successfully used by Israeli apologists to discredit and bury it, again illustrating a preference for deflection as opposed to substance.

Even such global moral authority figures as Archbishop Desmond Tutu and Jimmy Carter have been called anti-Semites because they dared to raise their voices about the wrongs that Israel has inflicted on the Palestinian people, specifically identifying the discriminatory legal structures of the occupation as an incipient form of apartheid.

In the unpleasant course of being myself a frequent target of such vilifying techniques, I have discovered that it is difficult to make reasoned responses that do not have the effect of accentuating my plight. To fail to respond leaves an impression among some bystanders that there must be something to the accusations or else a reasoned and well-evidenced response would be forthcoming. To answer such charges is to encourage continuing attention to the allegations and provide the accusing side with another occasion to repeat the charges by again cherry-picking the evidence. NGOs such as UN Watch and UN Monitor specialize in managing such hatchet jobs.

What is more disturbing than the attacks themselves is their resonance among those holding responsible positions in government and international institutions, as well as widely respected liberal organizations. In my case, the accusations reached the UN Secretary-General, the U.S. ambassadors at the UN in New York and Geneva, the British prime minister, and the Canadian foreign minister, not one of whom bothered to check with me as to my response to the defamatory allegations or, apparently, took the trouble to check on whether there was a credible basis for such damaging personal attacks. Even the liberal, mainstream human rights powerhouse Human Rights Watch buckled under pressure from UN Watch, invoking a long-neglected technical rule to obtain my immediate removal from a committee, and then lacked the decency to explain that my removal was not a "dismissal" when UN Watch claimed "victory," then proceeded to tell the UN and other bodies that if Human Rights Watch had expelled me, surely I should be expelled elsewhere. I learned, somewhat bitterly, that Human Rights Watch has feet of clay when it comes to standing on principle. I have been the victim of repeated calumnies because of an effort to report honestly and accurately on Israeli violations of Palestinian rights that generate sharp critical attacks on Israel.

Auspices–Messenger: A favorite tactic of those practicing the politics of deflection is to contend that the auspices from which criticisms are issued are biased, and thus whatever substantive criticisms might issue from such an organization should be disregarded. Israel and the United States frequently use this tactic to deflect criticism of Israel in the UN system, especially if it emanates from the Human Rights Council in Geneva or the General Assembly. The argument is reinforced by the similarly diversionary claim that Israeli violations are given a disproportionately large share of attention compared to worse abuses in other countries, especially those in sub-Saharan Africa. Also, there is the complementary complaint that some of the members of the Human Rights Council themselves have appalling human rights records that disqualify them from passing judgment, thereby exhibiting the hypocrisy of criticisms directed at Israel.

It is tiresome to respond to such lines of attack, but important to do so. First of all, in my experience, the UN has always made fact-based criticisms of Israeli policies and practices, appointed individuals with strong professional credentials and personal integrity, and painstakingly reviewed written material prior to publication to avoid inflammatory or inaccurate criticisms. Beyond this, Israel is almost always given an opportunity to review material critical of its behavior before it is released and almost never avails itself of this chance to object substantively. In my experience, the UN, including the Human Rights Council, bends over backward to be fair to Israel and to take account of its arguments even when Israel declines to make a case on its own behalf.

Further, the heightened attention given to Palestinian grievances is a justified result of the background of the conflict. It needs to be remembered that it was the UN which took over historic Palestine from the United Kingdom after World War II, decreeing a partition solution in General Assembly Resolution 181 without ever consulting the indigenous population, much less obtaining their consent. The UN approach in 1947 failed to solve the problem, consigning Palestinians to decades of misery due to the deprivation of their fundamental rights as of 1948, the year of the *Nakba*, a national experience of catastrophic dispossession. Through the years the UN has provided guidelines for behavior and a peaceful solution of the conflict, most notably Security Council Resolutions 242 and 338, which have not been implemented. The UN has for more than a decade participated in the Quartet tasked with implementing the "Roadmap" designed to achieve peace but has not followed it, allowing Israel to encroach more and more on the remnant of Palestinian rights via settlement expansions, wall construction, residence manipulations, apartheid administrative structures, land confiscations, and house demolitions. The UN has been consistently frustrated in relation to Palestine in a manner that is unique in UN experience, making the issue a litmus test of this body's credibility to promote global justice and overcome the suffering of a dispossessed and occupied people.

Usually, the attack on the sponsorship of a critical initiative is reinforced by scathing screeds directed at anyone prominently associated with the undertaking. The attacks on the legendary Edward Said, the one Palestinian voice in the United States who could not be ignored, were rather vicious, often characterizing this humanist among public intellectuals as the "Professor of Terror." The most dogmatic defenders of Israel never tired of trying to make this label stick by showing a misleadingly presented picture of Said harmlessly throwing a stone at an abandoned guard house during a visit to southern Lebanon not long before his death, as if this was a heinous act of violence against a vulnerable Israeli soldier. This effort to find something, however dubious, that could be used to discredit an influential critic disregards the ethics of fairness and decency. My own most mean-spirited detractors have endlessly relied upon an accidentally posted cartoon with an anti-Semitic angle, although any fair reading of my past and present scholarship, together with the blog post in which it appeared, in which Israel is not even mentioned, would conclude that their sole purpose of highlighting the cartoon was to defame, and by so doing, deflect. UN Watch also harps on my supposed membership in the ranks of 9/11 conspiracy theorists, an allegation that I have constantly explained to be contrary to my frequently articulated views on the 9/11 attacks. It makes no difference what the target says or what the facts are once the defamatory attack has been launched.

In like manner, Israel has successfully manipulated the use of the label "terrorist" in relation to Hamas to avoid dealing with its presence as the elected governing authority in Gaza or with its offers of long-term coexistence, provided the blockade of Gaza is ended and Israeli forces withdraw to 1967 borders. The Hamas demands are really nothing more than a call for the implementation of international law and UN Security Council resolutions, and thus highly reasonable from the perspective of fairness to both sides, but Israel is not interested in such fairness and hence avoids responding to the substance of the proposals by insisting that it is unwilling to respond to a terrorist organization. Such a stubborn position is maintained by Israel and supported by the United States and EU despite Hamas's successful participation in an electoral process, its virtual abandonment of violent resistance, and its declared readiness for diplomatic accommodations with Israel and the United States.

If the messenger delivering the unwelcome message lacks prominence or the campaign of vilification does not altogether succeed, then at governmental levels, Israel—and the United States as well—will do its best to show contempt for criticism for the whole process by boycotting proceedings at which the material is presented. This has been my experience at recent meetings of the Human Rights Council and the Third Committee of the General Assembly, where I present reports on a semiannual basis: Israel and the United States make it a point to be absent. There is an allocation of the work of deflection: At the governmental end, substance is often evaded by pretending not to notice while pro-Israeli NGOs pound away, shamelessly repeating over and over the same quarter-truths, which often are not even related to their main contention of biased reporting.

Diplomatic Deflection: The entire Oslo peace process, with its periodically revived negotiations, has served as an essential instrument of deflection for the past twenty years. It diverts the media from any consideration of Israel's expansionist practices during the period in which the parties are futilely negotiating and succeeds in making critics and criticism of Israel's occupation policies seem to be obstructing the overarching goal of ending the conflict and bringing peace to the two peoples.

Geopolitical Deflection: Although not solely motivated by the goals of deflection, Israel's bellicose focus on Iran's nuclear program has made Iran seem so dangerous for the region and the world that Palestinian grievances appear trivial by comparison. It has also led outside political actors to believe that it would be provocative to antagonize Israeli leadership in relation to Palestine at a time when there are such strong worries that Israel might attack Iran or push the United States in such a direction. To a lesser extent, preoccupation with the effects of the Arab Spring upheavals, especially in Syria and Egypt, have had the incidental benefit for Israel of still further diminishing regional and global pressures relating to Palestinian grievances and rights. This distraction, a kind of spontaneous deflection, has given Israel more time to consolidate its annexationist plans in the West Bank and Jerusalem, which makes the still-lingering image of peace through a two-state solution a convenient mirage—no more, no less.

Overall, the politics of deflection is a repertoire of techniques used to shift the gaze away from the merits of a dispute. Israel has relied on these techniques, with devastating effects for the Palestinians. The purpose of my analysis is to encourage Palestinians in all settings to do their best to keep the focus on substance and respective rights. Perhaps it is time for all of us to learn from the brave Palestinian hunger strikers whose nonviolent defiance of Israeli detention abuse operated with laser-like intensity to call attention to prison and administrative injustice. Unfortunately, the media of the world was silent, including the self-righteous liberal pundits who for years urged the Palestinians to confront Israel nonviolently, then sat back and watched the response from Tel Aviv with satisfaction. Waiting for Godot is not a matter of patience, but of ignorance.

Israel's Politics of Fragmentation
October 10, 2013[6]

Background
If the politics of deflection exhibits the *outward* reach of Israel's grand strategy of territorial expansionism and regional hegemony, the *politics of fragmentation* serves Israel's *inward* moves designed to weaken Palestinian resistance and induce despair and de facto surrender. In fundamental respects, deflection is an unwitting enabler of fragmentation, but it is also its twin or complement.

The British were particularly adept in facilitating their colonial project all over the world by a variety of divide-and-rule tactics. These haunted anticolonial movements almost everywhere, frequently producing lethal forms of postcolonial partition, as in India, Cyprus, Ireland, Malaysia and Singapore, and of course Palestine, and deadly ethnic strife elsewhere, as in Nigeria, Kenya, Myanmar, and Rwanda. Each of these national partitions and postcolonial traumas has produced severe tension and long-lasting hostility and struggle, although each takes a distinctive form due to variations from country to country of power, vision, geography, resources, history, geopolitics, and leadership.

An additional British colonial practice and legacy was embodied in a series of vicious settler-colonial movements that succeeded in effectively

---

6. Originally published at http://richardfalk.wordpress.com/2013/10/10/
   israels-politics-of-fragmentation/.

eliminating or marginalizing resistance by indigenous populations, as in Australia, Canada, the United States, and somewhat less so in New Zealand, and eventually failing politically in South Africa and Namibia, but only after decades of barbarous racism.

In Palestine the key move was the Balfour Declaration, which was a colonialist gesture of formal approval given to the Zionist project in 1917, tendered at the end of Ottoman rule over Palestine. This was surely gross interference with the dynamics of Palestinian self-determination: at the time the estimated Arab population of Palestine was 747,685 (92.1 percent of the total), while the Jewish population was an estimated 58,728 (7.9 percent). It was also a decisive stimulus for the Zionist undertaking to achieve supremacy over the land, embraced by the British mandate to administer Palestine in accordance with a framework agreement with the League of Nations. The agreement repeated the language of the Balfour Declaration in its preamble: "Whereas recognition has thereby been given to the historical connection of the Jewish people with Palestine and to the grounds for reconstituting their national home *in that country*." To describe this encouragement of Zionism as merely "interference" is a terribly misleading understatement of the British role in creating a situation of enduring tension in Palestine, which was supposedly being administered on the basis of the well-being of the existing indigenous population, what was called "a sacred trust of civilization" in Article 22 of the Covenant of the League of Nations, established for the "well-being and development" of peoples "not yet able to stand by themselves under the strenuous conditions of the modern world."[7] The politics of fragmentation manifested here as a bundle of practices and an overall approach that assumed the form of interethnic and interreligious strife during the almost three decades the mandate arrangements were in effect.

At the same time, the British mandate was not the whole story by any means. The fanatical and effective exploitation of the opportunity to establish a Jewish homeland of unspecified dimensions manifested the dedication, skill, and great ambition of the Zionist movement; the lack of comparable sustained and competent resistance by the indigenous population abetted the transformation of historic Palestine; these developments were then strongly reinforced by the horrors of the Holocaust and the early complicity of the liberal democracies with Nazism, which led the West to lend its support to the settler-colonial reality that Zionism had become well before the 1948 War. The result was the tragic combination of statehood and UN membership for Israel and, for most Palestinians,

---

7. League of Nations, "Covenant of the League of Nations," December 1924, full text available at http://avalon.law.yale.edu/20th_century/leagcov.asp.

the *Nakba,* involving massive dispossession creating forced refugees and exile and leading after 1967 to occupation, discrimination, and oppression of those Palestinians who remained either in Israel or in the 22 percent of original Palestine.

It should be recalled that the UN solution of 1947, embodied in General Assembly Resolution 18, after the British gave up their mandatory role, was no more in keeping with the ethos of self-determination than the Balfour Declaration, decreeing partition and allocating 55 percent of Palestine to the Jewish population and 45 percent to the Palestinians without the slightest effort to assess the wishes of the population resident in Palestine at the time or to allocate the land in proportion to the demographic realities at the time. The UN solution was a new rendition of Western paternalism, opposed at the time by the Muslim and Middle Eastern members of the UN. Such a solution was not as overbearing as the mandate system, which was devised to vest quasi-colonial rule in the victorious European powers after World War I, yet it was still an Orientalist initiative aimed at the control and exploitation of the destiny of an ethnic, political, and economic entity long governed by the Ottoman Empire.

The Palestinians (and their Arab neighbors) are often told in patronizing tones by latter-day Zionists and their apologists that the Palestinians had their chance to become a state but squandered their opportunity, forfeiting their right to a state of their own by rejecting the UN partition plan. In effect, the Israeli contention is that Palestinians effectively relinquished their statehood claim by refusing to accept what the UN decreed, while Israel, by nominally accepting the UN proposals, validated its sovereign status, which was further confirmed by its early admission to full membership in the UN. Ever since, Israel has taken advantage of the fluidity of the legal situation by pretending to accept the UN approach of seeking a compromise by way of mutual agreement with the Palestinians while doing everything in its power to prevent such an outcome by projecting its force throughout the entirety of Palestine, by establishing and expanding settlements, by the ethnic cleansing of Jerusalem, and by advancing an array of maximalist security claims that have diminished Palestinian prospects. That is, Israel has publicly endorsed conflict-resolving diplomacy but operationally has been constantly moving the goal posts by unlawfully creating facts on the ground, then successfully insisting on their acceptance as valid points of departure. In effect, and with American help, Israel seems to have given the Palestinians a hard choice, one tacitly endorsed by the United States and Europe: accept the Bantustan destiny we offer or remain forever refugees and victims of annexation, exile, discrimination, statelessness.

Israel has used its media leverage and geopolitical clout to create an asymmetric understanding of identity politics as between Jews and

Palestinians. Jews are defined as a "people without borders" who can gain Israeli nationality no matter where they live on the planet, while Palestinians are excluded from Israeli nationality regardless of how deep their indigenous roots in Palestine itself. This distinction between the two peoples exhibits the tangible significance of Israel as a "Jewish state" and why such a designation is morally and legally unacceptable in the twenty-first century even as it is so zealously claimed by recent Israeli leaders, none more than Prime Minister Benjamin Netanyahu.

Modalities of Fragmentation

The logic of fragmentation is to weaken, if not destroy, a political opposition configuration by destroying its unity of purpose and strategy and fomenting, to the extent possible, conflicts between different tendencies within the adversarial movement. It is an evolving strategy that is interactive and that by its nature becomes an important theme of conflict. The Palestinians publicly and constantly stress the essential role of unity, along with reconciliation to moderate the relevance of internal differences. In contrast, the Israelis fan the flames of disunity, stigmatizing elements of the Palestinian reality that are relevantly submissive and pushing the agenda and framework devised by Tel Aviv, refusing priorities set by Palestinian leaders. Over the course of the conflict from 1948 to the present, there have been ebbs and flows in the course of Palestinian unity: maximum unity was achieved during the time when Yasser Arafat was the resistance leader; maximum fragmentation has been evident since Hamas was successful in the 2006 elections and managed to seize governmental control from Fatah in Gaza a year later. Another way that Israel has promoted Palestinian disunity is to favor the so-called moderates operating under the governance of the Palestinian Authority while inflicting various punishments on Palestinians who adhere to Hamas.

Zionism, the Jewish State, and the Palestinian Minority

Perhaps the most fundamental form of fragmentation is between Jews and Palestinians living within the state of Israel. This type of fragmentation has two principal dimensions: pervasive discrimination against the 20 percent Palestinian minority (about 1.5 million people) affecting legal, social, political, cultural, and economic rights and creating a Palestinian subjectivity of marginality, subordination, and vulnerability. Although Palestinians in Israel are citizens, they are excluded from many benefits and opportunities because they do not possess Jewish *nationality*. Israel may be the only state in the world that privileges nationality over citizenship in a series of contexts, including family reunification and access to residence. It is also worth observing that if demographic projections prove to be reliable, Palestinians could be a majority in Israel as early as 2035 and would almost certainly outnumber Jews in the country by 2048. Not only does this pose the familiar choice for Israel between remaining an electoral democracy and retaining its self-proclaimed Jewish character, but it also shows how deeply inappropriate it is at this stage of history to insist that the Palestinians and the international community accept Israel as a Jewish state.

This Palestinian entitlement is validated by international human rights law prohibiting all forms of discrimination, especially structural forms embedded in law that discriminate on the basis of race and religion. The government of Israel, reinforced by its Supreme Court, endorses the view that only Jews can possess Israeli nationality, which is the basis of a range of crucial rights under Israeli law. What is more, Jews have Israeli nationality wherever they are located, even if they lack any link to Israel, while Palestinians (and other religious and ethnic minorities) are denied Israeli nationality (although given Israeli citizenship) *even if indigenous to historic Palestine and to the territory under the sovereign control of the state of Israel.*

A secondary form of fragmentation is between this minority in Israel and the rest of the Palestinian corpus. The dominant international subjectivity relating to the conflict has so far erased this minority from its imaginary of peace for the two peoples, or from any sense that Palestinian human rights in Israel should be internationally implemented in whatever arrangements are eventually negotiated or emerge via struggle. As matters now stand, the Palestinian minority in Israel is unrepresented at the diplomatic level and lacks any vehicle to express its grievances.

Occupied Palestine and the Palestinian Diaspora

Among the most debilitating forms of fragmentation is the effort by Israel and its supporters to deny Palestinian refugees (and Palestinians living in the diaspora) their right of return as confirmed by General Assembly Resolution 184. Between 4.5 and 5.5 million Palestinians are refugees or living in the diaspora, as well as about 1.4 million residents in the West Bank and 1.6 million in Gaza.

The diplomatic discourse has long been shaped by reference to the two-state mantra. This includes the reductive belief that the essence of a peaceful future for the two peoples depends on working out the intricacies of "land for peace." In other words, the dispute is falsely categorized as being almost exclusively about *territory* and *borders* (along with the future of Jerusalem), not about *people*. There is a tacit understanding, which seems to include the officials of the Palestinian Authority, to the effect that Palestinians' refugee rights will be "handled" via compensation and the right of return—not to the place of original dispossession, but to territory eventually placed under Palestinian sovereignty.

The same disparity that exists between the two sides is again encoded in the diplomacy of the "peace process," ever more so during the twenty years shaped by the Oslo framework. The Israel propaganda campaign was designed to make it appear to be a deal breaker for the Palestinians to insist on full rights of repatriation, as this would, it alleged, entail the end of the promise of a Jewish homeland in Palestine. Yet such a posture toward refugees and the Palestinian diaspora cruelly consigns several million Palestinians to a permanent limbo, in effect repudiating the idea that the Palestinians are a genuine "people" while absolutizing the Jews as a "people" of global scope. Such a dismissal of the claims of Palestinian refugees also flies in the face of the right of return specifically affirmed in relation to Palestine by the UN General Assembly in Resolution 194 and more generally supported by Article 13 of the Universal Declaration of Human Rights.

The Two Warring Realms of the Occupation of Palestine: The Palestine Authority versus Hamas

Israel and its supporters have been able to drive ideological wedges between the Palestinians enduring occupation since 1967. With its initial effort to discredit the PLO, which had achieved control over a unified and robust Palestinian national movement, Israel actually encouraged the initial emergence of Hamas as a radical and fragmenting alternative to the PLO when it was founded in the course of the First Intifada. It later strongly repudiated Hamas when it began to carry armed struggle to pre-1967 Israel, most notoriously engaging in suicide bombings that involved indiscriminate attacks on civilians, a tactic it has repudiated in recent years.

Even though Hamas entered the political life of occupied Palestine with U.S. encouragement, winning an internationally supervised election in 2006 and taking control of Gaza in 2007, Israel and the Western powers continue to categorize it as "a terrorist organization" and give it no international status. Israel also relies upon this "terrorist" designation to impose a blockade on Gaza, a form of collective punishment in direct and flagrant violation of Article 33 of the Fourth Geneva Convention. The Palestinian Authority, centered in Ramallah, has also (despite occasional rhetoric to the contrary) refused to treat Hamas as a legitimate governing authority, to allow it to operate as a legitimate political presence in the West Bank and Jerusalem, or to insist on its inclusion in international negotiations addressing the future of the Palestinian people. This refusal has persisted despite Hamas's more conciliatory tone since 2009, when its leader, Khaled Mashaal, announced a shift in the organization's goals:

Hamas agreed to accept Israel as a state beside Palestine as a state and discontinue armed struggle, provided Israel agreed to withdraw fully to 1967 borders and implement the right of return for refugees. Mashaal also gave further reassurances of moderation by indicating that Hamas's earlier goal of liberating the whole of historic Palestine, as proclaimed in its Charter, was a matter of history that no longer described its political program.

In effect, the territorial fragmentation of occupied Palestine is reinforced by ideological fragmentation, with Israel seeking to somewhat authenticate and privilege the Palestinian Authority's secular and accommodating leadership while repudiating Hamas's Islamic orientation. In this regard, Israel cynically reproduces the polarization of such countries as Turkey and Egypt as part of its overall occupation strategy. This includes a concerted effort to make it appear that material living conditions for Palestinians will be much better if the Palestinian leadership cooperates with the Israeli occupiers than if it continues to rely on a national movement of liberation and refuses to play the Oslo game.

Israel's propaganda on Hamas has emphasized the rocket attacks on Israel launched from within Gaza. There is much ambiguity and manipulation of the timeline relating to the rockets in interaction with various forms of violent Israeli intrusion. We do know that casualties during the period of Hamas control of Gaza have been exceedingly one-sided, with Israel doing most of the killing and Palestinians almost all of the dying. We also know that when ceasefires have been established between Israel and Gaza, there is a good record of compliance on the Hamas side; it was Israel that provocatively broke the truce and then launched major military operations on a defenseless and completely vulnerable population in 2008–9 and 2012.

Cantonization and the Separation Wall:
Fragmenting the West Bank
A further Israeli tactic of fragmentation is to make it difficult for Palestinians to sustain a normal and coherent life. The several hundred checkpoints throughout the West Bank seriously disrupt Palestinians' mobility and make it impossible for them to avoid long delays accentuated by a variety of humiliations. It is better for them to remain contained within their villages, a restrictive life reinforced by periodic closures and curfews that are extremely disruptive. Vulnerability is accentuated by nighttime arrests, especially of young male Palestinians, 60 percent of whom are detained in prisons before they reach the age of twenty-five, and by the sense that the IDF and settlers, often working jointly, enjoy impunity for their violence.

The Oslo framework not only delegated to the Palestinian Authority the role of maintaining "security" in Palestinian towns and cities, but bisected the West Bank into Areas A, B, and C, with Israel retaining a residual security right throughout occupied Palestine. Area C, where most of the settlements are located, comprises more than 60 percent of the West Bank and is under the exclusive control of Israel.

This administrative fragmentation at the core of the Oslo framework has been a key element in perpetuating Palestinian misery. It is rigid and discriminatory, allowing Israeli settlers the benefits of Israel's rule of law while subjecting Palestinians to military administration with extremely limited rights and denying them even the right to enjoy the benefit of rights. Israel also insists that since it views the West Bank as disputed rather than "occupied" territory, it is not legally obligated to respect international humanitarian law, including the Geneva Conventions. This fragmentation between Israeli settlers and Palestinian residents is so severe that it has been increasingly understood in international circles as a form of apartheid, which the Rome Statute governing the International Criminal Court denominates as one type of "crime against humanity."

The separation wall is an obvious means of separating Palestinians from one another and from their land. A supermajority of 14–1 in the International Court of Justice declared it a violation of international law in 2004, but to no avail; Israel has defied this near-unanimous reading of international law by the highest judicial body in the UN with no adverse consequences. In some West Bank communities Palestinians are surrounded by the wall; in others, Palestinian farmers can only gain access to and from their land at appointed times when wall gates are opened.

Fragmentation and Self-Determination

The pervasiveness of fragmentation is one reason why there is so little belief that the recently revived peace process is anything more than one more turn of the wheel, allowing Israel to proceed with its policies designed to take as much of what remains of Palestine as it wants so as to realize its own conception of Jewish self-determination. Just as Israel refuses to restrict the Jewish right of return, so it also refuses to delimit its boundaries. When it negotiates internationally it insists on even more prerogatives under the banner of security and counterterrorism. Israel approaches such negotiations as a zero-sum dynamic of gain for itself and loss for Palestine, a process hidden from view by the politics of deflection and undermining through the politics of fragmentation the Palestinian capacity for coherent resistance.

The Emergent Palestinian Imaginary
January 10, 2014[8]

Remarks at the Second Annual Conference of Research Centers in the Arab World, "The Palestinian Cause and the Future of the Palestinian National Movement," Doha, Qatar, December 7–9, 2013.

"There is no tomorrow in yesterday, so let us advance."

—Mahmoud Darwish, "Mahmoud Darwish Bids
Edward Said Farewell," translated by Mona Anis

It is a welcome development that such a major conference as this one should have as its theme "the future of the Palestinian movement," so well articulated in the opening address by Azmi Bishara.

It is often overlooked that, as early as 1988 and possibly earlier, the unified Palestinian leadership has decisively opted for what I would call a "sacrificial" peace. By sacrificial I mean an acceptance of peace and normalization with Israel that is premised upon relinquishing significant Palestinian rights under international law. The contours of this image of a resolved conflict consist of two principal elements: a Palestinian sovereign state within the 1967 "green line" borders and a just resolution of the refugee problem. This conception of a durable peace is essentially an application of Security Council Resolutions 242 and 338 and is the foundation of the initiative formally endorsed by the Palestine National Council in 1988.

It is sacrificial in both dimensions of what was declared in advance to be acceptable. It involves a territorial delimitation of less than half of what the UN partition plan offered in 1947, which was reasonably rejected by the Palestinian leadership at the time, as well as by the neighboring Arab governments, on the grounds that it was imposed in defiance of the will of the Palestinian people and offered the Jewish residents of Palestine 55 percent of the territory, even though its land ownership was only 6 percent of the total and its population share was estimated to be 31 to 33 percent of the total. In effect, Palestinian acceptance of the 1967 borders overlooked Israel's unlawful acquisition of territory by forcible means in the 1948 War. It also seemed to signal readiness to negotiate a solution for the dispossessed Palestinians that fell short of the right of return affirmed by the General Assembly in

---

8. Originally published at http://richardfalk.wordpress.com/2014/01/10/
   the-emergent-palestinian-imaginary.

Resolution 194. From an international law or global-justice perspective, it can be argued that the rights of the Palestinian people were severely violated by the Balfour Declaration in 1917. It would seem that fully implementing the Palestinian right of self-determination would involve questioning this colonialist origin of the state of Israel. For political and prudential reasons, and in view of Israel's acceptance as a member of the United Nations, these legal and moral arguments have not been officially insisted upon in Palestinian diplomacy. Also ignored are the rights of the Palestinian minority living within pre-1967 Israel, who have neither received equal treatment nor had their human dignity respected, especially to the extent that Israel not only grants Jews throughout the world an unlimited *right of return* but also insists on being a "Jewish state"—what the Jewish leader Henry Siegman has labeled an "ethnocracy"—and is no longer entitled to claim to be a democratic state.

The Arab peace initiative of 2002 reaffirmed this regional acceptance of such a solution, and the Palestinian Authority in recent years has exhibited a willingness to compromise still further in relation to the Israeli settlement blocs and even the prospect of having the capital of Palestine in East Jerusalem. Israel, on its side, has never clearly signaled a similar readiness to establish peace on a sustainable basis that included an acknowledgement of Palestinian *rights,* despite strong indications that such a solution would produce security for the state of Israel, which was always invoked as Tel Aviv's primary demand. In effect, over the years, by a series of interlinked policies, especially the settlement movement, the separation wall, and the annexation and enlargement of the city of Jerusalem, Israel has been unwilling to reach peace on the basis of the 1988 Palestinian offer and has enlarged the concept of security to include its various strategic and national goals. These extravagant security demands have continuously escalated and are reinforced by occupation policies in violation of the Fourth Geneva Convention, including apartheid structures of administration, illegal interferences with mobility via checkpoints and closures, ethnic cleansing in East Jerusalem, house demolitions, and various devices to subvert Palestinians' residence rights.

It is notable and revealing that neither Israel nor the United States has ever even acknowledged this unilateral expression of willingness on the part of Palestine to accept peace on terms that fall far short of the legal and moral entitlements embedded in international law. What is more, there have been no direct or indirect Israeli moves that could qualify as reciprocal gestures. Instead, Israel has persisted with its relentless establishment of "facts on the ground" in violation of international humanitarian law and has even persuaded the United States, most formally in the 2004 exchange of letters between Ariel Sharon and George W. Bush, to accept the core of these facts as establishing a new baseline for devising a formula to fulfill the promise of "land for peace."

Overall, it is best to view this background as constituted by Israel's continuous inflation of security expectations, to be realized by the steady diminution of Palestinian rights. In effect, the *Nakba* associated with the dispossession and dispersal of Palestinians in 1948 should be regarded as a *process*, not just a catastrophic event. Such a national trauma as has been inflicted on the Palestinian people is unprecedented during this historical era of decolonization and self-determination.

Three Palestinian Disillusionments

For more than sixty-five years, as Palestinian hopes have languished, there have been many efforts to constitute, sustain, and build a national movement with the capacity to achieve liberation and realize fundamental Palestinian rights. In the present period there is a clear effort to find a viable post-Oslo strategy and vision that will help restore Palestinian collective identity, which has been shattered ever since the 1993 Oslo Accords, reinscribed as the Roadmap of the Quartet in 2003. The consensus among Palestinians that the Oslo approach is dead is rejected by governmental actors, above all the United States, which pushed successfully for the resumption of direct negotiations between the Government of Israel and the Palestinian Authority. In contrast, undertaking a reformulation of the Palestinian national movement proceeds from the experience of three disillusionments:

(1) International Law and the Authority of the United Nations

Especially in the early years after the end of the 1948 War, Palestinians put hope in the authority of international law and the support that their struggle seemed to gain at the United Nations, especially in the General Assembly. This support remains important in identifying the contours of a just and sustainable outcome, which needs to reflect a balance of *rights* rather than a bargaining mechanism that depends on a balance of *power*, including "facts on the ground." The disillusionment arises because having international law on the side of Palestinian grievances relating to the occupation, borders, Jerusalem, refugees, water, settlements, and more has yielded no results on the level of *practice*. On the contrary, despite the backing of international law and organized international society, Palestine's position has continuously deteriorated, especially with respect to the underlying goal of exercising the inalienable right of self-determination.

(2) Armed Struggle

The Palestinian national movement, despite its current fragmentation, has for the past seven years or so become generally disillusioned with reliance upon armed struggle as the basis for attaining primary goals of an emancipatory character. This abandonment has not involved a principled shift to a politics of nonviolence and continues to claim the prerogative of relying on force for defensive purposes, as when Israel launches an attack on Gaza or settlers violently attack Palestinians in the West Bank. As Nelson Mandela made so clear in the South African struggle against apartheid, the commitment to nonviolent forms of resistance to an oppressive order allows the oppressed to use whatever instruments they find useful, including violence, although limited by an ethos of respect for civilian innocence. Most of the anticolonial struggles legitimated as "wars of national liberation" relied on violence, but achieved their victories by the effective reliance on soft-power means of social mobilization and unconditional commitment to sustained opposition by popular forces. Recent historical transformations of an emancipatory kind have happened as a result of "people power" rather than through superiority in "hard power." This historical interpretation of recent trends in relation to conflict has profound tactical and strategic implications for the Palestinian struggle.

(3) Traditional Diplomacy

The learning experience for those supporters of the Palestinian struggle of the last twenty years is that intergovernmental diplomacy is not a pathway to a just peace, but rather a sinkhole for Palestinian rights. The Oslo–Quartet process has facilitated Israel's expansionist designs as it continues confiscating land, building and expanding settlements, and changing the demographics of the occupation, especially in East Jerusalem. Periodic breakdowns of this diplomatic charade help the Israelis realize their goals at the expense of Palestinian prospects. The long period of gridlock has lowered Palestinians' expectations, as articulated by their formal representatives in Ramallah. From the outset the process has been one-sided and flawed, fragmenting the Palestinian remnant of historic Palestine into areas A, B, and C, relying on the United States as the intermediary despite its undisguised alignment behind Israel, and remaining deeply responsive to inflated Israel security claims while ignoring Palestinian grievances and claims based on international law.

Those who insist on special "security" arrangements usually fear losing what they possess, while those who call for "rights" are normally seeking what is their entitlement from a position of deprivation and dispossession.

From a Palestinian perspective, the framework and process have been biased in Israel's favor, the substantive promises have been unfulfilled, and despite such disappointments, it is the Palestinians who get the lion's share of the blame when the diplomatic negotiations break down.

This disillusionment means that the Palestinian outlook should be by now clearly post-Oslo, given the failure of direct negotiations to produce positive results. This contrasts with the intergovernmental consensus of the United States, Israel, and the Palestinian Authority which insists that such diplomacy is the *only* road to peace, despite its record of failure. This spirit of "Oslo is dead, long live Oslo" is clearly defeatist and manifests the deficiencies of Palestinian representation via Ramallah.

Israel's Strategic Posture and Regional Developments

In part, Palestinian disillusionment has been prompted by Israel's hard-power dominance, recently reinforced by regional developments. To the extent that such disillusionment is interpreted in a defeatist spirit, it ignores Palestinian opportunities to pursue a soft-power approach to realizing self-determination and other rights so long denied. In effect, to interpret the conflict from a hard-power perspective is to indulge in false political consciousness, given recent historical trends, and leads to unwarranted pessimism about Palestinian prospects. This is a time to take stock and to reformulate a vision and strategy to guide the Palestinian struggle. As the future is unknowable, such a call for strategic reset is not an occasion for optimism; it is rather a time for the renewal of struggle and for a deepening of solidarity on the part of those of us who seek justice for the Palestinian people. Yet we must be as realistic as possible about the elements in the national, regional, and global context that pose challenges to the movement.

Several adverse developments need to be noted. First and foremost, Israel has successfully maintained—perhaps extended—its hard-power dominance, including acquiring the latest weapons systems (e.g., Iron Dome) and becoming an arms supplier for many countries around the world ensuring a measure of political spillover. Second, Palestinian fragmentation and vulnerability have been accentuated by a series of policies: the split between Fatah and Hamas; the Oslo bisection of the West Bank; the various divisions between refugees and persons living under occupation; between West Bank and Gaza, between East Jerusalem and West Bank; between those dispossessed in 1948, 1967, and subsequently; between the Palestinian minority within the 1967 "green line" and those living either under occupation or in exile. Third, the perpetuation of unconditional support by the U.S. government, especially Congress, gives Israel little reason to feel bound by international law, UN authority, and international morality and has resulted in Israel refusing with impunity to abide by international criminal law.

In effect, Israel has been able to rely on its capacity to contain Palestinian resistance by employing a mix of hard-power capabilities backed up by a range of soft-power instruments of control. Such an approach has included reliance on state terror to crush Palestinian resistance and a sophisticated *hasbara* campaign of disinformation and propaganda to obscure the structures of violence and oppression that have been constructed to weaken, and if possible destroy, the Palestinian national movement.

This Israeli approach has been also extended to its relations with the Middle East in general, especially with respect to neighboring countries. Israel has used its hard-power dominance and diplomatic skills to encourage fragmentation and to impart a disabling sense of utter vulnerability to any leadership in the region that dares challenge or threaten Israel. Iran has been the principal target of this tendency to punish disproportionately and violently those that stand in the way of or exhibit hostility to the Israeli national project. Syria illustrates the sort of fragmentation that weakens a neighboring country in a hostile or conflictual relationship with Israel. That Israel welcomed the Egyptian coup that displaced the democratically elected government with an oppressive military leadership further discloses its conception of its security interests.

Israel has achieved a strong sense of security, with little incentive to make concessions relating to Palestinian goals, grievances, and rights. The inadequacy of such realism to comprehend the failures of hard-power superiority to sustain national security is the foundation of a hopeful future for the Palestinian people. Hope rests on the commitment to struggling for what is right, not the assurance of victory, which is to embrace an unwarranted optimism about the future.

The Palestinian Shift to Legitimacy War: Acknowledgement and Affirmation

I believe a crucial shift in Palestinians' understanding about how to progress toward their goals has been taking place during the last several years, and is being implemented in a variety of venues around the world. Indeed, the contributions at this conference reflect this shift in the direction of what I call a "legitimacy war" or "legitimacy struggle" being waged by the Palestinian people so as to secure their fundamental rights. The essence of this globally oriented struggle is to gain control over the discourse relating to international law, international morality, and human rights as it relates to the Israel–Palestine conflict. The discourse is embedded also in a revised tactical agenda that relies on two main elements: reliance on nonviolent initiatives of a militant character and the social mobilization of a global solidarity movement committed to achieving self-determination for the Palestinian people. Such tactics range widely, from hunger strikes in Israeli prisons to efforts to break the blockade on Gaza to pressures brought to bear from various constituencies on corporations and banks to break commercial connections with unlawful Israeli settlements.

In effect, the legitimacy struggle being waged seeks to rely on soft power to exert mounting pressure on the Israeli government, creating incentives for Israel to reassess its interests and policy alternatives, including acknowledging that past overreliance on hard-power superiority has brought about new threats to Israel's well-being and even to security, as understood in a wider sense as encompassing the ingredients of a peaceful and productive life.

Legitimacy struggles shift the emphasis from *governments* and *governing elites* to *people* and *civil society* as the principal agents of historical change and, at the same time, subordinate hard-power forms of resistance to soft-power tactics. There is no inherent commitment to nonviolence; it is rather a matter of seeking an effective strategy in a particular context. This follows the guidance of Nelson Mandela and others that liberation movements should select their tactics on the basis of their perceived *effectiveness*. Even if it would seem that violence has a part to play, as was certainly the case for the Israeli movement against the British mandate, there are still legal and ethical questions associated with selecting appropriate targets and avoiding operations directed at civilians, especially women and children. What appears to be the case now in relation to Palestine is a definite move toward the adoption of a legitimacy-struggle conception of how to interpret the Palestinian national movement.

It seems important to understand, especially for non-Palestinians, that it is the Palestinians who should retain control over the discourse on their struggle, vision, and strategy. It is up to the rest of us, those who side with the Palestinians in the struggle to uphold their rights, that we not encroach on this political space and appreciate that our role is secondary: to aid and abet, to accept a responsibility to act *in solidarity*. It is this kind of activist solidarity that will move a victorious trend in the legitimacy struggle into the behavioral domain wherein change takes place. This important distinction between *resistance* and *solidarity* is a key to a successful embodiment of this shift.

It should be remembered that ever since this encounter originated, the Palestinian people have been victimized by outsiders deciding what was in their best interest. If we go back to the Balfour Declaration, the British mandate, the UN commission that devised the partition plan, and the various U.S. formulations of how to resolve the conflict, the Palestinians have been the objects, not the subjects, of the "peace process." Beyond this, such paternalism, whether well-meaning or not, has contributed to rather than overcoming or even mitigating the Palestinian tragedy.

Intergovernmental solidarity is also important for turning success in legitimacy struggles into appropriate political outcomes. In this regard, it is regrettable that so few governments in the Middle East have exhibited solidarity in concrete and relevant forms in relation to this latest phase of the Palestinian national movement. It is not in the Palestinian interest to act as if the Oslo framework or the Roadmap are credible paths to a sustainable and just peace. The Palestinian people are entitled at this stage to more relevant forms of support in their struggle; the people of Gaza, especially, should not be left to languish in an unfolding humanitarian catastrophe while diplomats dither in luxurious venues.

Finally, it is worth noting the historical trends since the end of World War II. By and large, the militarily superior side has not prevailed. This is true of the major anticolonial wars. It is also true in the state–society struggles in Eastern Europe and the Soviet Union and most of all in South Africa, where a legitimacy-struggle strategy was largely responsible for the remarkable outcome that defied all expectations. U.S. military dominance in Vietnam over the course of a decade did not produce victory, but a humiliating political defeat. True, in the First Gulf War of 1991 the military superiority of coalition forces overwhelmed Saddam Hussein and produced a political surrender, but that was a conflict in which the defensive response was wrongly rooted in contesting vastly superior Western and regional forces on a desert battlefield, where popular forms of resistance were irrelevant. It is when the people become centrally engaged in a struggle that the political potency of soft-power instruments is exhibited. Even when this involvement is centrally present, it does not guarantee victory in the political struggle, as such cases as Tibet, Chechnya, Kashmir, and many others illustrate. What the turn toward legitimacy struggle does achieve is to significantly neutralize hard-power advantages in a political struggle involving such fundamental rights as that of self-determination. In this sense, it is most relevant to a reinterpretation of the vision and strategy of the Palestinian national movement.

This relevance is increasingly acknowledged by Israel itself, which has shifted its concerns from Palestinian armed resistance to what it calls the "delegitimation project" or "lawfare," terms to which it gives a negative spin as efforts to destroy Israel by relying on law and challenges to Israeli legitimacy such as the BDS campaign. In effect, Israel contends that it is being victimized by an *illegitimate* legitimacy struggle, an argument U.S. political leaders have seemed to accept.

There are likely to be many developments in coming years as to the viability and effectiveness of the Palestinian engagement in a legitimacy struggle against Israel. As of the end of 2013, it appears to be the one vision capable of restoring collective unity to the Palestinian national movement and, by doing so, bringing hope for a brighter Palestinian future.

7

Fragments of the Whole

The posts comprising this section address different aspects of the Palestine–Israel struggle that are important but do not fit with any of the previous themed clusters of commentary. I think the issue of language used in this political discourse, addressed in the opening selection, is a particularly neglected topic. There are several distinct modes of discourse, aside from the partisan encounters of adversary positions. There is the misleading pro-Israel Western media, which makes it extremely difficult for a conscientious citizen to assess the claims and counterclaims being made. For instance, rocket fire from Gaza is generally discussed in isolation from a timeline that includes Israeli provocations, without noting the comparative casualty and damage statistics, and with disproportionate attention to the trauma endured by civilians on the Israeli side of the border and complete inattention to the far greater trauma experienced by the Gazan civilian population.

Then there is the UN public discourse, which tends to be legalistic and technical in ways that obscure the realities of the situation. For instance, to speak of "occupation" as if it is a temporary reality when it has lasted since 1967 is to obscure its annexationist character, at least in part. To talk of the military administration of the West Bank without noting the discriminatory application of regulatory authority between the Israeli settlers and Palestinian residents is to occlude from view the apartheid nature of the governing regime. Language can either be disclosing or obscuring, and sometimes it is a mixture.

The second post takes note of some controversial issues, such as the annual observance of the *Nakba*, the catastrophic dispossession of the Palestinians that took place in 1947 and 1948. I have argued, along with many others, that the *Nakba* is best conceived as an ongoing process rather than a historical event. Further posts in this section discuss some ways the Palestinian struggle is perceived in the minds of others, with the last selections focusing on the shifting perceptions of the conflict itself.

The Politics of Language and the Israel–Palestine Discourse
November 25, 2010[1]

The politics of language raises delicate issues in the setting of assessing the Israel–Palestine conflict as the year 2010 draws to an end. A neutral and objective terminology associated with the abusive Israeli occupation of the West Bank, East Jerusalem, and Gaza seems consistent with the spirit of accommodation and eventual reconciliation, but it also clouds the mind and obscures the daily ordeal of the Palestinians, who are enduring multiple privations with no end in sight after more than forty-three years of occupation and some sixty-two years of dispossession. If it were possible to attach any hope to the possibility that a just outcome to intergovernmental negotiations could be forthcoming, then it might be best to avoid inflaming emotions by escalating the rhetoric of exposition. If, in contrast, the negotiations are far more likely to lead nowhere or entrap the Palestinian side, then it seems preferable to call attention to what seems to have taken place under the misleading rubric of temporary belligerent occupation, a presence that seeks and acquires no longevity.

In my opinion, there is an important issue of language that arises from the cumulative effects of multiple severe Israeli violations of international humanitarian law, human rights law, and criminal law. It becomes increasingly misleading to treat these violations as distinct behavioral instances disconnected from broader consequences that are either designed by intention, representing the motive for the violations, or the natural outcome of accumulating circumstances (so-called "facts on the ground"). These concerns about language are accentuated because Israel is the stronger party in all diplomatic settings and generally enjoys the unconditional support of the United States. Unlawful Israeli behavior that starts out as "facts" is gradually and deliberately over time transformed into "conditions" that are treated as essentially irreversible, which is true of several aspects of the occupation, including at a minimum the "settlement blocs"

---

1. Originally published as "Politics of Language: Israel/Palestine Discourse" at http://richardfalk.wordpress.com/2010/11/25/ politics-of-language-israelpalestine-discourse.

and the "separation wall." To perceive the effects and implications of these unlawful patterns and their attempted de facto legalization requires stronger expository language to understand better the assault of Palestinian rights and prospects for meaningful self-determination. It is against this background that I believe the time has come to "call a spade a spade" and use such terms as "annexation," "ethnic cleansing," "apartheid," "colonialist," "settler colonialism," and "criminality." Although admittedly emotive, and requiring a finding by a court of law to be legally conclusive, such robust language in my view more accurately describes the unsavory realities of the occupation at the present time than does the more neutral-seeming language beloved by diplomats and welcomed by defenders of the established status quo. The language litmus test in the relationship between Israel and Palestine is the infamous G-word, which I am not ready to apply as a moral, political, or legal term of art, but if the more ambiguous "genocidal" is invoked to identify the tendencies implicit in this kind of prolonged and invasive occupation, I would not disagree.

Observing the *Nakba*: 2012
May 17, 2012[2]

There are parallel hunger strikes currently taking place in Israeli prisons that have captured the imagination of Palestinians around the world, giving the word "solidarity" a new urgency. The crisis produced by these strikes makes this year's observance of Nakba Day a moral imperative for all those concerned with attaining justice and peace for the long-oppressed Palestinian people, whether living under occupation or in exile. The Palestinian mood on this May 14 is inflamed by abuse and frustration but also inspired by, and justly proud of, exemplary expressions of courage, discipline, and nonviolent resistance on the part of imprisoned Palestinians, who are mounting the greatest internal challenge that Israel has faced since the Second Intifada. Even as the strikes seem on the verge of ending due to a series of Israeli concessions, their impact and significance remains a shining light in an otherwise dark sky.

It all started when a lone prisoner, Khader Adnan, initiated a hunger strike to protest his abusive arrest and administrative detention on December 17—which happens to be the exact anniversary of the day that

---

2. Originally published as "The Nakba: 2012" at http://richardfalk.wordpress.com/2012/05/17/the-nakba-2012.

the Tunisian vendor Mohamed Bouazizi, set himself on fire. His death led directly to a wave of uprisings across the region that became known throughout the world as the Arab Spring. Adnan gave up his strike after sixty-six days, when Israel relented somewhat on his terms of detention. What Adnan did prompted other Palestinians to take a similar stand. Hana Shalabi, a few weeks, later experienced a horrible arrest and was returned to prison without charges or trial. She too seemed ready to die rather than endure further humiliation; she too was also eventually released but, punitively, "deported" to Gaza. Other hunger strikes followed and now two types of hunger strike are under way, each influenced by the other.

The longer of the strikes involves six protesting Palestinians who are in critical condition, with their lives at risk for at least the past week. Bilal Diab and Thaer Halahleh have now refused food for an incredible seventy-six days, a sacrificial form of nonviolent resistance that can only be properly appreciated as a scream of anguish and despair on behalf of those who have been suffering so unjustly and mutely for far too long. It is a sign of Western indifference that even these screams seem to have fallen on deaf ears. By now as many as two thousand prisoners are reported to be refusing all food until a set of grievances associated with deplorable prison conditions are satisfactorily resolved. The remaining several thousand nonstriking Palestinian prisoners in Israeli jails have already pledged to join the strike if there are any deaths among the strikers. This heightened prisoner consciousness has already been effective in mobilizing the wider community of Palestinians living under occupation and beyond.

This heroic activism gives an edge to the 2012 *Nakba* Day observance and contrasts with the apparent futility of traditional diplomacy. The Quartet, tasked with providing a roadmap to a peaceful resolution of the Israel–Palestine conflict, seems completely at a loss and has long been irrelevant to the quest for a sustainable peace, let alone the realization of Palestinian rights. The much-publicized efforts a year ago to put forward a statehood bid at the United Nations seem stalled indefinitely due to the crafty backroom maneuvers of the United States. Even the widely supported and reasonable recommendations of the Goldstone Report have been permanently consigned to limbo. And the situation is even worse for the Palestinians than this summary depiction suggests. While nothing happens on the diplomatic level, other clocks are ticking: forty thousand additional settlers have begun living in the West Bank since the temporary freeze on settlement expansion ended in September 2010, bringing the overall West Bank settler population to about 365,000—well over half a million if East Jerusalem settlers are added on.

Is it any wonder then that Palestinians increasingly view the *Nakba* not as an event frozen in time back in 1947, when as many as seven hundred thousand fled from their homeland, but as describing an historical process? It is this understanding of the *Nakba* as a living reality with deep historical roots that gives the hunger strikes such value. Nothing may be happening when it comes to the peace process, but at least, with heightened irony, it is possible to say that a lot is happening in Israeli jails. The resolve of these hunger strikers is so great as to convey to anyone paying attention that the Palestinians will not be disappeared from history. Merely saying this has renewed a sense of engagement on the part of Palestinians the world over and their growing number of friends and comrades, a feeling that this Palestinian courage and sacrifice and fearlessness will bring eventual success and that, in contrast, the governmental search for deals and bargains built to reflect power relations, not claims of rights, seems so irrelevant that its disappearance would hardly be noticed.

By and large, the Western media, especially in the United States, has taken virtually no notice of these hunger strikes, as if there was no news angle until the possibility of martyrdom for the strikers began at last to stir fears in Israeli hearts and minds of a Palestinian backlash and an international public relations setback. Then and only then was there speculation that maybe Israel could and should make some concessions, promising to improve prison conditions and limit reliance on administrative detention to situations where a credible security threat existed. Beyond Israel's frantic quest to find a last-minute pragmatic escape from this volatile situation, posed by both hunger strikers on the brink of death and a massive show of solidarity by the larger prison population, is this sense that the real message of the *Nakba* is to underscore the imperative of self-reliance, nonviolence, and ongoing struggle. The Palestinian future will be shaped by the people of Palestine or by nothing. And it is up to us in the world, Palestinian or not, to join in their struggle to achieve justice from below, sufficiently shaking the foundations of oppressive structures of occupation and the exclusions of exile to create tremors of doubt in the Israeli colonial mindset. As doubts grow, new possibilities suddenly emerge.

For this reason, the *Nakba* should become important for all persons of good will, Palestinian or not, in Israel or outside, as an occasion for displays of solidarity. This might mean a global sympathy hunger strike on May 17, an added commitment to the BDS campaign, or signing up to join the next voyage of the Freedom Flotilla. Certainly the *Nakba* is a time for remembrance of the historic tragedy of expulsion, but it is equally a time for reflection on what might be done to stop the bleeding and to acknowledge and celebrate those who are brave enough to say: "This far and no further."

What Is New in the Israel–Palestine Conflict
May 25, 2012[3]

Undoubtedly transfixed by the extraordinary developments throughout the Arab world since Mohamed Bouazizi's self-immolation on December 17, 2010, from Tahrir Square to the NATO intervention in Libya to bloody confrontations in Syria, Yemen, and Bahrain to the eerie quiet in Algeria to the relative and temporary calm in Morocco, a widespread few have noticed that the Israel–Palestine conflict has changed its character in fundamental respects during the last couple of years.

Some may have noticed the first of these transformative developments sooner, but now almost everybody knows—except for those in high places, especially in Washington and Tel Aviv, who seem to have a political need not to know. The stark fact is that both Israel and Palestine have no hope that international negotiations between governmental representatives have any chance of reaching an agreement that will end the conflict. Israelis, especially those backing the Netanyahu government, never desired or believed in the possibility of a diplomatic solution. The "peace process" that started in Oslo back in 1993 has steadily deteriorated Palestinian prospects while enhancing those of Israel; it has been worse than gridlock for the Palestinians and a smokescreen for Israelis to carry out their expansionist plans while pretending to be pursuing a political compromise. The sequel to Oslo, the Quartet's Roadmap, has been a pathetic enterprise, a charade at which Israel has scoffed while representatives of the Palestinian Authority seemed to believe that it was worth playing along, working within the confines of the occupation to establish governmental institutions that could claim statehood by unilateral self-assertion. The Palestinian Authority did seize this option last September when President Mahmoud Abbas made his historic plea to the UN General Assembly, but was stymied by the U.S. exerting its geopolitical muscle on Israel's behalf. At this point even the Palestinian Authority seems to have abandoned its effort to challenge a supposed status quo that should no longer be called "occupation"; it is more realistically comprehended as a toxic mixture of annexation and apartheid.

Apparently to please Washington, and to a lesser extent the EU, neither Tel Aviv nor the Palestinian Authority has openly repudiated diplomacy; both continue to give lip service to a readiness to talk yet again, although the Palestinian Authority has at least the dignity to insist that no further

---

3. Originally published as "What Is New in the Israel/Palestine Conflict" at http://richardfalk.wordpress.com/2012/05/25/what-is-new-in-the-israelpalestine-conflict.

negotiations can occur until Israel agrees to halt settlement expansion in the West Bank. To demand that Israel discontinue unlawful activities that affect what is being discussed should be a no-brainer, but it is treated by the world media as though the Palestinians were seeking a huge concession from the Israelis—and in a way it is, if we acknowledge that the Netanyahu government is essentially a regime under the control of the settlers.

The second of these under-observed developments in the conflict is a definite shift toward nonviolence by the Palestinians. There are several different manifestations of this turn to nonviolence and a global solidarity movement. The following instances are illustrative and should have been treated as major news, but because Israel refuses to be challenged, even nonviolently, the world media have been silent and offered very little overall analysis. Among the forms of nonviolent opposition are: repeated village demonstrations in the West Bank against the continued building of the separation wall; strong support and some impressive results for a growing worldwide BDS initiative modeled on the global anti-apartheid campaign that was so effective in inducing the collapse of the racist regime in South Africa; and the Freedom Flotillas, in which humanitarian activists from many countries challenged the five-year Israeli blockade of Gaza, which in May 2010 led to an ugly confrontation when the Turkish ship *Mavi Marmara* was assaulted in international waters by Israeli naval commandos, killing eight Turks and one Turkish American.[4] Most impressive of these nonviolent challenges by Palestinians civil society has been a dramatic series of hunger strikes in Israeli jails that has reignited the Palestinian moral and political imagination. These hunger strikes mobilized widespread support among Palestinians and an enthusiasm that contrasts with the bitter disillusionment directed at the failed peace talks.

The Western mind does not grasp hunger strikes in their full significance. Such voluntary actions are an extreme form of nonviolence. The striker sacrificially forgoes violence against the other, seeking to awaken the conscience of those accused, bear witness to abusive behavior, and appeal for solidarity from the wider affected community. Such extended hunger strikes send a moral message to both the oppressed and the oppressor, although the latter is likely to turn away in cynical disregard, as the Israelis have.

The third major development is the shift in the regional balance in favor of the Palestinians. Arab public opinion is strongly supportive of the Palestinian struggle and deeply alienated by the kind of Egyptian

---

4. After more than four years in a coma, a tenth Turkish victim of the Mavi Marmara attack died. See http://richardedmondson.net/2014/05/24/ death-of-tenth-mavi-marmara-victim.

collaboration with Israel typified by the Mubarak regime. Turkey, once a strategic ally of Israel, is now its antagonist as well as an avowed backer of Palestinian claims. In light of these changes, I would have supposed that Israeli realists would be devoting their utmost energies to finding ways to reach a sustainable peace agreement that is sensitive to Palestinians' rights under international law. Israeli realists, however, may have sought refuge underground to avoid humiliation or worse in an Israel so firmly under the thumb of Netanyahu extremists, who refuse to read this ominous writing on the regional wall. This refusal is applauded by a U.S. Congress ready to sacrifice American security at the altar of Israeli militarism. Such an unnatural geopolitical relationship is currently unchallengeable in the United States, which is itself sad and dangerous.

These three sets of developments should lead us to reimagine the Israel–Palestine struggle and to channel our hopes and resources accordingly. The Israeli government and its strategic think tanks are clearly more threatened by this turn toward militant nonviolence than by armed resistance. Israel has the weaponry and the skill on the battlefield, but fortunately its formidable propaganda machine has been unable to stem the rising tide of public opinion hostile to Israel and supportive of the Palestinian struggle.

For What? A Pledge to the Palestinian People
July 20, 2012[5]

Being disinclined to look in mirrors, not only to avoid evidences of aging but also because of an autobiographical deficit, I have recently started to question the vectors of my motivation—not to raise doubts but to seek some understanding of "for what?" I am especially wondering about the reasons behind my solidarity with the struggles of distant strangers—why such solidarity is not more widely shared with like-minded friends and why the inevitable priorities as to what is emphasized and what is ignored have the shape they do. Most pointedly, why am I giving the Palestinians so much more attention and psychic energy than the Kurds, Tibetans, Kashmiris, or a host of other worthy causes? And how do I explain to myself a preoccupation with the unlawful, immoral, and imprudent

---

5. Originally published as "For What?" at http://richardfalk.wordpress. com/2012/07/20/for-what.

foreign policy of the U.S. government, the sovereign state of my residence, upon whose governmental resources I depend upon for security and a range of rights?

There are rational answers that tell part of the story, but only a part, and probably the least illuminating part. I was drawn to the Palestinian struggle as a result of friendship with prominent Palestinian exiles while still a student. I formed a well-evidenced belief that the U.S. government and the organized Jewish community were responsible for the massive and enduring confiscation of Palestinian land and rights. With this awareness came some added sense of responsibility. "Just don't sit and stare: do something." And with this modest kind of engagement came pressures to do more by way of public identification and witnessing, which led to a somewhat deeper awareness, greater familiarity, and a dumpster full of harsh criticism. After many years of speaking and writing, the opportunity and challenge to do more in relation to the Palestine–Israel conflict came my way unexpectedly, in the form of an unsolicited invitation in 2008 to become the next Special Rapporteur for Occupied Palestine on behalf of the UN Human Rights Council.

I never sought such a position, and I realized that it would expose me to an escalating onslaught of vicious personal attacks and threats, an expectation that has been amply fulfilled. It is always uncomfortable to be the target of toxic language; it is even more scary and disturbing to expose my closest partner in life and love to such calumny. Besides the hotly contested terrain that exists whenever Israeli policies are subject to *objective* scrutiny and criticism, a position within the UN hierarchy is both burdensome and often frustrating. True, being a Special Rapporteur is essentially a voluntary post, without salary or civil service affiliations, although "compensated" to some degree by institutional independence within the UN (which I have discovered in my four years, can be a considerable blessing). There is little doubt in my mind that if I had been a paid employee, I would long ago have been handed a pink slip. As it is, I have merely endured a barrage of slanderous insults, including from the Secretary-General and Susan Rice, the U.S. ambassador to the UN in New York.

Lest I protest and complain too much, I hasten to add that there are also deep and moving satisfactions. I find particularly satisfying the extent to which my two reports each year on the Israeli occupation of Palestine provide a truthful witness to the unspeakable ordeal of this prolonged and harsh occupation. Actually, it is less and less an occupation and more and more an apartheid-style form of annexation, aggravated by continuous land grabs, various instruments of ethnic cleansing, and a range of gratuitous cruelties. Bearing witness, giving the Palestinians an authentic voice with which to formulate their grievances, and having the means to issue press releases calling attention to particular incidents of abuse makes me feel as though my time is well spent, even if the bodies keep piling up on the Palestinian side of the border. Part of the challenge in such a role is to realize the discouraging constraints on what can be achieved. Governments mainly don't listen, and even when they do, their actions and policies are rarely informed by moral imperatives—so nothing changes, however much the evidence is present.

The devastating impact of the Gaza blockade has been known and lamented for years by political leaders, yet the costs of doing anything about it have seemed so great that even those who complain most loudly in the chambers of the UN are silent or worse when it comes to doing something. Someone at my level must shout to be heard amid the clamor that prevails in the diplomatic discotheques of New York and Geneva and, even when heard, must learn to expect nothing to be done or else despair, even madness, will soon follow.

Beyond this rational balance sheet of gains and losses is a deeper, less accessible convergence of feelings and impulses which cannot be explained, only acknowledged. I am not sure why direct exposure to victimization has such a powerful animating effect on my behavior, but it does. I do feel that a sense of responsibility emerges with such knowledge, especially knowledge derived from direct contact with the suffering of victims caught in some historical trap not of their own making. Whether visiting North Vietnam as a peace activist during the Vietnam War or seeking to understand the Iranian Revolution by talking with its leaders as the extraordinary process was unfolding in Tehran, I felt a meta-professional obligation to share this privileged exposure by talking and writing about it, however inadequately—particularly, as seemed generally to be the case, since the mainstream media distorted and manipulated their presentations of such historic happenings through a Western optic of (mis)perception.

Somewhere in this agonizingly slow formation of my character, there was being constructed a self that took the shape of "engaged scholar" and "citizen pilgrim." In retrospect I think I was reacting somewhat dialectically to my academic colleagues, who mostly felt it inappropriate to speak out on controversial issues, although they viewed it as entirely professional to consult with the government and quite all right to avoid the public sphere altogether by packaging themselves as experts who should not be expected to take public stands on partisan issues that divided the polity. I felt, increasingly with age, the opposite. I came to believe that it was an organic part of my integrity as teacher–scholar to create a seamless interface between the classroom and sites of political struggle—in truth not entirely seamless, a faculty member must always treat the classroom as a sacred space. It should be maintained as a sanctuary for the uninhibited exchange of views, however diverse and antagonistic, in an atmosphere of disciplined civility. I have always felt that the primary duty of a teacher is to establish sufficient trust with students—that is, permission and encouragement of openness of expression, with a clear understanding that performance will be objectively assessed and not affected by agreement or disagreement with what the teacher happens to believe. This is a delicate balance, yet far more conducive to learning than a sterile, journeyman insistence that what people beyond the campus are dying for can be usefully addressed with sanitary dispassion.

In the end, this vital domain of conscious pedagogy and unconscious morality is spiritually validated by an unmediated and uninterrogated sense that this or that is "the right thing to do." It certainly helps to remain as free as possible of vested interests and career ambitions that tend to crush the implicit pledge of truthfulness upon which authentic witnessing depends. Beyond witnessing there exists an iron wall of moral obligation: caring about the future, doing what I can to make the world a better place for human habitation and coevolution with nature. I have understood the latter as a species obligation that has been made historically urgent ever since an atomic bomb was exploded over the Japanese city of Hiroshima and is now also deeply connected with protecting the planet from the multiple hazards of global warming hopelessly embedded in our carbon-dependent lifestyles, as promiscuously promoted in disastrous directions by the greed of super rich fossil-fuel billionaires and their far-too-powerful corporate allies.

I have not rested these life commitments on the teachings of any particular religious tradition or institution, although I have long found that the great world religions, Eastern and Western, despite their menacing contradictions and multiple readings, provide me with the most profound sources of wisdom and guidance. It is the basis of my ecumenical longing for human solidarity, along with my feelings of awe produced by contact with cosmic and natural wonders, which deeply inform my sense of the spiritual ground of the human adventure. These sentiments are reinforced in my case by a commitment to an emergent form of cosmopolitan citizenship that owes allegiance to the ethics and praxis of human sustainability, the individual and collective dignity of all human beings, and a respectful kinship with and love of our nonhuman co-inhabitants of the planet. Such perspectives, I believe, respond to our historically precarious situation as a species. Here in the United States this concern is accentuated, for this is a country with a surfeit of moral and political pretensions. It exhibits *hubris* to an alarming degree and in extravagant ways, and is endangering itself along with the rest of the world by refusing to heed the warning it sees in the geopolitical mirror of reflection.

2014: International Year of Solidarity with the Palestinian People
December 31, 2013[6]

In a little-noted initiative, the UN General Assembly voted on November 26, 2013, to proclaim 2014 the International Year of Solidarity with the Palestinian People. The UN Committee on the Exercise of the Inalienable Rights of the Palestinian People was requested to organize relevant activities in cooperation with governments, the UN system, intergovernmental organizations, and significantly, civil society. The vote was 110 to 7, with 56 abstentions, which is more or less reflective of the sentiments now present in international society. Among the seven opponents of the initiative, in addition to Israel, were—unsurprisingly—its three staunchest supporters, each once a British colony: the United States, Canada, and Australia, with the addition of such international heavyweight states as Micronesia, Palau, and the Marshall Islands. European and other assorted states around the world were among the fifty-six abstentions, with virtually the entire non-West solidly behind the idea of highlighting solidarity with the Palestinian people in their struggle for peace with justice based on rights under international law.

Three initial observations: those governments that are willing to stand unabashedly with Israel in opposition to the tide of world public opinion are increasingly isolated, and under mounting public pressure from their own civil societies to seek a balanced approach that is rights-based rather than power-dominated; the West, in general, is dominated by the abstaining governments that seek the lowest possible profile, to be seen as neither for or against, even in those countries where civil society should now be capable of mobilizing more support for the Palestinian struggle; and the non-West that is, as has long been the case, rhetorically in solidarity with the Palestinian people has yet to match its words with deeds seems ready to be pushed.

Also revealing are the arguments of UN Watch and others who denounce this latest UN initiative because it unfairly singles out Israel and

---

6. Originally published at http://richardfalk.wordpresscom/2013/12/31/ 2014-international-year-of-solidarity-with-thepalestinian-people.

ignores countries that have worse human rights records. Always forgotten here are two elements of the Israel–Palestine conflict that justify singling it out among others. First, Israel owes its existence, to a significant degree, to the organized international community, starting with the League of Nations, continuing throughout the British mandate, and culminating with the partition plan of 1947. The latter overrode the decolonizing principle of self-determination with a solution devised and imposed from without; such antecedents to the current Israel–Palestine situation also expose the colonialist foundations of the current struggle as well as calling attention to the settler-colonial elements associated with Israel's continuous expansion of territorial, resource, and ethnocratic claims far beyond what the Western-dominated international community proposed and then approved of after the end of World War II.

To be sure, there have been delicate and complex issues all along that make the problematic role of the international community somewhat more understandable. Up to 1945 there was a generalized acceptance of European colonial administration, although in the Middle East colonial legitimacy was balanced for the first time against an obligation on the part of the colonial powers to prepare a dependent people to stand eventually on its own, an ambivalent acknowledgement of the ethos of self-determination, if not yet in the form of a legal norm. This affirmation of self-determination as an alternative to colonial rule was the special project of U.S. president Woodrow Wilson, who insisted that such an approach was a moral imperative, especially in dealing with the regional aftermath of the Ottoman Empire, which had long ruled over many diverse ethnicities.

Beyond this, the Jewish experience during the reign of fascist regimes throughout Europe, culminating in the Holocaust, created a strong empathetic urge in Europe to endorse the Zionist project for a Jewish homeland in Palestine. This empathy, although genuine in many quarters, also exhibited a deferred sense of guilt on the part of the Western liberal democracies that had done so little to challenge the genocidal policies of Hitler and the Nazis, refusing to act at all until their national interests were directly engaged by German aggression. European support was also forthcoming because the Zionists' proposed solution for the "Jewish problem," long present in Europe, could be enacted *elsewhere*, that is, at the expense of non-Europeans. This "elsewhere" was far from empty and was coveted by others for various reasons. Palestine was a land long lived in mainly by Muslim Arabs, but also by some Jews and Christians, and associated centrally with the sacred traditions of all three monotheistic religions. Normally, in the modern world, the demographics of residence trump biblical or other claims based on national tradition, ethnic identity, and ancient historical presence. Yet, despite these factors, there were ethical reasons in the aftermath of such extreme victimization of the Jewish people to lend support to a reasonable version of the Zionist project as it had evolved in the years since the Balfour Declaration, even if from a variety of other perspectives it was deeply unfair to others, disruptive of peaceful relations, and, throughout its implementation, produced an unfolding catastrophe for most non-Jewish Palestinians.

Taking account of this historical and moral complexity, what seems evident is the UN's failure to carry out its responsibility effectively and responsively to the human circumstances prevailing in Palestine. The UN's overall record is quite disappointing if considered from the perspective of accommodating these contradictory clusters of consideration in a manner reflective of international law and global justice. The military prowess of Zionist forces in Israel inflicted a major defeat on the Palestinian people and neighboring Arab governments, and in the process expanded the territorial dominion of Israel from the 55 percent decreed by the UN in its partition plan to 78 percent where the green line established an armistice arrangement in 1948. Such an outcome was gradually endorsed by a geopolitical consensus, exhibited through the admission of Israel to the UN without any solution to the underlying conflict, leaving the Palestinians out in the cold and allowing Israel to constitute itself within borders much larger than what the UN had a mere year earlier decreed as fair.

This situation was further aggravated by the 1967 war in which Israel occupied all of the remaining territory of historic Palestine, purporting even to annex East Jerusalem while greatly enlarging the area of municipal Jerusalem by incorporating land belonging to the West Bank. Since 1967 this Palestinian territorial remnant has been further decreased by the massive settlement phenomenon, including its network of settler-only roads, carried out in flagrant violation of international humanitarian law; by the separation wall constructed and maintained in defiance of the International Court of Justice; and by a variety of moves to change the demography of East Jerusalem. In other words, Israeli forces on the ground in what had been Palestine have undermined the vision set forth in the partition plan, which was itself a controversial UN solution to the conflict that was rejected by Palestinians and neighboring countries.

Despite much propaganda to the contrary, the Palestinian leadership, has over most of the period of its struggle, shown an unusual readiness to abandon maximal goals and put forward forthcoming proposals that recognize the unfavorable realities of the situation. Palestinian willingness, expressed formally since 1988, to accept Israel as a legitimate state within the green line borders of 1967 remains, more than twenty-five years after its articulation, an unacknowledged and unreciprocated major initiative for peace. That such a proposal has been ignored and continuously undermined by Israel with de facto Western acquiescence and in the face of feeble rhetorical objections displays UN's inability to fulfill its responsibilities to the people of Palestine.

As might be expected, Palestinians have long become disillusioned about the benefits of having UN authority and international law on their side. Over the years, the backing of international authority has failed to improve their life circumstances and political position. The UN is helpless—and designed to be helpless—whenever a UN position is effectively resisted by a combination of military force and geopolitical alignment. Israel's military capabilities and U.S. geopolitical leverage have completely nullified the expressed will of the United Nations, but have not overcome the sense of frustration or excused the UN from its failure to act responsibly toward the Palestinian people.

In light of this background, the wonder is that the UN has done so little to repair the damage—not that it has done so much or more than it should in relation to Israel–Palestine. Arguably, yes, there are a variety of other situations in which the abuse of human rights has been worse than what is being attributed to Israel, but the rationale for focusing on Palestine is not only a question of the denial of rights: it is also an issue of fundamental justice, of the seemingly permanent subjugation of a people, partly due to arrangements devised and endorsed over a long period of time by the organized international community. Yet witnessing the dire emergency of the people of Gaza makes it perverse to contend that the human rights challenge facing this large and vulnerable Palestinian community is not among the worst in the entire world, and makes us wonder anew why the UN seems unwilling and unable to do more.

We can hope, at the dawn of 2014, that the UN will be vigorous in giving the International Year of Solidarity with the Palestinian People a political meaning that goes beyond words of empathy and support. There is an opportunity to do more. The UN resolution calls for working with civil society. Recent moves in the United States to join boycotts of Israeli academic institutions, and in Europe to hold corporations responsible under international law for dealing commercially with Israeli settlements, are major successes of civil society activism, led by a BDS campaign that has the important legitimating virtue of Palestinian leadership and backing. The UN can help build a momentum in the global solidarity movement that encourages the kinds of nonviolent, militant forms of coercive action that alone can give "solidarity" a good name.

Palestinians are starting to win their struggle for legitimacy and rights against unlawful Israeli policies. The turning point in world public opinion can probably be traced back to the way Israel waged the Lebanon War of 1982, especially its avowed reliance on disproportionate force directed at residential neighborhoods such as south Beirut, a tactic that became known as the Dahiya doctrine. The tipping point in shifting the Israeli collective identity—from one of victims and heroic underdogs to lawless perpetrators of oppressive warfare against a totally vulnerable people—came in Operation Cast Lead, Israel's sustained, three-week high-tech assault on the people of Gaza (December 27, 2008–January 18, 2009). After these developments the Palestinians were understood more widely to be a victimized people engaged in a just struggle to gain their rights under international law, who need and deserve an international movement of support to offset Israel's hard-power and geopolitical dominance.

Israeli leaders and think tanks try their hardest to discredit this Palestinian legitimacy struggle by falsely claiming that it is directed against the legitimacy of Israel *as a state* rather than against *the unlawful policies* of the Israeli state. This is a crucial difference, and the distinction seems deliberately obscured by Israeli propaganda that inflates what Palestinians are seeking so as to make their activism appear hyperbolic, with unreasonable and unacceptable demands. This makes it easier to dismiss than would critically addressing Palestinian grievances in their actual form. It is to be hoped that the work of the International Year of Solidarity clarifies this distinction between Israel as a state and Israeli policies. Within such a framework, the UN will deserve credit for contributing to victories throughout the world that advance the legitimacy agenda of the Palestinian people and, by so doing, move the debate somewhat closer to the realization of a just and sustainable peace for both peoples.

Nelson Mandela's Inspiration
December 9, 2013[7]

Fifteen years ago I had the extraordinary pleasure of meeting Nelson Mandela in Cape Town while he was serving as president of South Africa. It was an odd occasion. I was a member of the International Commission on the Future of the Oceans, which was holding a meeting in South Africa. It happened that one of the vice chairs of the commission was Kader Asmal, my cherished friend and a member of the first Mandela cabinet, who himself played a major role in writing the South African constitution. Kader had arranged for Mandela to welcome the commission to

---

7. Originally published at http://richardfalk.wordpress.com/2013/12/09/
   nelson-mandelas-inspiration.

his country and asked me if I would prepare some remarks on his behalf, which was for me an awesome assignment but one that I undertook with trepidation, not at all confident that I could find the words to be of some slight help to this great man. Compounding my personal challenge, the Brazilian vice-chair of our commission became ill, and our chair asked me to respond to Mandela on behalf of the commission in his stead. I had the thrill of hearing 90 percent of my text delivered by Mandela, which, years later, I remember much better than my eminently forgettable words of response to the president.

What moved me most, and has led me to make this rather narcissistic introduction, is the conversation after the event. Mandela thanked me for my efforts and proceeded then to talk with each of our forty commission members, making a specific reference to circumstances of relevance and concern in each of their particular countries. He went from person to person with such grace and composure as I had never encountered before on the part of a public figure of renown. It was above all Mandela's *spiritual* presence that created such a strong impression of moral radiance on the part of all of us fortunate enough to be in the room. I was reinforced in my guiding belief that political greatness presupposes a spiritual orientation toward the meaning of life. This is not necessarily expressed by way of a formal religious commitment, but always implies living with an unconditional dedication to values and faith that transcend the practical, the immediate, and the material.

The political imaginary that accompanies such a life also has an integrity that challenges the proprieties and associated boundaries of conventional liberal thought. It is easy for almost everyone now to celebrate Mandela for his long struggle against South African apartheid, which included twenty-seven years in jail. It is less common to recall that, as late as the 1980s, leaders in Britain and the United States were condemning Mandela as a "terrorist" and "revolutionary" who deserved to be indefinitely jailed, if not worse. It is even less often remembered that Mandela rejected early offers to obtain his release from prison if he would "renounce violence" and call for an end to "armed struggle." Although Mandela is justly honored for his role in achieving a nonviolent transition to multiracial constitutionalism in South Africa, he was never willing to say that those who were oppressed must renounce whatever means was available to them to gain their freedom. Indeed, as leader of the African National Congress, Mandela endorsed the creation of its military wing and at one stage supported armed resistance to obtain liberation and overcome the racist crimes the apartheid regime was committing on a massive and systematic basis.

The Palestinian people, in the midst of their seemingly endless ordeal, have particularly reason to esteem the exemplary life of Nelson Mandela and the solidarity he exhibited for their cause. Mandela's words reflected a deep intuition that what the Palestinians were seeking had a deep affinity with his own struggle: "We know too well that our freedom is incomplete without the freedom of the Palestinians."[8] In a comment with a strong resonance in the present debate about whether Israel is not responsible for repeating the crime of apartheid in its occupation of the West Bank, Mandela's words are strong: "Never in the darkest days of South Africa's apartheid have there been separated roads for blacks and whites."[9] In Israel's apartheid there exists a network of separated roads for Israeli settlers and the Palestinians, as well as a discriminatory dual legal administrative structure.

Mandela regarded Yasser Arafat as a "comrade in arms." He identified Arafat as "one of the outstanding freedom fighters of his generation," adding that "it is with great sadness that his and his people's dream of a Palestinian state has not been realized." By affirming Arafat, Castro, and even Qaddafi, Mandela made plain to the West (in reaction to criticism) that "our enemies are not your enemies."[10] Such a voice of peace, which never submitted to Western liberal notions of good behavior, was fully appreciated by Indian followers of Gandhi, who regarded Mandela as a natural political heir to their national hero because Mandela stood so firmly for dignity, independence, and the end of colonial domination in all its manifold forms.

Mandela's journey, like that of Gandhi, was not without its major disappointments. To gain the political end of apartheid, Mandela deferred challenges to social and economic apartheid. Part of his legacy to South Africa is to carry forward this mission to free the great majority of the country from the many disadvantages and burdens of their still-segregated, subordinated, and humiliating reality.

It is also notable that Marwan Barghouti, confined to an Israeli jail for five consecutive life sentences, looked to Mandela for inspiration, writing an open letter from his prison cell not long ago. He wrote, "From within my prison, I tell you that our freedom seems possible because you reached

8. Nelson Mandela, "Address by President Nelson Mandela at the International Day of Solidarity with the Palestinian People," African National Congress, December 4, 1997. http://anc.org.za/show.php?id=3384.

9. AFP, "Palestinians draw on Mandela Legacy for Inspiration," December 6, 2013, *Breitbart*, http://www.breitbart.com/Big-Peace/2013/12/06/Palestinians-draw-on-Mandela-legacy-for-inspiration.

10. A. Akbar Muhammad, "A Man of Character and Principle," *The Final Call*, December 12, 2013, http://www.finalcall.com/artman/publish/Perspectives_1/article_101039.shtm.

yours." Beyond this he hailed Mandela, whose torch of freedom burned so brightly as to cast universal light: "You carried a promise far beyond the limits of your country's borders, a promise that oppression and injustice will be vanquished, paving the way to freedom and peace. All sacrifices become bearable by the sole prospect that one day the Palestinian people will also be able to enjoy freedom."[11] Barghouti is Palestinians' strongest symbol of collective identity in resistance and struggle; a comparison to Mandela's lifelong journey is inevitable, including Barghouti's clear turn toward embracing militant forms of nonviolent resistance.

I believe that when Israel is ready for a sustainable and just peace, it will signal this to itself, to the Palestinians, and to the world by releasing Barghouti from prison and by treating Hamas as a political actor with genuine grievances and aspirations that needs to be included in any diplomacy of accommodation that deserves the label of "peace process." Until that most welcome moment arrives, the Palestinian march toward victory in its ongoing legitimacy struggle must continue with renewed vitality and dedication.

---

11. Ma'an News Agency, "Barghouti: Mandela Gave Palestinians Hope for Freedom," December 6, 2013, http://www.maannews.net/eng/ViewDetails.aspx?ID=654797.

A Concluding Note

There is a bewildering mixture of continuity and rupture in the Palestinian reality. The continuity is mainly exhibited in Israel's relentless effort to extend its hold over the West Bank and Jerusalem and to maintain its punitive regime of occupation, especially as it affects Gaza and its people. This continuity is disguised by proclaiming a commitment to peace, even a rhetorical willingness to envision coexisting with a Palestinian state. Such proclamations are less and less credible, making Israel's true expansionist intentions increasingly transparent to all those who will open their eyes. There is also an increasingly thinly disguised embrace of what might be called a *soft* Israeli one-state scenario, offering Palestinians the prospect of greatly improved economic and living conditions and a relaxed occupation administration with eased mobility, but an end to any illusions of negotiated withdrawal or realization of Palestinian rights, including self-determination. In effect, Israel is asking Palestinians to go gently into the long dark night of political surrender to what purports to be an inevitable outcome of the national struggle to control the whole of historic Palestine.

On the Palestinian side, the central continuity is a refusal to submit to such a dismal future and a determination to sustain resistance both to the occupation and throughout the Palestinian regional and global dispersal. Sadly, for many Palestinians living under oppressive occupation or in miserable refugee camps from birth to death, it has meant enduring Israeli state terror for generations, with no end in sight.

Despite these grim circumstances, Palestinians in all settings continue to hold their heads high. Many have powerfully narrated their experiences through song, art, music, poetry, novels, commentary, and scholarship. Few liberation movements can boast of such dedicated and universal voices as the Palestinians have possessed; Mahmoud Darwish and Edward Said are only two of the most luminous members of the vibrant Palestinian creative community whose legacy of inspiration keeps their memory alive. Among those now active many could be mentioned; by naming those who have exerted a direct influence upon my engagement with the Palestinian struggle, I do not mean to overlook many others who equally deserve such recognition. In this spirit I have been personally moved and inspired by the fiction and poetry of Susan Abulhawa, the filmmaking of Hany Abu-Assad, and the singing of Mohammed Assaf. I have also benefited from the extraordinary contributions of Raji Sourani (of the Palestine Center of Human Rights), Hassan Jabareen (of Adalah), and Raja Shehadeh (founder of Al-Haq and a gifted author).

When it comes to ruptures, they are mostly on the Palestinian side. It might be claimed that the Israeli internal drift to the right crossed a line so consequential as to be designated a rupture; my own view is that there is no clear evidence that this rightist political trend represents anything more than a shift in tone, a reduced willingness to genuflect before the altar of diplomatic accommodation. Even during the supposedly halcyon days after the signing of the Oslo Accords, Israel never ceased building settlements or acknowledged the deep injustices wrought by the *Nakba*, nor did it express willingness for Israeli Jews to live in genuine equality with the Palestinian people. In retrospect, what emerges from a look back at the unfolding of the Zionist project is its settler-colonialist ethos of dominating and dispossessing the indigenous population and extinguishing its cultural traditions. As Israeli expansion has proceeded under the aegis of the settler movement, there is more transparency relating to the full scope of its territorial and political ambitions, but no fundamental revision of the settler-colonial ethos.

On the Palestinian side, there have been ruptures in leadership and political consciousness. One such rupture was produced by the death of Yasser Arafat who, for all of his failings, embodied Palestinian unity and struggle as an iconic figure of resistance. Since Arafat's death in 2004, the Palestinian movement has been without an inspiring leader capable of gaining the confidence of the broad spectrum of Palestinian opinion. In one respect, even while Arafat was alive, the intifada of 1987 represented a sea change in the tactics of resistance, shifting the emphasis from the exiled PLO leadership (then in Tunis) to the Palestinian people living under the oppressive heel of occupation. The memory of the First Intifada remains the most charismatic moment in the whole long story of Palestinian resistance.

In addition, shifts in Palestinian political consciousness have been so fundamental as to constitute a rupture. In the early years after 1947, Palestinian hopes rested on the prospect of liberation *from without and above*, that is, through the belligerent actions of neighboring Arab governments fighting against the Israeli presence in Palestine. This hope was shattered by a series of lost wars, culminating in the 1973 Yom Kippur War, which led the Palestinian national movement to realize that Israel was too strong militarily to be defeated through the collective efforts of the Arab world. Palestinians would henceforth have to depend mainly on themselves. This realization led to a variety of actions designed to create effective armed resistance while under occupation, including recourse to the tactics of insurgent terrorism; hijacking and destroying planes; taking hostages; suicide bombings; and launching crude, indiscriminate rockets. Israel was skillful in managing Palestinian resistance and in its manipulation of antiterrorist public opinion, especially in the United States and Europe, to build international support and sympathy for its portrayal of the conflict. Beyond this, the Palestinians were hampered by the absence of any territorial base that would allow them to form an effective armed insurgency.

Over the course of the last decade, the Palestinian national movement has made a decisive shift in the direction of seeking legitimacy for its struggle, which is the unifying theme of the posts that make up this volume. The shift has had three main elements: (1) an emphasis on nonviolent modes of resistance, from prison hunger strikes to a global civil society campaign including actions such as the Freedom Flotilla to break the Gaza blockade and deliver humanitarian aid and the BDS initiative, designed to exert pressure on Israel of the sort that eventually broke the back of South Africa's apartheid regime; (2) reliance on civil society activism for leadership, organization, and the partial displacement of the PLO and governmental authority; and (3) the mobilization of a robust global solidarity movement that continues to grow and is dedicated to peace with justice for both peoples. These three elements are the new face of the Palestinian liberation movement and the basis for hope that the future will not resemble the past.

It remains to observe that current developments need to be interpreted in relation to these basic forces that remain in contention. There have been, in mid-2014, some positive steps on the Palestinian side. The collapse of the Kerry peace talks in April 2014 reminded close observers that Israel is defiantly disinterested in reaching a solution to the conflict, even if arranged on pro-Israeli terms mediated by the United States. Such an appreciation means that the two-state mantra should be abandoned, especially by statesmen and -women and by media gurus who deep down have long understood that Israel has no intention of allowing a viable Palestinian state to be established and has acted for many years to undermine the conditions that might at one time have allowed a partitioned Palestine to become a viable reality.

There have been, at long last, some signs of life in Ramallah. Palestine began, although hesitantly, to act in some ways like a state, having been formally acknowledged as such by the UN General Assembly on November 29, 2012. The Palestinian Authority adhered to fifteen international treaties and, in May 2014, formed a unity government that ended the split with Hamas and promised elections of a new leadership within six months. It is hard to tell whether the PLO–Hamas reconciliation will hold up under a variety of pressures from within and without. Israel has thunderously repudiated this development, insisting that it will never make peace with a Palestinian political leadership "backed by Hamas." Interestingly, the U.S. government, while indicating its disapproval, distanced itself from Israel at least temporarily by saying that it would continue to work with the new Palestinian Authority governing authority, supposedly consisting of nonpartisan technocrats, so long as Hamas was not exercising "undue influence," whatever that means. What it could mean—if all goes well—is some Palestinian progress toward reducing the leadership deficit, although Mahmoud Abbas, however benign his intentions, seems like a colorless manager, failing to project a sense of urgency and dedication.

The Middle East is fraught with uncertainties in this period, the resolution of which might be helpful or harmful to the unfolding Palestinian struggle. If the Iran diplomacy succeeds in removing the threat of war, it could be helpful in clearing the air and could allow some new phase of creative conflict resolution. The same could be true if the Syrian war comes to an end. The ebb and flow of political currents in the turbulent aftermath of the Arab Spring is certain to exert a variety of influences on Palestinian prospects. Important as well is the degree to which BDS and other global solidarity initiatives exert sufficient pressure on Israeli leadership and public opinion to induce a recalculation of Israel's options, including even questioning the viability of a Jewish state confronting a Palestinian population that will, sometime in the coming decades, constitute a majority.

It is impossible to divine the future on the basis of such complexity. The obstacles facing the Palestinian people seeking justice and rights under international law have never been as formidable. Yet the reorientation of the Palestinian struggle, together with the increasing expression of solidarity throughout the world, creates a new reality—the legitimacy of hope. This hope rests on the liberating potential of militant nonviolence when combined with mobilized movements of national resistance and global solidarity. It was the realization of such hopes in the two decades after World War II that unexpectedly led to the worldwide collapse of European colonialism. Israel, while a unique political reality and lacking in any overseas affiliation that can be compared to the relations between colony and metropole, has established a process of governance that in many ways resembles the colonial rule that preceded its existence. The Palestinians are engaged in a conflict that, in its essential features, appears to be the last major anticolonial struggle.

Acknowledgments

I started to write posts for a blog shortly after my eightieth birthday. It was a present from my daughter Zeynep and her digitally skilled husband Andre, to whom this book is gratefully dedicated.

I say "gratefully" with reluctance. Living in the blogosphere brings me its share of torments along with satisfactions. Because I have articulated views on controversial issues and have a certain public presence because of my role as Special Rapporteur on Palestine for the UN Human Rights Council, it has been a gold mine for those determined to do their best to destroy my reputation. It made it possible to quote my views out of context or spin their meaning in provocative directions.

What has been disturbing, but on reflection not so surprising, is the willingness of supposedly responsible public officials to heed such defamatory commentary. In this regard, my peace of mind as well as my reputation fell under attack from such luminaries as Ban Ki-moon, Susan Rice, Samantha Power, Ken Roth, and a host of others, not one of whom bothered to check out the allegations that I was a "bigot," an "anti-Semite," a "9/11 conspiracy theorist," and on and on. I would stake my life on the truthfulness of denying the substance of such attacks on my character and worldview. This avalanche of abuse all stemmed from the perception that I was sharply critical of Israel; rather than address my message in the form of debate and refutation, the most organizationally dedicated defenders of Israel, above all UN Watch (spearheaded by its notorious leader, Hillel Neuer), carried on an incessant campaign of defamation.

Such is the terrain that must be traversed by anyone willing to bear witness to the Palestinian ordeal and the Israeli state crimes that are mainly responsible for this tragic reality. I am not alone in such a journey. Anyone who has tried to shine the light of truth and bestow the warmth of compassion upon what the Palestinians experience is subject to such an onslaught; many have suffered in tangible ways far worse than my experience. I think, for instance, of Norman Finkelstein's denial of tenure and Joseph Massad's long struggle at Columbia. Many like me have endured hurtful insult, including such luminaries as Edward Said, Noam Chomsky, Alice Walker, and even Archbishop Desmond Tutu and President Jimmy Carter, each a person whose work and commitment have inspired me.

Yet the satisfactions of inhabiting the blogosphere these past years have far outweighed the torments. Blogging has brought me into creative contact with many thoughtful and compassionate people from all corners of the planet. It has widened my horizons and taught me to be a better listener. Although it is challenging to maintain a flow of posts through all four seasons, it is also a discipline that rewards by keeping my aging sensibility better attuned to the twists and turns of what seems worth noticing and commenting upon.

This collection has been selected to reflect my preoccupation with Israel–Palestine during this period. It will be complemented by a companion volume devoted to the Middle East, whose contents exhibit my intense interest in Turkey, Iran, Egypt, and the aftermath of the Arab Spring. I want to thank my research assistant, Sergey Saluschev, for his devoted assistance in selecting and compiling the posts that comprise both volumes.

This entire undertaking is really a collaborative venture with Helena Cobban and her wonderful team at Just World Books. It was Helena's responsiveness to the idea of doing these books and my excitement about working with such a congenial publisher, whose list I so admire, that converged to make the challenge of producing a coherent book a happy undertaking and one I very much hope is worth the effort. I thank Helena not only for her infectious enthusiasm but for her deep understanding of what it takes to mold an array of posts into a readable book. I would not deny that she is demanding, but I am convinced by the justness of her demands!

The outcome was also immeasurably blessed, and I mean blessed, by the superb editorial work of Sarah Grey, whose contributions were so far beyond the norm as to leave me without a vocabulary that includes words sufficient to express my deepest appreciation.

My work on Israel–Palestine in this period reflects the influence of friends and colleagues. Never far from my political consciousness is the looming gigantic figure of my cherished friend Edward Said, and in the foreground, among the many who have influenced my views and touched my heart, I would single out Raji Sourani. The person to whom I owe the most by way of help, ranging from practical wisdom to spiritual guidance, herself a distinguished writer on all that is addressed here, is Phyllis Bennis.

As always, I thank those whom I love the most, just for being there.

Lightning Source UK Ltd.
Milton Keynes UK
UKOW03f0022021014

239466UK00004B/206/P